Emotional Healing FOR DUMMIES®

by Dr David Beales and Helen Whitten

WILEY

A John Wiley and Sons, Ltd, Publication

Emotional Healing For Dummies®

Published by
John Wiley & Sons, Ltd
The Atrium
Southern Gate
Chichester
West Sussex
PO19 8SQ
England

E-mail (for orders and customer service enquires): cs-books@wiley.co.uk

Visit our Home Page on www.wiley.com

For general information on our other products and services, please contact our Customer Care Department within the U.S. at 877-762-2974, outside the U.S. at 317-572-3993, or fax 317-572-4002.

For technical support, please visit www.wiley.com/techsupport.

Wiley also publishes its books in a variety of electronic formats. Some content that appears in print may not be available in electronic books.

British Library Cataloguing in Publication Data: A catalogue record for this book is available from the British Library

ISBN: 978-0-470-74764-3

Printed and bound in Great Britain by TJ International, Padstow, Cornwall

10 9 8 7 6 5 4 3 2 1

WILEY

About the Authors

Dr David Beales, FRCP MRCGP DCH Dip Psych, is a faculty member of the Royal College of Physicians, Royal College of General Practitioners and the Royal Society of Medicine. He was formerly Chief Medical Officer of the Bristol Cancer Help Centre and has more than 30 years' experience in the field of medicine. David lectures, conducts workshops and has an individual practice.

David works within the speciality of mind-body medicine and aims to help clients understand and relieve the impact of sustained stress. When this gets locked into body-mind an over-revved state is created where signals of distress need to be interpreted and relieved. Symptoms may range from anxiety and depression to functional syndromes like irritable bowel, fibromyalgia and chronic pain. These disturbances of inner balance can be resolved by creating the mind-body tool kit that allows the recovery of health and well being. David's aim in this book is to distil the fruits of his experience, culled from many disciplines.

Helen Whitten is a personal and executive coach, accredited by the Association for Coaching. She is founder and Managing Director of Positiveworks Ltd and is also a practising facilitator, mediator, trainer and writer. She is trained in cognitive-behavioural psychology and neuro-linguistic programming, and applies cognitive-behavioural coaching models to personal and professional development, enabling individuals to develop confidence, break through old patterns of behaviour and achieve greater potential in their lives and their careers.

Helen is the author of *Cognitive-Behavioural Coaching Techniques For Dummies,* is a member of the Association for Coaching, the International Stress Management Association and the CIPD and is a CEDR Accredited Mediator. She has a degree in history and a postgraduate in personnel management.

Helen's career began in publishing and historical research. In mid-life she decided to pursue her interest in people and psychology, went to university as a mature student and changed career. This transition required her to face many of her own fears, healing personal issues so as to develop the self-knowledge required to work with others. Helen believes that people have the potential to enhance every aspect of their life, relationships and happiness when given the right support, encouragement, tools and techniques.

Author's Acknowledgements

We would like to say a special thank you to our clients and all those who have shared their stories with us. We have been inspired and honoured to have worked with some wonderful and courageous people who have shared their personal experiences and challenges with us and found the resilience to move towards healing.

We would like to thank our sons, families, friends and colleagues who have put us through our paces over the years and no doubt taught us some of the lessons we needed to learn! We recognise that there are plenty more lessons to come.

Thanks also to Steve Edwards and the team at John Wiley, for their editorial comments, encouragement and support in bringing this book to publication. And to Anna Rawlinson for her technical expertise.

Are you ready to take a whole new look at emotions? This book tackles them from every angle – mind, body and spirit – explaining why they are an essential part of human nature, and how to live in lively harmony with a full spectrum of emotions. I don't believe there is anyone who couldn't learn something from this comprehensive little book.

- David Peters, Professor of Integrated Healthcare at the University of Westminster

This book will show you how to re-channel all the energy you unknowingly used to cause yourself pain and suffering into healing yourself. By simply becoming aware of the power of breathing to influence all aspects of physical, mental and emotional health you can awaken to a new life experience which will be yours to nurture and enjoy. I have pulled myself out of a 30-year self-destructive pattern by applying the principles covered in this book and cannot praise its authors highly enough.

- Diana Bellinger, Client of David Beales

Publisher's Acknowledgements

We're proud of this book; please send us your comments through our Dummies online registration form located at www.dummies.com/register/.

Some of the people who helped bring this book to market include the following:

Commissioning, Editorial,
and Media Development

Project Editor: Steve Edwards

Content Editor: Jo Theedom

Commissioning Editor: Wejdan Ismail

Assistant Editor: Jennifer Prytherch

Development Editor: Brian Kramer

Copy Editor: Andy Finch

Technical Editor: Anna Rawlinson

Proofreader: David Price

Production Manager: Daniel Mersey

Cover Photos: © Image Source Pink/Alamy

Cartoons: Ed McLachlan

Composition Services

Project Coordinator: Lynsey Stanford

Layout and Graphics: Joyce Haughey

Proofreader: Jessica Kramer

Indexer: Ty Koontz

Special Help

Brand Reviewer: Jennifer Bingham

Contents at a Glance

Table of Contents

Introduction

*E*motional healing relates to every human being: no one has a perfect life. You have probably, like everyone else, been hurt or misunderstood, been in conflict or in love, experienced acceptance or rejection, and suffered losses, including bereavement. Most of the time you're able to dust yourself down and carry on, but at other times certain experiences result in wounds that linger on, negatively influencing your life.

Unhealed emotions can result in dysfunctional relationships, depression and physical and mental illness. Unresolved issues and emotional trauma can be locked deep inside your body and mind, creating disturbed bodily responses, emotional reactivity leading to problematic thinking and behaviour. Therefore, taking time to explore your own issues is extremely worthwhile, so that you can release them and move forward.

Emotional healing is required when you hold on to memories or feelings that still cause you pain. Your underlying drive as a human being is to seek pleasure and avoid pain. As you transition through many different life events this goal can become easier because you get better at identifying things that make you happy and more adept at avoiding things that cause you pain. You also develop resilience and develop ways to manage your emotions more effectively. Yet certain memories and events may still disturb you even as you face old age and death. Finding a way to make peace with past pain and grievances enables you to heal.

This book can help you explore and achieve emotional healing in problematic areas of your own life. We recognise that doing so takes great courage on your part, and we salute you for the step you're taking in picking up the book. We want to help you free yourself of past burdens, take control of your life and find ways to enjoy aspects of it that you may have had difficulty enjoying before.

About This Book

Our aim in writing this book is to give you the opportunity to heal yourself or work with others in their emotional healing. We have extensive experience of working with people to address mental, emotional and physical problems. We're sharing with you the models and processes that have helped our clients – and us in our own lives.

We offer you a wide variety of methods to transform the way you think about and manage the events, memories and concerns of your life. We hope that these options enable you to heal and come to terms with areas of your life that have not worked out the way you wanted.

Inevitably, people encounter a huge range of diverse emotional experiences, from the everyday irritations and disappointments of life to major traumas and tragedies. We can't cover every situation in this book. We're fully aware of, and a little in awe of, our responsibility to those of you who have the courage to face your difficulties. We very much hope that you can adapt the models and stories we share with you to suit your own specific situations and begin to find healing.

Conventions Used in This Book

To help you gain the most from this book and be able to pick up information and suggestions as quickly as possible, we use certain conventions:

- ✔ We refer to those individuals who have come to us for support as *clients*. Nearly all the information in this book can relate to any reader, and so we sometimes refer to a client as 'he' and sometimes as 'she'. For general examples and those in which clients aren't named, we use male gender in odd-numbered chapters and female in even-numbered chapters.

- ✔ The personal stories and examples come from specific experiences within our coaching and counselling practices, but they aren't direct representations of any one client or event.

- ✔ Sometimes we use the term 'feeling' and other times we use 'emotion'. We refer to a feeling when it is a more direct bodily experience and the word emotion when we discuss a situation where action is necessary.

Foolish Assumptions

We assume, though we may be wrong, that some of the following statements apply to you:

- ✔ You're seeking to address and release emotional pain.
- ✔ You want some methods, tools and techniques to support your healing.
- ✔ You may be working to help others achieve emotional healing.

✔ You may connect with some of the stories and examples we use and be able to apply the lessons to your own life.

✔ You're willing to explore the subject of emotional healing in order to enhance your own life or that of someone you know.

How This Book Is Organised

We divide the book into six parts, and each part has a specific focus. The Table of Contents gives you an overview of how we divide chapters and topics. Although we cover many aspects of emotional healing throughout the book, you don't have to read it from start to finish. You can skip or refer directly to any section that may resonate with your own life.

Part 1: Introducing Emotional Healing

We introduce you to the subject of emotional healing and how you can tune into your own emotions. When you understand how your mind, body and emotions are closely linked, you can pick up on your body's warning signals that your emotions are disturbed. We introduce you to the Emotional Healing Process, which provides you with steps to stop, breathe and take space to observe how you're responding to life challenges. We share with you ways to recognise your physical symptoms and make good decisions about how to take actions that reflect your personal needs and goals.

Part 11: Emotions and Your Body

Recognising that your mind, body and emotions are a finely tuned and integrated system is essential to creating balance and wellbeing in the future. We help you consider how your body is responding to your emotional experiences and give you strategies to care for yourself and encourage good health. We show how your breath is the conductor of your emotions, signalling when you're disturbed and providing you with the key to rebalancing and achieving emotional equilibrium.

Part III: Emotional Healing for Real Life

Get ready to review your own life, exploring childhood influences and life events that may have been difficult or traumatic. You discover the role of expectations in your response to emotional situations and find the courage to identify and move through past pain so that you can forgive yourself and others. We help you to understand the phases of loss and grief so that you can be patient with yourself in your healing process and let go of past pain. You even find tips and strategies to prepare for life's transitions and imperfections.

Part IV: The Emotional Healing Toolkit

We introduce you to four specific clusters of approaches that help you to heal yourself emotionally now and in the future. We give you thinking strategies to ensure that your mind focuses on optimistic, rational and constructive thoughts. We focus on mindfulness – sharing our favourite practices to relax and quieten body and mind through a variety of strategies, including breathing techniques – and provide suggestions for lifestyle strategies that you can practise every day in order to maintain emotional balance. In addition, we describe several practices and behaviours that you can adopt to become an emotionally healed person.

Part V: Taking Your Healing to New Levels

We help you begin to think about your future as well as the emotional health of people around you. We show you how to ensure that you don't fall back into old behaviours and instead enjoy and move through the next stages of your life. Your emotional state impacts other people, and so we describe how you can use your own knowledge to help others heal, including your children.

Part VI: The Part of Tens

In the Part of Tens, we share quick tips and stories that serve as speedy reference points. You find strategies to heal your emotional wounds and develop good lifestyle practices and activities that help you maintain your health and positivity.

Appendix

This resource lists contact details of organisations that can further support your healing. We include websites that lead you to specific information and share a booklist of titles that enable you to discover even more about emotional healing.

Icons Used in This Book

We use the following icons in this book so that you can immediately identify which parts of the book can be helpful to you:

This icon highlights practical advice that you can apply in your own life.

Bear in mind the crucial information under this icon while reading the book – and throughout your life in general.

Take a second look at material under this icon; it may well help you avoid a pitfall.

Read this story or short case study based on one of our real-life clients to discover some specific truths of the emotional healing process.

Time to get going! Do these activities and get ready to reap the rewards of emotional healing.

This icon indicates a topic or question that you need to stop and consider in order to ask yourself whether this sort of thing happens in your own life.

Where to Go from Here

We suggest that you take a good look at the Table of Contents and have a quick flip through the book in order to get an overview of the subjects we cover. Then take some time – perhaps have a walk outside or a few minutes to just sit and think – to reflect quietly on how the topics you noticed impact your own life.

Of course, you can skip to any part of the book that you feel is most relevant, but if possible, start by reading Part I because this part introduces you to many of the basic concepts that we touch on again and again in the book. After that, feel free to read the book in exactly the way you choose.

You may find that this book and its activities churn up past wounds. Be gentle with yourself and take a little time out. Talk with a friend or counsellor about the issues that are raised. Getting professional help can provide you with a safe environment in which to discuss your feelings and find a way through to healing.

Part I
Introducing Emotional Healing

'All right, Gerald, no one had a perfect childhood, but for goodness sake, you can't live forever in the past!'

In this part . . .

Take a moment and think about what healing yourself emotionally may mean for you personally. In this part, you discover how your body uses physical symptoms to alert you to emotional disturbance and how you can begin to tune in to these messages so you can take action to address your emotional problems.

We share information about the biology of emotions and how it impacts your body's self-healing system. We also give you specific techniques that help you re-balance and re-set your body's stress response.

Chapter 1

Understanding Emotional Healing

- -

In This Chapter

▶ Uncovering your emotional needs

▶ Using thoughts to feel better

▶ Getting out of stuck states

▶ Releasing yourself from past pain

- -

Certain events in your life – bereavement, accidents, divorce or the negative emotional responses of other people – can affect you deeply. As a result, you may experience anger, fear, guilt, anxiety, hurt and a host of other painful emotions. You can probably name some people who become bitter after a minor disappointment and other people who suffer trauma and yet manage to smile again. Although time can play its part, the difference is in the way you think about your situation and in the support you receive.

Emotional healing occurs when events in your life no longer disturb you when you recall them or limit you from enjoying life. Clinging to misery and holding onto negative emotions isn't virtuous. You can unburden yourself and move forward with a lighter step. This book is your opportunity to review how you're thinking and feeling about these events in order to move on and heal your wounds.

The key to healing emotions lies not in what you experience but in how you respond. The quality of your life depends more on your emotional state than on specific events. You can ease or adjust any feeling by adopting a different perspective.

This chapter introduces you to the main ingredients of emotional healing. We help you recognise how your emotions are impacting your life and identify what actions you can take to heal them. You can get unstuck from old memories or current challenges and free yourself to lead life unimpeded by the chains of the past. Life is for living in a positive way; we show you how to focus on managing and enjoying the present and future.

Appreciating the Role of Emotions

Emotions are designed to help you survive. They express your deepest desires and act like a compass to remind you of the things you most care about. They direct you to take action that keeps you emotionally happy and physically secure.

Your biological make-up consists of chemicals, including hormones, that drive you to protect both your physical security and your sense of self. A complex mix of chemistry fuels your energy when you're in physical danger and also drives you towards meeting your emotional need for love, recognition, intimacy and connection with others (see Chapter 2). Your instinct is to avoid pain and to seek pleasure. No one's life, however, is without some pain.

Sending signals to yourself

Your emotions demand your attention through the signals that you feel. Hence, you feel happy in situations that are good for you. These signals also make you feel uncomfortable when something isn't in your best interests. Similarly, you may feel anxious, grumpy, overwhelmed, miserable or fatigued when your personal security is threatened.

Emotions act like a silent and wise navigation process. Emotional messages remind you of your values and personal truths. When you don't listen to these cues, emotional and physical disturbances occur. How often have you said to yourself, 'I knew that there was going to be a problem with this job' or 'I always had a bad feeling about this relationship' or 'I get a headache after talking to Bill'? When you tune into these signals, you can take action to adjust the situation to better meet your needs.

Negative feelings upset the balance of your body. The chemicals that give you the strength or speed to respond to physical threat reduce the effectiveness of your immune system to keep you healthy when threat or stress persists too long. If you don't address your emotional messages, you may become physically ill. In worst cases, ignoring your needs can result in mental breakdown, depression or serious illness. Chapter 2 gives more information in this area.

You need to acknowledge, name and express your emotions in appropriate ways, otherwise you hold them in a locked-in state within your body. In Chapter 3, we discuss ways in which you can consciously monitor your feelings and interpret the messages you're receiving. Throughout the book, we show you how to take action and focus on those aspects of life that make you feel good.

Assessing your basic needs

Your health and happiness are disturbed when your basic needs aren't met. The needs that matter most to you are unique to you personally but all humans share some basic universal needs. Your family, friends and physical and social environment all influence your needs. Identifying and expressing your emotional needs appropriately enables you to maintain emotional well-being.

Your needs change over your lifetime. Continually review them using the following Needs Review activity.

1. **Think about and prioritise your basic emotional needs.**

   Read the descriptions of basic emotional needs that appear in the first column of Table 1-1. Which are most important to you? Which least important? No wrong answers exist here. You're just getting reacquainted with your emotional needs. If you have needs that don't appear in Table 1-1, you can add them.

   In the second column of Table 1-1, place in rank order each need, from 1 (the most important to you) to 14 (the least important to you).

2. **Assess whether each emotional need is currently being met.**

   In the third column, use a scale of 0 to 10 (10 indicating that the need is being well met and 0 that it isn't being met at all). See the later section 'Considering whether your needs are being met' for more on this topic.

3. **Consider actions that you can take to meet more effectively the needs you find most important – or that you discover aren't being met.**

   In the fourth column, list any thoughts that come to mind with regard to how you can get your needs met more effectively. If filling out the fourth column is a challenge for you, plan to read the chapters in Part III.

Table 1-2 shows an example of a partly completed review of emotional needs.

Table 1-1   Reviewing Your Emotional Needs

Emotional need	How important is this need to me?	How well is this need being met (on a scale of 0–10)?	What actions can I take to better meet this need?
Love: experiencing emotional intimacy; loving, being loved			
Connection: finding emotional support within social groups, family, friends and wider community			
Personal growth: sensing challenge and adventure, continuous discovery and curiosity; having goals to aim for			
Recognition and status: being affirmed, seen, understood and accepted for who I am and what I do			
Purpose and contribution: making a difference; having a sense of meaning; contributing to the wider community			
Self-acceptance: appreciation that I have unique needs and fallibilities; accepting myself even when I make mistakes			
Hope and optimism: having a vision of a future that's good; believing that I can improve things			

Emotional need	How important is this need to me?	How well is this need being met (on a scale of 0–10)?	What actions can I take to better meet this need?
Trust and flexibility: having faith in myself and others; accepting life's imperfections; feeling able to manage the ups and downs			
Sense of autonomy and control: being independent and free; making my own decisions and choices; seeing myself as capable and competent			
Expression: communicating my unique needs honestly; sharing what I believe in			
Physical balance and wellbeing: caring for the health of my mind and body; eating well; enjoying a mix of work, play and rest			
Sense of security: feeling safe within a territory, family, space and with personal possessions			
Privacy and reflection: taking part in space and time alone to be quiet and reflect			
Spiritual needs: experiencing my personal sense of the sacred and divine			

Table 1-2	Example of a Needs Review		
Emotional need	*How important is this need to me?*	*How well is this need being met (on a scale of 0–10)?*	*What actions can I take to better meet this need?*
Recognition and Status. *No one sees all that I do at work.*	3rd priority	4	Arrange a feedback appraisal with my boss
Connection *I'm feeling lonely now my sons have left home.*	2nd priority	3	Find outside sources of connection in my community

After you complete the Needs Review, ask yourself this big question: does your life at the moment reflect your personal priorities? List ten things you love to do that support your emotional needs. Star the five items that you love the most and begin planning how you can act on them. (Chapters 14 and 15 offer strategies about changing your behaviour.)

Considering whether your needs are being met

You can easily be so busy with 'important' things that you overlook whether your needs are being met. You may:

✔ Suppress your own emotional unhappiness for the sake of harmony within your family, your circle of friends or your workplace.

✔ Engage in lots of activity – such as working long hours or watching hours of television – to avoid confronting difficult emotions.

✔ Experience *secondary emotions* about your primary emotion. In these complex situations, you may feel really cross with yourself for being so anxious, or you may feel helpless and depressed when you think about how angry you are with someone.

Often, the easiest thing you can do when a need isn't being met is to ignore addressing uncomfortable issues. Unfortunately, if you take no action when you feel unacknowledged, unsafe or unloved, you simply reinforce the lack of another need – your sense of personal control in your life.

Have the courage to take action and express your needs. Even if the outcome isn't exactly what you want, action gives you a greater sense of self-care and self-esteem. Take a look at Chapter 8 for how to take action appropriately.

Linking Thoughts and Feelings

As we explore in greater depth in Chapter 2, how you think impacts how you feel. Every thought has a chemical reaction in your body and changes how you feel. Every feeling changes the way you think. The two states are interlinked.

Anxious thoughts trigger your emotional brain to assume that you're under physical threat, preparing you to fight or to run away. Persistent negative thoughts drive you into despair, depression and helplessness. Focusing on the positive aspects of your life lifts your spirits. Positive emotions also have the benefit of boosting your immune system so that you're likely to experience better health as well as increased happiness.

You may consider yourself to be a thinking person who feels, but neuroscientists argue that biologically – because you're a human being – you're a feeling creature who thinks. The human evolutionary journey indicates that your emotional brain developed *before* your thinking brain (see Chapter 2 for more detail on the brain and emotions).

Stand back and become an evaluator of the situations you're facing. Doing so isn't as easy as it may sound. In fact, people can be surprisingly bad at evaluating their own lives, placing themselves again and again in situations that upset them. Chapter 13 helps you develop an inner observer and evaluator to better identify the factors that support your emotional wellbeing.

Conditioning your emotional responses

When you're young, you pick up messages from your family about what's good or bad, and what's likely to make you happy or sad. As a child you received *rewards* (for instance, receiving a treat for good behaviour) and *punishments* (being sent to your room). Surprisingly quickly, your brain begins to associate certain actions with reward and others with punishment, a process known as *conditioning*. As you grow up, your responses become automatic and drive behaviours that may no longer be appropriate for you as an adult. For example, if you were frequently sent to your room as a child, you may find that you now link being alone with feeling bad.

An internal reward system regulates your brain, leading you towards pleasure and away from pain. This system releases 'feel-good' chemicals, such as dopamine, when you have pleasurable experiences such as eating chocolate or feeling loved. Research shows that being able to recognise and manage your internal reward system has a more significant impact on your success and happiness than having a high IQ. Emotional maturity comes from using your thinking brain to review your emotions and behaviours, so that you can consider which actions help you to feel happy and allow you to live the life you desire.

Every decision in life has costs and benefits – whether you're choosing to divorce your partner, starting a new job, talking to someone about an emotional problem or letting go of past pain. Even simple decisions involve costs and benefits. For example, eating chocolate may be delicious and provide you with a quick reward, but over-indulging can lead to becoming overweight, which can counteract the initial, momentary pleasure. Only you can decide the cost versus the benefit of each decision you take.

Helpful and unhelpful emotions

A difference exists between a helpful emotion and an unhelpful one. Begin to notice and distinguish between the two. For example:

- **Feeling grief and sadness after a bereavement is natural.** However, if these feelings incapacitate you for a number of years, you can regard them as unhelpful because you've become stuck in negative feelings (such as guilt) that complicate your recovery. (Check out Chapter 10 for more on acceptance and how to move on.)

- **Feeling angry that your partner is unfaithful is natural.** But feeling jealous because you imagine that your partner may one day cheat on you is unhelpful because the event may never happen. Distrust can interfere with the progress of your relationship, setting up an unhelpful suspicion.

- **Feeling pain and anger when your partner rejects you (at the end of a relationship or marriage) is natural for a period of time.** However, if you're still feeling angry after several years, you may be struggling to accept and move on. Everyone experiences rejection from time to time. Not coming to

terms with the pain is unhelpful and will interfere with your long-term happiness and ability to make new relationships.

- **Feeling guilt about a past misdemeanour may help you consider what you want to do differently next time.** However, what's done is done; harbouring guilt and regret over a long period is unhelpful, simply prolonging your unhappiness.

- **Feeling low as a result of an event such as a redundancy or domestic upheaval is natural.** But feeling depressed for a long period means that you're focusing only on the negatives in life and ignoring the positives. Adjust this balance by listing what is working and the people who do support you. Planning how to raise your spirits in future is more helpful.

Constantly review the emotions you're experiencing and consider whether you may be stuck in unhealthy emotions that you need to address. Identify thoughts and behaviours that can help you move forward through acceptance and action.

The *cost-benefit model* can help you to assess the pain and the pleasure associated with a decision, and then identify the actions that benefit you. Table 1-3 shows an example of a cost-benefit analysis on whether to start going to the gym to exercise. You can use a similar model to help you make good decisions in your own life.

Table 1-3	Cost-Benefit Analysis – Going to the Gym
Costs	**Benefits**
Exercising requires effort.	I'll get fit.
Exercising takes time.	I'll be able to get into that outfit if I slim down a bit.
Joining the gym costs money.	I'll feel much better about myself.
I'll have to get up early.	I'll improve my long-term health and happiness.

Recognising your mental models

Over your lifetime, you develop *mental models* of how you would like the world to be, how you prefer others to treat you and what standards you want to live by. A mental model is a representation of your own preferred reality derived from your personality, experience and ideals. Your models may or may not be realistic. You can easily allow your personal preferences to become universal rules of expectations of yourself and others, which can lead to pain and disappointment when a mismatch occurs.

Your mental models can negatively impact your thinking in three main ways:

✔ **High internal standards:** You see yourself as competent at what you do. You believe that your competency is a major (or perhaps the only) reason why people love and appreciate you. Failing to meet your standards is therefore awful because it signifies that you're a worthless, unlovable individual. This type of thinking results in lowered self-acceptance and increased anxiety; self-loathing and depression often follow.

✔ **Blaming others:** You believe that others must treat you fairly. When they don't, they're rotten people. Of course, you overlook the fact that your definition of 'fair' may not tally with other people's. This type of thinking leads to increased judgement, criticism, irritation, conflict and self-pity.

✔ **High expectations of life:** You believe that you must experience pleasure rather than pain in life. You expect life to turn out the way you want it to, and you get upset when it doesn't. This type of thinking leads to increased frustration, anger and disillusionment.

All the preceding mental models can result in you feeling blame, self-pity and a sense of helplessness when things don't turn out as you expect.

Although being able to manage everything perfectly sounds great, you're a human being and, like all other human beings, you're going to make mistakes over your lifetime! Accepting life's unpredictability and your own imperfections is realistic. Acknowledging that your perspective represents just one viewpoint takes courage, but doing so also releases you to acknowledge other views and find new ways to manage things. Chapter 12 includes more strategies to gain a broader perspective.

Setting idealistic rules for yourself and others isn't always helpful. These types of rules can easily morph into perfectionist demands that end up upsetting you if they don't work out. Being optimistic is great, but maintain your optimism as your *preference*. Tell yourself, 'I'd prefer if things worked out the way I want, but I can manage when they don't.'

Recognising How Emotions Influence Actions

Your feelings have direct consequences on life choices, and by extension how you act or don't act.

Think about the last time you considered buying or renting a house or flat. If you're like most people, you probably knew within a couple of minutes of walking through the front door whether the location was right for you. You may have felt instantly emotionally comfortable or 'at home' in the new place. From that moment on, you probably tried to rationalise your emotional response to sign the contract!

Acting sensibly – or not

You make very different decisions depending on the mood you're in. If you're feeling happy, you're likely to be bolder in your decisions than if you're feeling low. You may choose to go for an adventure holiday or push for a promotion. Conversely people sometimes make radical decisions to relocate or chuck in their job due to an emotional event.

Emotions can drive you to do crazy things. In fact. when you're in love the state of your brain is very similar to the delusion of paranoia! People who are jealous can stalk or hound their partners and normally mild-mannered people can turn into maniacs behind the driving wheel.

Become aware of the impact that your emotions have on your life decisions. Check yourself when tempted to make a decision at a time when you know your emotions are out of kilter. Take advantage of the moments when you know that you feel balanced. Gradually, utilising the techniques in this book, you can take control of your emotions to ensure that you're in an optimal emotional state when you need to make the wisest possible choices.

Every action has a consequence. Become aware of how your emotions influence you and try to make sure that you aren't just jumping into a habitual response where your negative emotions are shaping your behaviour. Use your thinking brain to manage your emotions in a given situation.

Getting stuck in old pain

Many people get stuck in pain and allow it to limit their enjoyment of life. Don't allow one experience to shape your reactions to other similar situations. For example, students failing an exam can become so stuck in the pain of that failure – and the fear of failing again in the future – that they give up pursuing career goals. Or an actor who forgets his lines once may decide that he can never be successful and goes on to experience dreadful stage fright each time he performs.

These people are allowing one bad event to colour their experiences in further situations. Their emotional brains are automatically connecting one situation to other situations that are similar, which may be totally irrational. Read more about this process in Chapter 3.

One bad event or experience doesn't logically mean that you're going to encounter problems every other time in the future.

For example, rejection by a partner or in a job can lead you to feel resentment, anger and depression. The problem can be two-fold:

- ✔ You take the situation too personally and consider yourself a failure or unlovable as a result of the rejection.

- ✔ You blame another person for being 'unfair' or 'unreasonable' for having rejected you, instead of realising that other people have a right to make choices based on their own emotional needs.

In these cases, you're thinking about the situation in generalised terms, rather than basing your views on the specifics of the situation. You may judge another person as 'inconsiderate' even though he was only inconsiderate to you in one instance. You may exaggerate the situation by thinking, 'I can't stand him' or 'How dare he treat me in this way?', when in reality you can put up with a lot and he only treated you that way once.

What? Other people think they're right too!?

Other people involved in any situation have their own mental models (see the section 'Recognising your mental models'). They may consider themselves to be acting fairly within their world views. Just because you have different models doesn't make these people unreasonable.

All individuals are endeavouring to seek happiness in their own ways. Personal perceptions and needs inevitably lead to disharmony from time to time. Take personal responsibility for your own reaction. Then realise that you have the option to change your reaction by evaluating whether it's realistic and logical. Remind yourself that although you may prefer life to meet your needs, you can manage when things go wrong.

When you generalise, you stop yourself from moving on. Instead, try to assess each situation and behaviour on its own objective merits rather than writing off the whole human being. Being rejected on one occasion, whether in your personal or work life, doesn't logically mean that you're unlovable or incompetent. (Besides, this way of thinking can lead you to self-pity, which negatively affects your ability to move forward.) Turn to Chapters 6, 7 and 10 to discover how to relate to old pain more constructively.

Unsticking yourself

If you feel stuck in emotional pain, take time out to consider the underlying causes. Ask yourself the following useful questions:

- ✔ What emotions are holding me back?

- ✔ Have I experienced this emotional situation before? Am I associating the current challenge with a previous challenge? Just because the previous event didn't go well, does that mean that this event will also go badly?

- ✔ How can I think differently in order to let go of this pain? Can I focus on a positive emotional state, for example transforming fear into confidence?

- ✔ Is it logical to assume that everyone would see the situation in the same way as I do?

See Chapter 6, 7, 8 and 10 for more helpful strategies to get unstuck emotionally.

One of the biggest mistakes people make is relying on others for their own happiness. This expectation creates dependence and disempowers you. Ultimately, as an adult, your happiness is your own responsibility, not that of anyone else.

Two Zen monks

Two Zen monks were on a pilgrimage to another monastery. They had both taken strict vows not to touch other people and to remain silent at all times. They came to a river where a beautiful peasant girl asked if they would carry her across because the water was too deep. The first monk said 'All right' and carried her safely to the other side. They continued their journey but the second monk brooded until finally he burst out, 'Why did you do that? You know we're not allowed to touch or speak to anyone!'. 'Let it go,' said the first monk. 'It is you who are still carrying her.'

Encountering Obstacles

Life events, whether major or minor, are those episodes that leave an imprint on you. Life events shape the pattern of how you respond to everyday challenges now and in the future. Wherever you are in your life, past events have an ongoing emotional impact. These events may include bullying, bereavement, divorce or a row with a friend or neighbour. Of course, you've experienced emotions such as happiness, fulfilment and contentment, too.

Your body's cells store emotional information as body memory. Your brain checks every piece of sensory information and assigns to it an emotional impact. Situations that are highly emotionally charged create a state of physiological arousal, which your body-mind system holds and automatically reactivates when you find yourself in a similar predicament. For example, deep inside, your brain remembers that your muscles tensed up when you argued with your partner last week, as well as the fact that you relaxed when on holiday in Spain. Chapter 3 helps you begin uncovering the connection between past experiences and emotions, and Chapter 7 guides you deeper into your upbringing and past experiences.

If you're a human being (and we hope you are!), you'll experience a number of losses in your lifetime. These losses may be as simple as moving house and losing friends, or as tragic as the death of a loved one. The common thread is that you become attached to something or somebody and you lose that connection. Any one of these situations leaves an imprint mentally, emotionally and physically. However small or large your experience, you may feel *grief* – deep and poignant distress over a loss.

No fixed formula exists for a speedy recovery from grief, although Chapter 10 gives you some important first steps and the Appendix offers some relevant contacts for professional and group help with grief.

Journeying through the Emotional Healing Process

All the tips and techniques in this book connect to the *Five-Step Emotional Healing Process*, an integrated method that brings together a variety of approaches into a structured model. We developed this model (based on our professional work involving Cognitive Behavioural Therapy and Emotional Freedom techniques, as well as David's medical background in mind-body medicine) to help you stop and review your emotional responses to situations and consider how to release disturbed or locked-in feelings – by letting them go or by expressing them.

In the emotional healing process you:

1. **Experience (or re-experience) any situation that caused or continues to cause you disturbing physical or emotional sensations and experiences.**

2. **Notice the mental, emotional, physical, behavioural and lifestyle impacts of the experience on your life.**

   Emotions have a physical impact. (Think about your sweaty hands and tight shallow breathing before you give a presentation.) The internal chemistry that causes these physical changes also alters your behaviour. (Hence you become impatient or can't sleep.) Over time, these behavioural changes can affect your overall lifestyle (for example, you start drinking excessively the night before a big presentation to calm your nerves). See Chapter 2 for more on the interconnectedness of emotions and behaviours.

3. **Take a breathing space to evaluate, observe, analyse and choose a response to the experience and your initial response.**

   Developing your inner observer and evaluator – the part of you who takes time to stop, observe yourself and consider what's happening and what needs to happen – is the focus of Chapters 10 and 12.

4. **Take four types of action.**

   These include thinking strategies (as we discuss in Chapter 12); emotional interpretation and expression (Chapters 7, 8 and 9); physiological actions (Chapters 2, 6, 13 and 19) and breathing and other behaviour changes (Chapters 10, 14, 15 and 16).

5. **Release held-in emotional energy so you achieve further healing and re-connect to your sense of conscious choice so that you move forward with ease and confidence.**

Deciding to be happy

After 15 years of marriage, Peter's wife unexpectedly left him for another man. For many months, he felt depressed and had difficulty feeling positive about anything in his life. When we asked him what his daily experience of life was like, he said, 'I have a grey pit in my stomach, the world is deadened, the sky is grey and everything is pointless.' Obviously, he wasn't in a very cheery place to live every day!

He was asked to imagine what it would be like if he felt happy. He replied, 'I would feel light in my stomach as I wake up, the birds would be singing and the sky would be blue. I'd see my friends and take an interest in life. It would be like switching the world on again.'

As he spoke, Peter's body language changed, and he became visibly happier. He noted these changes himself and began to realise that happiness was within his own control.

Happiness doesn't depend on the outside situation; it's a decision you make. With this new understanding and after experiencing happiness just by talking about it, Peter was able to begin building new habits by focusing on enjoyment. He identified and took action to bring positive experiences back into his life, which sustained his renewed feelings of happiness and helped him rebuild a new life.

We advise that you move through the Five-Step Emotional Healing Process in a linear manner because each builds on the one before it. However, in the midst of overwhelming stress, you may need to take a break, re-connect with a sense of inner calm and return to clear thinking *before* taking action. You can go through this five-step process alone. However, if you find yourself in a predicament in which you're unable to switch out of an emotionally aroused state, you need to find external support from a professional such as a doctor, counsellor or psychologist. The Appendix includes contact details for caring professionals.

You're building your emotional 'muscle' to help you manage difficult situations in a more balanced way. You may not be able to change or control your situation, but you can change and control the way you think and feel about it.

Chapter 2

Exploring the Physiology of Emotion

· ·

· ·

*Y*ou're an integrated system of mind, body and emotion. What you feel emotionally is immediately experienced chemically in your body. Emotional wellbeing represents a state in which you're confident and positive. When this state is threatened, your *physiology* – your body's combined biology and chemistry – alerts you to take action to protect yourself. Your brain monitors your physical safety and your emotional needs such as love, social significance and emotional connection. Your body's response to threat is essentially the same whether you're being attacked by a mugger in the street or receiving a phone call from an irate family member or business colleague.

Your physiology seeks to keep you alive, monitoring your internal chemistry and maintaining for your good health. Perhaps you've experienced a sudden surge of an emotion such as sadness or anger that swamped you when you least wanted this to happen. Signals such as butterflies in the stomach or shivers of excitement alert you to your underlying emotional state. You can develop the ability to recognise and interpret these signals and then take action to restore and maintain your wellbeing.

In this chapter we explore the reasons why emotions are such powerful guides and why they can kick in with such force. We help you to identify the situations and feelings that trigger your own physiology and to recognise physical symptoms of emotion, so that you can act in ways that are appropriate and in your best interests. The inevitable successes and disappointments of life then become a roller coaster that you ride with greater ease, in the knowledge that you have the tools to bring yourself back into emotional balance.

Understanding the Threat Response

Your brain is on constant alert to protect you, which is essential, of course, when you're in real danger – facing a mugger in a dark alley or hurtling towards a brick wall in an out-of-control car. Your body and mind kick into overdrive and work furiously to save you from harm. But sometimes your body-mind can get a bit carried away and put you into an unnecessary state of overdrive.

We use the term *body-mind* here and elsewhere in the book because a continuous interchange, or *feedback loop,* is happening between the physiological responses to threat within your body and your mind.

Looking at the brain's reactions to threats

Fifty thousand years ago, primitive humans took a big leap forward on the evolutionary path, moving from ape-ancestors to modern man. Humans began walking upright, making tools and communicating with language. In order to hold all this extra information, the human brain developed an enlarged thinking section.

The threats affecting you in the modern world are very different from those of primitive humans. But your brain still carries the primitive responses of ancestors: any perceived threat, affecting survival and safety, sets off an automatic physiological response.

Modern humans respond to threats to their social status and sense of emotional security. For example, whether at work or within the family, you may feel threatened when:

- You don't feel that your social position is being recognised.
- You don't feel in control.
- You don't get what you want or expect.
- You don't feel loved.

When threatened, your body-mind picks up the message of alarm, switching on the stress response. This response is known as the *fight, flight or freeze response* and gives you the strength to fight or the speed to run away from the threat. Stress can also lead to paralysis, when you freeze rather like a rabbit in the headlights. This reaction can be appropriate when avoiding drawing attention to yourself in a dangerous situation, but it can incapacitate you if it happens when you're making a presentation at work!

You may experience an 'adrenaline rush' before a big event; for example, when you're just about to take a rollercoaster ride, do a parachute jump, make a presentation or sit an exam. This response is your sympathetic system kicking into gear as a result of your anxiety about the event. Figure 2-1 illustrates how your body feels during the fight, flight or freeze response.

For primitive humans all the changes associated with fight or flight ensured survival. But this primitive stress response isn't appropriate in the majority of situations that you face in today's world. Luckily you don't have to contend with too many woolly mammoths! Strength and speed can be useful if you're being mugged, but they aren't particularly helpful when you're managing a large workload or trying to negotiate with a truculent client or teenager.

Even more importantly, when you allow your automatic responses to take control without your more evolved thinking brain directing the process, your emotions take over – and your ability to think takes the back seat.

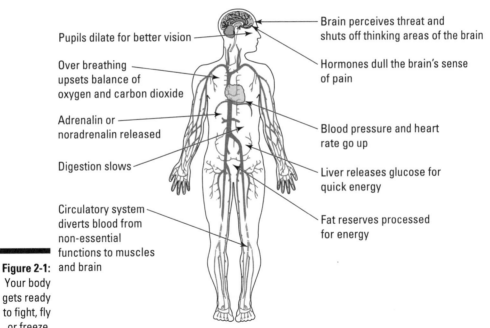

Pupils dilate for better vision

Over breathing upsets balance of oxygen and carbon dioxide

Adrenalin or noradrenalin released

Digestion slows

Circulatory system diverts blood from non-essential functions to muscles and brain

Brain perceives threat and shuts off thinking areas of the brain

Hormones dull the brain's sense of pain

Blood pressure and heart rate go up

Liver releases glucose for quick energy

Fat reserves processed for energy

Figure 2-1: Your body gets ready to fight, fly or freeze.

The Fight or Flight Response = Strength or Speed

Tackling the persistent stress response

Many people today are on continuous alert due to the pressures of the modern world: their threat response is overactive. Hormones such as cortisone and adrenaline continue to be released even though you're no longer in danger and dealing with specific physical threats. Although these hormones are helpful in the short term, they can be destructive in the long term, leading to:

- Circulation becoming sluggish
- Digestion slowing
- Growth and tissue repair being reduced
- Immune system becoming disturbed with a shift to an inflammatory pattern
- Reproduction being affected
- Stress responses occurring, such as insomnia, headaches and illness

Long-term stress, where you're feeling overwhelmed, leads you into a downward spiral of ill health and can result in burnout, taking the form of a physical or nervous breakdown.

Finding your position on the stress curve

A little bit of stress can be motivating and make you alert. (Indeed, too little arousal can also be physically and emotionally draining because your performance is low.) But too much stress occurs when the perceived pressure on you exceeds your ability to cope. Remember: motivation is pleasurable, whereas too much stress takes you into a state of struggle, triggering aggression, intolerance, impatience and the inability to think clearly about complex situations. Figure 2-2 shows how 'healthy tension' motivates performance, but too much stress results in a productivity down slope.

Take a look at Figure 2-2, think about your average day and figure out where you put yourself on this curve. Specifically:

- Are you on the down slope with too many demands?
- Are your mind and body signalling to you with irritability and difficulty relaxing?
- Are you experiencing sleep difficulties?
- Are you experiencing symptoms such as muscular tension, chest pain, abdominal discomfort or dizziness?
- What do you need to do to adjust your position on the curve?

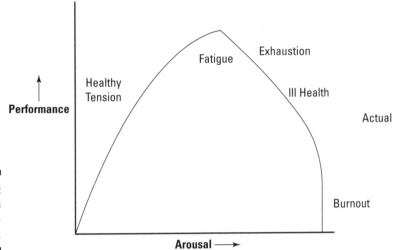

Figure 2-2:
How stress
impacts per-
formance.

Each person's stress symptoms differ: one person may experience headaches and another skin complaints. Become familiar with *your* body's symptoms and signals. Consider placing a copy of Figure 2-2 in your journal and marking where you fall on the curve over a period of several weeks. If you find yourself frequently towards the bottom levels of the down slope, we advise you see your medical practitioner.

Adjusting your position on the stress curve

To effectively deal with stress, you need to develop the ability to step back, see the bigger picture and take conscious control to rebalance your physiology via your thinking brain. Here are some ways to take your brain and body out of overdrive:

- ✔ Breathing exercises (see the section 'Tuning Into Your Breathing')
- ✔ Meditating and visualising yourself in a calm place (see Chapter 13)
- ✔ Taking exercise, which naturally reduces the body's stress chemistry (see Chapter 6)
- ✔ Thinking calm and rational thoughts to gain a sense of control and per- spective, such as 'I can manage this' (see Chapter 12)

You also need to develop strategies to minimise the physical consequences of fight, flight or freeze:

1. **Identify potential situations at home and at work that may cause you emotional stress.**

   Rate each situation from 0 to 10, with 10 being high stress and 0 low stress, so that you can easily identify your major problems.

2. **Consider why you find those situations so difficult.**

   Refer to Chapter 12 to understand your underlying thought processes. Your physiology is signalling that you need to change something, so identify what you need to do to meet your emotional needs.

3. **Develop a practical plan to manage the situation.**

   This may include constructive and calming thoughts, breathing techniques and behavioural changes such as assertiveness, managing time and making good decisions.

Become the inner observer of your life. Be alert to your body's symptoms and notice which situations trigger a feeling of stress. Stop and consider whether you're imagining that things are going to go wrong when in fact they may not. You may temporarily have lost perspective. See Chapter 12 for tips on how to regain perspective.

Ensuring reactions to threat don't hijack thought

Your fight, flight or freeze response gives you important messages that your thinking brain needs to read *before* acting. The alternative is that your primitive brain responds automatically and may lead you into inappropriate behaviour.

Your brain has both a fast track and a slow track to respond to danger. The fast track takes a fraction of a second to activate and is always associated with the physiology of fight, flight or freeze, triggering a physical reaction before your thinking brain has a chance to consider whether such a response is appropriate. Your rational brain is literally 'hijacked' by the automatic emotion.

The fast track can be appropriate to specific physical threats. But often you need to take some time to restore thinking before reacting to someone or something. You need to take control of this process and discover how to switch to the slow track, creating a gap between the situation and your response to the situation. This gap enables you to decide how best to respond.

Imagine that you have a fear of spiders. You suddenly come across one in your house. You notice your fear response, but instead of reacting, you're able to stop and think about your situation rationally. You control your emotions by reminding yourself that the spider is small and unlikely to be able to hurt you. Controlling your fear switches you to the slow track, so that you can decide logically what to do with the spider.

Developing the ability to switch to the slow track helps you to consider the situation in a more measured way. The slow approach becomes 'thought first and feeling second', whereas the fast track is a misplaced 'feeling first and thought second' approach.

Switching from fast track to slow track is like changing gears in a car. You can find neutral by grounding yourself, focusing on your feet, slowing your breathing, quietening your mind and watching yourself within the situation rather than reacting. You can also take a pause or go into a different room until you feel ready to respond to the challenge.

Only by recognising that you're in a state of emotional reactivity can you shift circuits and use ways to interrupt the sudden fast track response. Individuals who don't understand this process get overtaken by strong automatic emotions with unfortunate consequences, such as road rage.

John was devastated when his girlfriend, Jane – a colleague he'd been dating for some time – broke up with him and started seeing someone else from his office. One night, he was in a bar with colleagues when one of them made a remark about his ex-girlfriend and the new boyfriend. John suddenly and uncontrollably lashed out and hit the colleague who had spoken. The colleague was forgiving but John didn't trust himself to return to work.

When John sought counselling, he realised how quickly his fight response was activated. For him the first signal was rapid upper chest breathing. When he consciously moved his attention to the out-breath, slowed his breathing down and rehearsed the scene again, he found that his ability to think clearly returned. The counsellor then asked him to rehearse seeing his ex-girlfriend in different situations (including with her new boyfriend) and being able to control his reactions. John now understood how to direct his actions consciously to the slow track, allowing him to function effectively. He then successfully returned to work.

The emotional brain can lay down remembered automatic responses as fears and phobias. Chapter 8 contains information on techniques that can replace these automatic responses with more helpful ones.

Unravelling feelings from thinking

The Greek philosopher Epictetus wisely said, 'Man is not disturbed by events, but by the view he takes of them.' In other words, how you interpret the world influences your feelings.

For example, your thinking mind may expect your partner to take you out to a restaurant to celebrate your birthday. When she decides to cook you a meal at home, you may feel disappointed. This example shows how a specific expectation can stimulate your feelings and impact your emotions. Although you may expect your birthday to be noticed and celebrated, you don't have to have such a set idea about what form the celebration takes.

Review whether your thoughts are inappropriately driving your feelings. You may have conditioned emotional responses to situations that are more to do with how you're *thinking* about them rather than how you're really *feeling* about them. For example, whether or not your partner takes you out for dinner probably doesn't alter the fact that you love one another.

Your own expectations aren't the only things that shape your emotional responses; societal norms also have a part to play. For example, acknowledging and expressing your feelings openly isn't always easy to do. Certain expectations can shape how you manage emotions: boys are brought up to be tough, whereas crying is okay for girls. This conditioning can cause you to deny what you're feeling in order to conform to a social environment.

Become aware that a mismatch may exist between what you feel and how you respond to that feeling. Instead of denying or disguising an emotion, try to acknowledge and feel it. Listen to the message that the feeling brings you about an appropriate action; it may help you manage the situation in a better way.

Listening to Your Body Talk

Your body talks to you through physical symptoms. When things go wrong you often think things such as

- ✔ 'I'm sick to my stomach'
- ✔ 'You're a pain in the neck'
- ✔ 'Get off my back'

These expressions are examples of emotions unconsciously triggering *body talk*. Each emotion calls for you to act in a different way in an effort to release you from overload.

When you start to notice some of these phrases and symptoms, you can become an expert in the language of your body. Where do you hold tension when stressed and struggling? Are you someone who gets a headache, or do you hold tension in your neck? Perhaps you suffer from stomach pains or feel discomfort in your solar plexus? Maybe you get skin complaints or high blood pressure? Each of these symptoms is driving you to take action to solve a problem that's upsetting you on some level.

Your body is signalling that you need to pay attention and possibly take action. For example, if you're feeling sad, angry or guilty, you have a need to honour and understand the sources of these emotions. You may need to take action to release the feelings, for example by calling a friend, setting boundaries or forgiving yourself or another.

If you don't listen to the early signals that you're overloaded, your body can ramp up the symptom messages. You may come down with a vicious bout of flu that necessitates rest for several days. You may even fall and break a bone because you didn't heed your body's message to slow down.

Your body and mind are working together to prompt action that protects your wellbeing, and you need to listen. Conditions such as irritable bowel and fibromyalgia are often exacerbated in situations where the body is signalling that its needs aren't being met or are ignored. As you develop the habit of tuning into your body's signals, ask yourself: 'What is my body trying to tell me that requires me to act differently?'

Recognising how emotions manifest in the body

Painful feelings create different body states, signalling that all is not well. These emotions reflect the chemical changes going on within body cells. You may notice the physiological change before you tune into the emotion. Alternatively, you may realise that you're feeling physically exhausted or unwell because you're miserable about something.

Tapping into your body's signals helps you to recognise and heal emotional problems. It enables you to develop greater self-knowledge. Your body signals are providing the information you need in order to respond wisely and move forward with a greater feeling of control.

Sometimes, physical reactions to emotions are immediate. Here are some examples:

- **Anger:** Your skin gets itchy and your muscles tense when someone gives you a dressing down.
- **Fear/danger:** The hairs on the back of the neck bristle when you walk in a dark area of a town late at night on your own.
- **Hurt:** Your eyes well up, you look down at the ground and your shoulders drop when someone teases you.
- **Mistrust:** You get a 'gut sensation', perhaps of unease, as you feel that someone is about to mislead you or is lying to you.

Sometimes, your physical reaction to emotion isn't immediate. If you don't deal with the emotion, you hold it in your body where it can manifest in the following symptoms:

- **Cardiovascular:** Palpitations; missed beats; angina-like pains.

- **Dermatological:** Eczema; rashes; flushing; exacerbation of psoriasis.

- **Gastrointestinal:** Nausea; bloating; constipation; 'shaking inside'; dry throat; sensations of restricted swallowing.

- **Mental:** Anxiety/panic/defensive behaviour.

- **Musculoskeletal:** Cramps/stiffness; fatigue; undue tiredness on exercise; muscle twitches; painful joints; jaw clenching.

- **Neurological:** Dizziness; feelings of unreality; visual disturbance; headaches; 'pins and needles' in face or extremities; increased sensitivity to stimulation (for example, light, noise and pressure).

- **Respiratory:** Irritable cough; tight chest; sighing or yawning; breathlessness/lack of air.

- **Sleep-related:** difficulty getting to sleep, or early waking. (See Chapter 5 for specific information about sleep.)

Doctors call a variety of symptoms in different body areas that have no obvious medical cause 'medically unexplained'. Your body is warning you that a physical or emotional need exists that you have to address.

Consider the physical-emotional link in the following emotions, and what you can do to alleviate the symptoms:

- **Anger** leads to quick, tense, sudden or jerky body movements, the eyes become wide and the skin flushes. Identify what you're angry about.

- **Anxiety** may upset sleep, increasing your likelihood of illness as the immune system rebalances itself at night. More frequent infections may follow. Recognise that anxiety represents thoughts about an imagined future that may not be as bad as you suppose.

- **Depression** leads to your body feeling sluggish, as if your life energy is drained. Shoulders hunch and the back is bent, as if carrying a heavy load. Unreleased emotion slows you. Identify what's weighing you down.

- **Excessive guilt** can lead to self-blame and may show in the skin with rashes resulting from self-irritation. Self-criticism and self-blame may lead to self-harm. Consider how to accept your fallibility and forgive your mistakes.

- **Hurt and sadness** create sighing. The corners of the mouth turn down. The eyes may be dry with suppressed sadness, or tears may come easily. You may experience a heavy or uncomfortable sensation in your stomach or solar plexus. Identify what's causing you pain and what you can do about it.

Understanding where you hold emotions

If you become more familiar with your own physical responses, you can develop the ability to recognise and understand where your emotions are held in your body.

Write about a situation in which something happened to upset you. Using Table 2-1, examine the situation, your bodily sensations and your feelings. We provide an example at the top of the table to help illustrate the kinds of things to write.

Table 2-1 Connecting Physical Feelings with Emotional Ones	
Situation	
Being cut up by a car on the motorway.	Bodily Sensations
Quick response to protect me by swerving and braking. Tense and sweaty hands on the wheel, sudden flush to the skin, tense arms and shoulders. Later, stomach ache and loss of appetite, and then very tired.	Feelings
Fear as I swerved, and then anger.	

You can use this exercise to explore all your emotions – looking at situations that made you feel sad, scared, angry, hurt and guilty. By noticing which physical sensations accompany your feelings, you're better equipped to notice what your body is trying to tell you when it feels ill, in pain or tired.

When you're caught up in an emotional state without being able to interpret what you need to do, check whether you have physical symptoms that you can't explain. Can you identify an emotion that accompanies the symptoms? If so, can you take any action to address the situation and relieve the feeling? For example, if you're experiencing a headache, identify recent situations that may have upset you emotionally before the onset of the headache. Review the situation, name the emotion and consider what action may help you reduce the emotional intensity of the situation. If you can't immediately connect a cause to your symptom, try keeping a Symptom Diary in your journal for a few days, observing the symptom, the situation, the gap between your emotional needs and what happened, so that you can then identify what action you need to take.

Healing the cause and not just the symptom

You need to identify the source of your emotional and physical disturbance. Sometimes doing so is easy, and we suggest in the earlier section 'Tackling the persistent stress response' that you review your life to identify people and situations that cause you stress.

You may find that you have symptoms that you can't explain. The Body Scan Technique that follows helps you to identify the emotional issue that may be causing the symptoms. You calm down your mind by tuning into the wisdom and messages held in your body.

1. **Find a place where you aren't going to be disturbed.**

   Don't make yourself too comfortable. Perhaps sit upright on a chair. Allow the curve of your lower back to be concave, which happens naturally when you lock your hands behind your neck and press the elbows back. Then gently drop the arms by your side.

2. **Start by noticing your feet on the floor.**

   What does the contact feel like – are your legs heavy? Do you notice gravity pressing you down? Don't feel you have to do anything, just notice and observe the feelings and sensations.

3. **Move your attention up from your feet through your ankles, to the upper thighs.**

   Notice how the area feels. Can you detect tension or tightness?

4. **Move attention up through the back to the shoulders and then down the front.**

   Notice your breathing without trying to change it. How do your stomach, chest and heart feel?

5. **Go up to the throat, the mouth, the jaw, face and eyes and then to the neck and down once more to your back.**

   Focus on each area in turn, observing sensations.

6. **Now tune in to the breath by placing a hand on the lower stomach and feeling the hand expand as you breathe in.**

   Let the in-breath be gentle and the out-breath slower. Let the breath out with pursed lips; this may release as a hiss or sigh.

7. **Now that the body is quiet, return to the situation where you felt emotional pain.**

   What was happening then? Remember as much detail as possible and try to think of the situation in terms of a logical journey from start to finish. What were your feelings, bodily sensations, thoughts and behaviour? What did you do? What did you need to do? You gain insight into the cause and the emotion, but also what your body was telling you to do to heal the emotional wound.

8. **Make a note of what your body may have been signalling to you.**

What insights do you have about what was causing your distress? Consider what you may have done to express your feelings in a way that allowed you to be heard. How can you get your needs met in a better way for you and those involved? Consider how you can use this information when you face challenging situations in future.

You can record this technique onto a tape or CD so that you can relax and follow the process.

Knowing how to respond to body talk in words

Holding feelings inside can make you ill. Your body's production of illness-protecting cells actually goes down when you hold in emotion. Conversely, expressing your emotion, verbally or in written form, boosts your immune system. In one research study, simply writing about strongly emotional situations for 20 minutes a day for four days in a row improved participants' immune function.

Only by reflecting and asking what your body signals are expressing to you, can you begin to be aware of your needs. Finding a way to express your emotions appropriately takes time, reflection and planning. Turn to Chapters 6, 8 and 9 to find out how you can safely express your feelings.

Emotional symptoms aren't always simple. They need interpretation, which is why your brain has developed to allow you to express what you need using language. Although, genetically, humans are very similar to monkeys and apes, the use of language allowing people to express their feelings is a crucial aspect that separates humans from their earlier ancestors.

When feelings don't have an outlet, they can lead to illness, self-destructive behaviours or inner emotional upset. You can achieve a healthy body and happy mind by expressing how you feel.

Start to interpret the link between any unexplained physical symptoms you experience that have not been diagnosed as disease-related. Examine the connection between the signal and any potential underlying emotion disturbance. If you find a connection, then the next step is to express your emotional needs in an appropriate way.

How belief becomes biology

Increasing evidence exists of the power of mind over matter. Thinking can make you ill or make you better because your mind and body work in unison. The *placebo effect* (where a patient gets well while unknowingly taking a sugar pill rather than real medication) demonstrates the ability of the mind to heal you physically.

Optimism supports both health and emotional wellbeing. Any activity that makes you happy enhances immunity. Your tissues are intelligent. Your immune system has the capacity for memory and responds to positive feelings.

The most immediate way for you to help your immune system is by introducing positive and life-affirming responses to your situation, which reduce the body's state of hyper-arousal and stress. You're able to move feelings from defeat or despair to hope and action by changing the focus of your mind from the negative to the positive and creating a plan to have your needs met.

For example, research suggests that after being diagnosed with breast cancer, patients who increase hope for recovery with the clear intention to be positive about an effective future have better quality of life and, for some, improved recovery. Another study shows that when patients decrease their stress and quieten their bodies, they reduce their levels of the hormone cortisol and their prognosis improves. The Appendix contains details of organisations and books to help you find ways of living well with cancer and other life-threatening diseases.

Following are some body talk messages that you may be able to fit to your own situation.

My symptoms are telling me to:

- Stop allowing myself to be dumped upon and start saying no
- Stop bottling up my feelings and start letting them out safely
- Stop holding on to self-blame and self-criticism and start accepting myself
- Stop hurting and start living
- Stop putting off what needs to be done and start doing
- Stop trying to be perfect and start acting like I'm a fallible human being

Lyn, aged 45, developed severe tiredness and spent three months in bed. She was unable to sleep, all her muscles ached and she felt unbearably tense. These physical symptoms had developed after she had been working very hard as a social worker in a child protection team, helping abused children. Although she knew she was taking on too much, Lyn didn't want to let the children down.

Lyn's childhood had been marred by her alcoholic mother's neglect and abuse. In one-to-one counselling, she discovered that her body was holding on to the old feelings of childhood sadness and abuse. She realised that her compulsion, largely unconscious, was to stop other children being abused in the way she'd been. Through coaching she discovered her body was telling her that she needed to stop looking after other people and start looking after herself and her own needs. She was finally able to speak about her pain and then release the strong feelings her body was carrying in words. She began sleeping better and feeling more energetic and relaxed.

You may have developed a pattern during childhood of holding in negative feelings rather than expressing them. This situation can result in your serving the needs of others before yourself or becoming *co-dependent,* where you take care of others but also need them to take care of you and feel abandoned if they don't. As an adult, you need to take care of yourself and express yourself. This action is the responsible – not selfish – one to take. Chapter 11 helps you think about 'parenting' yourself and taking an adult role in life.

Dealing with depression

Depression occurs when you fail to address issues over a period of time and unhappiness builds. Feeling positive becomes difficult when you're depressed. You feel as if you're continuously under a dark cloud because you're carrying a physical and emotional load.

If you've stopped enjoying activities that used to give you pleasure or you feel continuously down or emotionally flat for two weeks, doctors are likely to consider depression as a diagnosis. Although antidepressants are still recommended for severe depression, modern research, supported by the UK government's National Institute for Clinical Excellence, doesn't recommend antidepressants as first line treatment in mild and moderate depression. Mindfulness-based treatment approaches (see Chapter 13) and cognitive behavioural thinking strategies (Chapter 12) are now recommended for initial and ongoing treatment of depression.

If you're depressed, you may also like to take a look at *Overcoming Depression For Dummies* (Wiley) by Elaine Iljon Foreman, Charles Elliot and Laura Smith. You can also seek professional support. Trained professionals such as counsellors or coaches can help you find positive emotions and meet your emotional needs.

One of the first steps in healing depression is to try to access memories from before your depression, to help you remember what happiness feels like. Recovery occurs when you can access good feelings again, so that the depression lifts. You then return to the sense that you have value as a person and that your life is worthwhile. Depression can provide you with an opportunity to review whether your current situation and your real emotional needs are mismatched. By dealing with your depression, you can relieve yourself of considerable physical and emotional load, allowing you to create a more fulfilling life.

Tuning Into Your Breathing

Breathing keeps you alive but people often take it for granted. Breath plays a crucial role not only in your physical survival but also in your emotional well-being. When you're upset, you tend to breathe in a way that hinders rather than helps you calm down. So focusing on your breathing is an excellent way to relieve emotional tension.

Understanding over-breathing

Breathing is about balance. You take in oxygen with your in-breath and release carbon dioxide with the out-breath. The levels of oxygen and carbon dioxide affect the blood supply in your brain.

- ✔ When you breathe in and out slowly using your diaphragm, you achieve good carbon dioxide levels and your body is happy.

- ✔ When you breathe too quickly and shallowly, as you do when under stress or emotionally upset, you're *over-breathing*. Your chest tightens and the breath moves away from the diaphragm in the abdomen and into the upper chest.

Your body doesn't function at its best when you over-breathe because carbon dioxide levels in your blood go down. As a result, your blood releases less oxygen to tissues in your body. Blood leaves your thinking brain and moves to the central areas of the emotional brain. When you over-breathe, you're truly more emotional and have difficulty thinking clearly.

Sometimes, when stress and emotional overload persists, over-breathing can become *hyperventilation*, when you breathe much too fast. This breathing pattern disorder is commonly associated with panic attacks. If you find yourself panicking and struggling to breathe calmly, breathe into a paper bag or your cupped hands. By re-breathing carbon dioxide, your carbon dioxide levels go up again, helping you to calm down. Think calming thoughts such as, 'This is just a panic attack. I can think and breathe calmly and it will pass.' (Some mind-body practitioners use *capnometry* to measure your breath's carbon dioxide levels and determine whether your breathing is appropriately balanced.)

Using the six-breaths-a-minute technique

Your breathing changes rhythm when you're emotionally upset. To notice this change, listen to the way your breath is flowing in and out. When you're tense, the rhythm of the breath becomes more uneven and usually moves into the upper chest. You notice more movement on the in-breath than the out-breath. When you're calm, you breathe into your diaphragm in your abdomen, and you breathe out for longer.

Practise the following simple six-breaths-per-minute breathing exercise to create a state of physical and emotional equilibrium:

1. **Wherever you are, stop and bring the focus of attention into your body.**

   Do the body scan exercise we explain in the earlier section 'Healing the cause and not just the symptom'. Calm your mind.

2. **Tune into your breathing and move the breath from your upper chest into your diaphragm or abdomen.**

   Notice the diaphragm descending and the abdomen expanding as you breathe in. The ribs move outwards.

3. **Take three breaths, breathing in for the count of 4 and out for the count of 6.**

   As you breathe in, draw in a remembered sense of a time and place where you felt peaceful and loving to yourself. As you breathe out, imagine the breath flowing through your body. Visualise that this breath is carrying oxygen back through all the tissues of your body.

Adjust this pattern to give you a ten-second cycle per breath, or six breaths per minute. Try to practise this rhythm for ten minutes each day as part of looking after yourself and staying emotionally and physically well.

You don't have to shut your eyes or go anywhere special to do this exercise: you can sit practising this breathing exercise at your desk, and no one will notice.

Using this breathing exercise doesn't just help you calm down from emotional distress. Calming your breathing can also help with health problems. Research shows that ten minutes of slow breathing is effective in reducing symptoms for people who have asthma or raised blood pressure.

If you feel you need more help to calm your breathing, you can try using a 'breathing pacer', a device that tracks your in-breath and your out-breath so that you can find the six-breaths-per-minute rhythm. Ask your GP or a mind-body professional about working with this device.

ANECDOTE

Overcoming performance anxiety

Research suggests that at least a third of musicians in top orchestras, despite having wonderful professional technique, suffer from troublesome symptoms and anxiety that interfere with their ability to perform. The research shows that their stress leads to over-breathing, affecting oxygen release in the brain and holding the performer in a state of struggle.

Sylvia plays in the violin section of a symphony orchestra. The schedule is heavy. She also has two small children who need reliable childcare. One day before a concert her usual carer became ill and Sylvia had to find a replacement at the last moment, which added further stress. When the concert started, she felt tired. With a mounting sense of panic, her fingers grew much stiffer.

Fortunately, Sylvia discovered anxiety-reducing techniques involving breath and visualisation.

During a quiet period of the concert, she practised a breathing space meditation we describe in Chapter 13. She centred her body and deliberately and calmly reviewed her posture. She felt her feet on the floor and moved her attention through each area of her body, starting with her feet. She noticed the stiffness and tension in her shoulders. She then settled her breathing, feeling her breath move from the upper chest panic-breathing down to her abdomen. She also substituted anxiety-inducing thoughts such as 'I can't do this' with 'I know this works well, and I know I can do it'.

Finally, she imagined an inner smile and the pleasure that she was sure to feel at the end of the concert. Her body responded and helped her perform well again.

Chapter 3

Tuning In to Your Emotions

- -

In This Chapter

▶ Recognising your emotions

▶ Getting comfortable with your emotional signals

▶ Rediscovering positive aspects of life

▶ Filtering out overwhelming feelings

- -

*T*uning into your emotions is an essential step towards emotional healing. Few people are taught about the nature of emotions. Most people learn through experience without any formal information on the subject. Perhaps you notice a parent who's upset, a teacher who's irritable or a friend who's anxious. You feel hurt when classmates leave you out of a game in the playground. You cry because you fall over, or get angry when things don't go your way. These events are a natural part of growing up. But teachers and parents rarely explain that your emotions signal what you need and provide messages about how to take care of yourself.

Most of the time you probably function reasonably well. But unresolved emotional issues can lie just beneath the surface of your consciousness, ready to shock you to attention. This reaction can happen when external pressures build up or when an event reminds you of previous overwhelming stress and you suddenly find yourself flooded by emotion. In order to avoid being caught by surprise, you need to tap into how you're really feeling.

The aim of this chapter is to share some methods for tuning in to your emotions. Using a variety of approaches, you discover just how you feel, and how your thoughts, expectations and experiences shape your emotional responses. We show you how useful and necessary your feelings are and help you to befriend them, and we help identify which situations enhance your mood so that you can make choices to focus on these in the future.

You may find yourself deliberately, or unknowingly, blocking or burying some emotions because they're too uncomfortable or painful. Although this response can be a practical solution to managing yourself within situations where expressing your feelings isn't appropriate – for example in the workplace – we don't recommend this strategy in the long term. Emotions can burst out when not acknowledged, and so you need to work in tandem with them to gain release from strong emotions that impede your quality of life.

Observing Your Emotional Gauge

Much of the time people are too busy doing tasks to observe how they're feeling. In order to develop a deeper understanding of your emotions, you need to become more focused on what you're feeling each day. The following sections help you to notice and accept your broad spectrum of emotions.

Starting out: I feel. . .

The following exercise helps you begin to get to grips with how you feel. Take a look at Table 3-1 and familiarise yourself with a range of emotions. Notice the ones that you experience and consider whether you feel these frequently, sometimes or rarely – for example, 'I feel happy sometimes'. Put F for those emotions you experience frequently, S for sometimes and R for rarely.

At this stage you're just information-gathering. You're tuning in. Don't try to rationalise, justify or judge the emotions. Let them just be there and observe them. Also, pay attention to which emotions you experienced more frequently in the past, what emotions you're feeling today and what emotions you may be anticipating in the future. For example, many people feel fear when considering a future event that in the past created anxiety.

Table 3-1	Emotional Awareness Exercise
I Feel. . .	*Frequently, Sometimes or Rarely*
Happy	
Sad	
Angry	
Anxious	
Resentful	
Guilty	
Jealous	
Hopeless	
Depressed	
Annoyed	
Vengeful	
Disappointed	
Afraid	
Inspired	

I Feel. . .	Frequently, Sometimes or Rarely
Calm	
Optimistic	
Ashamed	
Lonely	
Loving	
Loved	
Peaceful	
Disgusted	
Surprised	
Joyous	
Envious	
Regretful	
Frustrated	
Hurt	

Journaling emotions for self-discovery

In the preceding section, we ask you to name your feelings. Now you can begin to notice what stimulates your emotions, for example:

- Your own thoughts
- Other people
- Situations that don't work out the way you want them to

Keeping a journal in which to record your emotions is an excellent method to fathom precisely what influences your feelings. We suggest that you buy a special book for this activity and choose a specific time to make the entries: for example, first thing in the morning or last thing at night. Or you may want to buy a smaller book that you can put in your pocket or handbag so that you can jot down your experiences during the day.

Make feelings the focus of everything you write. Notice

- What mood you're in when you wake up, and whether that mood stays with you through the day.
- Which situations lift your emotions and which bring you down.
- Which people make you feel good and who drains your energy.
- Whether specific emotions trigger physical symptoms, and what those symptoms are – for example loss of energy, tension, butterflies.

Here are some sentences to help start you off:

- ✔ I enjoyed today because. . .
- ✔ I had a lousy day because. . .
- ✔ I was really upset when. . .
- ✔ I felt fantastic when. . .

Try to write non-stop for ten minutes, if possible without interruption. You're on a journey of self-discovery, reflecting on your experiences and how you're feeling within the situations you face that day.

We suggest you keep this journal every day for at least one month. Several of our clients make journal-keeping a lifetime's habit. They find it helps them to keep in tune with their emotions.

At the end of a week, review your writing and look for themes:

- ✔ Do you experience one emotion more than another?
- ✔ What situations cause you to feel more emotional than others?
- ✔ Did your own part in the situation cause you emotion or was the cause what other people said or did?
- ✔ Do you recognise the person you're reading about as yourself? Or do you hear the voices of your family or other influential characters coming out in how you're thinking and experiencing life?
- ✔ Do you notice trigger themes, thoughts or expectations that stir up your feelings?

At this stage you're doing no more than becoming familiar with yourself and the feelings you experience. Your emotions constantly signal you to be true to yourself and to take care of your personal needs. This discovery can be a revelation in itself, as the example of a client's journal in Figure 3-1 shows.

Emotions provide you with messages that lead you towards people, events and activities that meet your needs. Your feelings move you away from pain towards pleasure. Noticing who and what makes you happy or sad, energised or fatigued, enables you to take heed of the messages through action. If you're detached from your feelings you can't translate this inner wisdom.

Noticing your breathing signals

One of the simplest and most powerful ways of tuning into emotions is to become familiar with the signals that your breath is giving you. When you're upset, excited or disturbed, your breath tends to move into your upper chest, becoming shallow and quicker. Sometimes you notice that your voice becomes thin and high as the quality of your breathing depletes. The result can be embarrassing – particularly if you're trying to speak confidently on a subject, such as when making a sales pitch or giving a presentation.

Monday morning	Monday evening
Woke up feeling miserable. Grey skies, dreading the commute, I know I should have finished the presentation on Friday. My boss will be furious. I wish I could be more efficient. I also wish I could say 'no' – I just keep taking on more and more when I know I haven't got the time to finish it. If only I could just stay in bed and hide.	Looking at what I wrote this morning I realise that I was feeling helpless. The world seemed to be demanding too much of me and I seem unable to protect myself and rise above it. I just get cross with myself when I can't say no and then get bolshie with my boss and storm off home without finishing. I ended up with a headache. Reading this entry makes me realise that something has got to change. . .

Figure 3-1:
Example of a feelings journal.

Tune into your breathing from time to time during the day and notice where the breath is focused. If you find that you're breathing in your upper chest, ask yourself:

- ✔ What emotion am I experiencing?
- ✔ What's causing this emotion?
- ✔ What am I thinking or expecting here?
- ✔ Is this emotion helping me manage this situation?

To centre yourself and control your state, visualise moving the breath down from your chest to your stomach. For detailed breathing methods, see Chapter 2.

Becoming more familiar with your breathing signals enables you to get in touch with your emotions and analyse whether the feelings are appropriate to the current situation. Alternatively, you may choose to take action to change your emotional state in order to manage the situation more effectively. (See 'Cutting out the emotional noise' in this chapter and also Chapters 12 and 13 which cover this aspect in detail.)

Listening to the intuitive whispers

Emotions may send you signals through your intuition. Have you ever had a gut feeling about a person or situation but then tried to overrule it with your rational brain, only to regret that you didn't take heed of the intuitive whisper of your inner wisdom? Your intuition works through physical and emotional sensations. Have you experienced the following:

- A bad feeling from shaking someone's hand?

- The sense that someone is 'shifty' or not to be trusted?

- A feeling in your stomach that warns you not to go somewhere?

- The immediate knowledge from the tone of voice on the telephone that the person is going to try to sell you something?

- The suspicion that someone isn't telling you the whole truth?

- A strong drive to do something even though no apparent logic backs up your decision?

With practice you can discover how to tap into these whispers and decide more consciously whether they have a valid message for you. Checking your instincts with your rational brain is quite reasonable, but listen closely when you have a really strong sense that something is right or wrong. Here are some examples:

- Someone who has a premonition that something is going to happen.

- An entrepreneur who has a vision of building a business but no rational idea as to how to secure investment.

- Someone who feels that he must travel to a particular country and then meets his life partner on that trip.

Knowing where feelings manifest

As you work on acknowledging and accepting feelings, you aren't just looking for a particular emotion you feel inside. You find emotional signals on other levels too, such as:

- Thoughts: 'I'm really angry that my partner doesn't support me'.

- Behaviours: becoming defensive or aggressive.

- Actions: suddenly taking action without prior planning because your emotions have overwhelmed your rational mind.

- Physical symptoms: waking up with a sick feeling in your stomach.

As you hunt out your feelings, keep these other aspects of yourself in mind as well. You may just find that although you don't *feel* cross, you're certainly *behaving* as though you're cross, and though you don't think you're unhappy, your body says otherwise.

Ours may not always be to reason why. Life moves in mysterious ways and people can't always explain why they did or didn't do something. Intuitive whispers can be powerful life-savers – think of deciding not to get on a plane that crashed, or leaving a building that burst into flames seconds later – and can lead you towards the achievement of your dreams.

Can you think of times when your intuition gave you a message? Did you heed it? Spend the next month tuning into these messages. Keep a journal that tracks you feelings and events and see what you observe.

Making Friends with Your Feelings

The process of emotional healing is one that you can apply for a lifetime. You can work on healing past pain or hurt, but part of the human condition is to continue to experience ups and downs. The ability to tune in and make friends with your feelings helps you to understand the true nature of your own personality and needs.

Everyone has different *emotional personalities.* Some people are more prone to anxiety, others to anger. When you take some time to identify your characteristic personality – such as 'the anxious self' or 'the self-doubting self' – you may better understand some of your past decisions. Be gentle with your labelling; you're describing yourself with kindness rather than judgement.

Getting to know your 'anxious self" or 'self-doubting self' may help you discover the root causes of these feelings. For example, you may discover that that the predominance of your 'anxious self' was sparked by insecurity within your family. Befriending and empowering this aspect of yourself can allow you to heal and manage your anxious automatic memory responses to similar situations (see Chapter 2) and make more helpful choices about how you respond in the future.

Accepting your emotional responses

As you identify your emotions, you need to accept them as part of your character. Acknowledging and accepting your emotions takes practice because sometimes pretending that you feel fine even if you don't is easier. Many people are afraid of their emotions and try to do all they can to avoid feeling them. They worry that if they start to cry they may never stop, or if they allow themselves to express anger they may harm themselves or others. They may disguise difficult emotions with denial or *over-activity,* such as workaholism or obsessive tidiness. People can even be nervous of expressing happiness.

Your childhood and social conditioning can influence how easily you accept your emotions. In some families people visibly express emotions; in others they keep feelings under wraps as if emotions are something to be ashamed of. Actually, emotions are vital to your health. Telling yourself 'I shouldn't be feeling this' achieves nothing. Just accept your feelings rather than judge them as right or wrong. Your feelings just 'are'.

You can't control your feelings, but you can control how you choose to manage them. Having a feeling doesn't mean you have to act on it or express it. You can pause and check out the feeling before you automatically respond in a way you may regret. By tuning into yourself – noticing the emotion and accepting it before you decide whether or not to express it – you gain control of your behaviour.

Understanding that feelings are about meeting needs

Your emotions are a core part of you. They exist to work in your interests – to alert you to your needs and warn you when those needs aren't met. Some emotions aren't comfortable, which can lead you to avoid tuning into them. However, even anger, sadness and frustration give you valuable signals about something that isn't working for you. Tuning in allows you to become more familiar with these messages and become more aware of the following:

- ✔ Which emotions you've been experiencing but not acknowledging.
- ✔ Which activities and situations reward your sense of self and fulfilment.
- ✔ When you would benefit from staying calm.
- ✔ What you may need to say to someone and how to say it appropriately.
- ✔ Whether the emotions you're feeling are a genuine reflection of your present situation or coloured by past influences

Look for an acceptable balance here because your needs may not coincide with the needs of the people around you. For example, you may need closeness and they may feel the need for space; you may need to talk about a problem but they may prefer not to. Everyone has his or her own needs. When your emotional needs don't match your partner's or your social group's, simply choose to acknowledge the difference and seek a compromise solution that is acceptable to you both.

Things don't always go your way and this can leave you with a residue of disturbing emotions. Continue to honour these uncomfortable feelings because they show you that the situation isn't yet solved and requires further action. Discomfort remains until you either find a solution to the external event or find a way to resolve your own feelings about the situation. To find ways to make peace with difficult feelings, see Chapter 13.

Pattern matching to past emotional events

When you befriend your emotions, you discover that they're acting to protect you – but they may not always be relevant to you current situation. Your emotions may be a reflection of the past.

Emotional experiences earlier in life can shape your response to subsequent events. An emotional pattern can emerge in situations or relationships where a new experience sets off a previous memory. Your emotional brain is making a connection between the past event and the present situation. You can benefit from observing and analysing situations where you become emotional and check whether you're reacting consciously to the current challenge or responding automatically, triggered by something from the past.

For example, if your first boyfriend dumped you and didn't treat you the way you wanted, you may retain an irrational belief that 'all boyfriends are beastly and hurt you'. This emotional memory may protect you from being hurt by subsequent boyfriends, but it also may deny you the joy of making a good relationship later in life because you're too defensive to allow anyone in. You've set up a habitual pattern that needs understanding, challenging and changing for your future happiness.

What was useful once may not be useful today, so be alert to getting sucked into past dramas, pain, conflict or knee-jerk reactions to situations. Keep your thinking brain actively scanning for the messages that your emotions are giving you about what you need to do *today* to maintain your wellbeing.

To change a pattern, you can apply the Five-Step Emotional Healing Process that we introduce in Chapter 1 and summarise on the Cheat Sheet. However, if you suspect a current situation you're facing matches the emotional patterns of past emotional challenges, try the following pattern matching activity:

1. **Describe and explore the current situation that's creating emotional disturbance.**

   Notice who's involved, what's happening, when and where.

2. **Consider the impact that the current situation is having on you.**

   Consider four different aspects of how you're being impacted:

   - The physical symptoms and signals that you're experiencing (for example, breathlessness or fatigue)

   - The dominant emotion or emotions

   - The thoughts that are coming into your mind (for example, 'I just can't cope with the rudeness of my teenage daughter!')

   - How the situation impacts your behaviours and lifestyle (for example, you're more irritable with everyone and your marriage is suffering)

3. **Carve out some quiet time, calm your body and evaluate the situation.**

   Calming your body quietens your mind. The Body Scan method in Chapter 2 can help. When you're calm, quietly ask yourself some questions:

   - Is this situation a pattern match? How so? (For example, your teenager's rudeness may trigger memories of the hurt you felt when your elder sister persistently put you down.)
   - Am I behaving appropriately for today's situation?
   - What are my current options?
   - What precisely caused me to experience this feeling now?

4. **Switch out of the pattern-match response by taking action.**

   Stop a pattern-match response at four different levels:

   - Make physical changes (for example, you may develop the ability to calm yourself before responding).
   - Change your emotional state (perhaps you can move from irritation to being in control; see 'Cutting out the emotional noise' in this chapter for more ideas).
   - Develop new thinking strategies to use in the situation (for example, tell yourself 'I can manage and stay calm'; see Chapter 12).
   - Change your behaviour to respond assertively to express your feelings and needs (for example, find effective ways to state that rudeness is unacceptable – but you're able to listen).

Healing occurs as you let go of an old pattern that incapacitates you and develop the ability to step out of the situation, respond and act appropriately – without getting caught up in outdated reactivity.

Sally had experienced a fear of lifts since she was young. In coaching she recognised that she picked up this fear from her mother who was once stuck in a lift for nine hours during a power failure. This fear was driving Sally to walk 12 flights of stairs at her new office building, which was exhausting. She worked through the pattern matching action and decided to work on calming herself, rehearsing going into the lift, changing her thinking from 'I hate lifts' to 'I can stay calm and manage', and practising in incremental steps getting used to being in the lift (such as riding for 1 floor and then eventually all 12).

Focusing on the positives

When you're in touch with your feelings, you have the choice of which feeling to focus on. Strong negative emotions can interrupt your ability to notice the good things in life. Part of the process of emotional healing is to awaken your senses to what makes you feel good – and you do this by tuning into your positive emotions.

For a fortnight try to identify which situations and people help you to feel happy, relaxed and content. Make a list in your journal of the experiences that raise your mood. Table 3-2 gives you an idea of how to develop this list.

Table 3-2	The Positive Mood Identifier Notebook		
Situation	*People*	*Mood*	*Reason*
Eating my sandwich in the park	No one, just me	Peaceful	Not having to make conversation with anyone
Going to the pub on Friday night	Joe and Will	Light-hearted, jokey	They help me forget my problems

In order to create your list initially, you need to become more open and observant in order to identify what makes you feel good. Stick with it and when the sun is shining, the sky is blue or you notice a bird singing, jot down the small pleasures in life. Gradually, this will open your eyes to the good things.

The quality of your life is shaped by the quality of your focus. For example, some days you may get up in the morning and feel totally overwhelmed by all the things you have to do before you go to work, and end up tetchy with your partner, the children, yourself, the cat or the toaster for taking too long! Yet other days you do exactly the same tasks in the same amount of time and feel cheery. What makes the difference? The answer is likely to be the focus of your thinking. On the first occasion you concentrate on everything that upsets you; on the second you focus on aspects of the situation that help you to feel good – the smell of fresh coffee, the postman coming early or finding your car keys at the first attempt.

Develop the ability to focus on the positive and befriend those emotions that make you feel good. When you plan time with people and activities that boost your mood and the feeling of contentment with yourself and with life, your mind and senses become attuned to picking out those aspects of life that you enjoy. The quality of your life improves accordingly.

Charles's bedroom view

Charles doesn't get on well with his sister. They've argued from childhood and continue to battle over family matters even though they're now in their 50s. Charles describes how Christmas presents are exchanged reluctantly and says his sister is mean. 'She just chooses gifts that insult me and remind me that she doesn't love me,' he says. When asked what he did with these gifts, he comments that he has one gift – a magnet – on the radiator beside his bed 'just to remind me how awful she is'. When asked how this helps him to feel good about himself, Charles realises that by focusing on this magnet every time he goes to bed or wakes up, he's undermining his own happiness. He decides to throw the magnet in the bin and puts a glass bowl that he likes beside the bed so that he can focus on something he likes, and that makes him feel good.

Calling Time Out

Sometimes, tuning into emotions can be overwhelming. They can fill your head and interrupt normal thoughts and reactions. Occasionally, you just need a break, and that's okay.

Cutting out the emotional noise

Familiarising yourself with your feelings can help you work through

- ✔ Out-dated habitual responses that are no longer appropriate.
- ✔ Destructive behaviours that you fall into when in certain emotional states.

The trick is to become aware of the *triggers* that push you into the unhelpful emotional state. Triggers can be thoughts, situations or a particular person or group. When you notice your body changing and becoming tense, you need a way to quieten the noise of the mind so that you can gather your thoughts and decide calmly how to respond. This response gives you the ability to restore your sense of perspective.

The *Radio technique* helps you to become aware of your thoughts. Stop to notice what 'radio station' you're tuned in to. Here are a few you may discover:

- ✔ Panic FM: 'everything is going to go wrong . . . I can't cope'.
- ✔ The Regret Station: 'how could I have . . . why didn't I. . .'.

✔ Anger Blast: 'how could you have . . . how dare you. . .'.

✔ Irritable Shortwave: 'why on earth does this have to happen. . .'.

✔ Revenge LW: 'I'll get you back one day. . .'.

✔ Jealousy FM: 'I'm sure you're cheating on me. . .'.

✔ Poor Me DAB: 'I do so much for everyone else – and they don't do anything for me!'

When you know which station you're listening to, decide whether this behaviour is helping you to feel good and have a good day or is upsetting you. Thinking straight or making good decisions when you're overcome with emotional thinking is difficult. Always remember that you have the power to control the switch. By changing the focus of your thoughts, you can tune to

✔ Music FM: play or imagine calming music.

✔ Supportive FM: create a slow gentle voice in your head that supports and encourages you.

✔ Silence FM: where you're able to switch off and stop your thoughts for a period of time to gain some peace.

Set yourself certain times to check into your thinking and notice which station you're tuned to. Make sure that you tune in at least three times a day – perhaps every time you sit down for a meal.

Taking a break from overwhelming feelings

Getting in touch with your feelings can be scary stuff. You may feel nervous that, when released, your emotions are going to overwhelm you. Don't worry – just take each step towards emotional healing slowly and gently. You can always switch off from this work when you choose to do so by taking time out and focusing on something else. Here are some ideas:

✔ Go for a walk.

✔ Listen to an upbeat or calming piece of music.

✔ Talk to a friend.

✔ Take 5–10 minutes to practise your six-breaths-a-minute breathing exercise (which we describe in Chapter 2).

✔ Picture an uplifting image that your brain can focus on, such as a calm lake, a mountain or a sunset. Choose an image that makes you feel good and capture it in your mind, or carry a postcard or photo in your wallet.

Part II
Emotions and Your Body

'I've completely changed thanks to
finding new perspectives through
emotional healing, but nobody believes me.'

In this part . . .

*P*ay attention to what you eat and how you take care of yourself physically, because both activities reflect your underlying emotional state.

Healthy eating is key to your wellbeing. The food you consume affects how you feel and how you feel affects your choice of food. Get ready to re-engage with your own body rhythms, enjoy a good night's sleep and re-balance rest and activity. We also introduce you to some simple and practical activities to release emotional tension.

Chapter 4

Unravelling Feelings and Food: What's Eating You?

In This Chapter

▶ Connecting feelings and food

▶ Getting to grips with healthy eating

▶ Making plans to take care of your diet and wellbeing

*W*hat you eat influences how you feel and how you feel influences what you eat. When you feel good about yourself you usually find that eating healthily is easier. And when you feel depressed, fatigued or gloomy the temptation is to reach for foods that you know rationally aren't good for you but you think comfort you. You often feel worse afterwards, however, because this approach simply makes you aware that you haven't taken control of what you eat. In contrast, eating healthily helps you feel better both physically and emotionally.

Food keeps you alive; it is an essential part of what your body needs for energy. Taking heed of what you eat signifies that you feel your life is worthwhile; not bothering often signifies that you lack self-esteem and a sense of purpose. Food is therefore a physical reflection of your inner emotional state.

This chapter aims to help you think about your own relationship with food and whether your eating habits support good feelings. We provide exercises to help you review patterns of what and how you eat and provide you with tips to develop a nutritious diet that feeds mind, body and soul.

Identifying Emotional Undercurrents in Your Eating Habits

Biologically speaking, you eat to give your body the fuel it needs to function. But, of course, eating is also a lot more than that. Food is tied closely to emotion – what you eat influences your feelings, and your feelings influence what you eat. Recognising the relationship between food and feelings is the first step to eating healthily.

Considering how eating affects mood

Your brain links and associates certain foods and eating behaviours to pleasure and others to pain. Food is often given as a reward for good behaviour or a special occasion: 'If you're good you can have an ice cream'. We celebrate birthdays, weddings and anniversaries with cakes and candles. Couples share romantic meals together to help them feel more intimate. As a child, you may have been denied a favourite item of food 'because you didn't behave'. Even advertising agencies link specific foods to achievement or a positive emotion, such as love or comfort.

What you eat often changes your mood. Some foods make you sluggish; other meals energise you. For example, research shows that the Mediterranean diet of olive oil, fruit and vegetables is good for health; but equally important is to understand your own body's reaction to certain foods. You're unique.

Become aware of how certain foods make you feel, both physically and emotionally. For example, chocolate contains caffeine (a stimulant) and has been shown to elevate mood for many people – but not everyone. The experience of eating chocolate varies from one person to another and depends upon your unique metabolism. One person may feel energised, while another develops a headache. The emotional consequences of eating chocolate also vary. You may link chocolate to a previous experience and consider it a great reward – or guilty food you must sneak. Notice your own personal unique response to all the foods you eat so that you can create an extensive list of the foods that make you personally feel good.

Analysing how feelings affect eating habits

What you eat is coloured by feelings. If you're tense, your body prepares itself for action, and you feel the need to stock up with food to give you energy. If you're miserable, you may be less likely to notice the taste of food: it loses its flavour. Some people eat more and others eat less when depressed. Food can be used as a comfort and also as a punishment.

Create a section in your journal to use as a self-observation diary. Writing down the details of your eating experiences helps you tune in to the relationship between your feelings and your diet. Table 4-1 gives you an example to work from. In the first column, record what you eat, with whom and where. In the second column, note how you feel emotionally. Notice whether you feel differently when you eat alone or in company. In the third column, list any thoughts you experience while eating, or afterwards.

Table 4-1	Sam's Eating Habits Observation Log	
Eating Activity	*Emotional Climate*	*Reflection (Including Mood and Physical Feelings Before and After Eating)*
Breakfast at home, alone. Ate bacon and eggs with coffee.	Tired and tense.	Ate too much. Why? I wanted some comfort. Afterwards felt bloated and then guilty for eating so much. Remember that when I eat less I feel better in every way.
Lunch: Cheese sandwich eaten at my desk.	Time-pressured so stressed by deadline.	Ate in hurried fashion so didn't taste the food. Felt bloated and sluggish afterwards. Don't want to repeat this experience. Check whether cheese upsets me.
Dinner out at a restaurant with my girlfriend: Fish, salad and tiramisu. 2 glasses white wine.	Initially tense after work, then relaxed and enjoyed a tasty meal. Happy to be with her and happy in myself.	A good experience of a light and delicious meal in a good surrounding.

As you can see in Table 4-1, Sam had a variety of experiences over a day from which he can identify those foods and environments that help him feel good or bad. Based on his log, he specifically decided he didn't want to eat sandwiches at his desk again because this type of lunch doesn't energise him.

After a week of self-observation, you can start to see patterns that help you connect what you choose to eat with the emotional climate of your eating. You can then step back and determine whether your habits are helping your emotional wellbeing. If not, you can make new choices about food in the future.

Working through Feelings Relating to Food

All sorts of feelings may drive your relationship with food. To eat happily and healthily, you need to be aware of how your emotions and your background affect your diet.

Recognising that you deserve to eat well

Sometimes people just don't feel like looking after their bodies. Because of low self-esteem, they feel they aren't worth care and attention.

Sharon was a young mother with a daughter. She had been living with her boyfriend, but one day he and his sons moved out. She was sad at this loss. Her home seemed empty. She gave up eating properly after that and only ate the scraps off her daughter's plate. When asked why she didn't cook for herself she replied, 'What's the point?' She had to discover how to love herself in order to feel that she deserved a good meal.

At times of emotional stress you may choose less healthy foods that at other times you try to avoid, which tends to compound your negative feelings. Pay attention to the situations and moods that trigger bad habits. You may find that you feel:

- ✔ Tired and fed up.
- ✔ Not worth cooking for.
- ✔ Angry after a row with someone.

However you feel, your body and mind deserve nurture not punishment. Eating too much, too little or lots of unhealthy food punishes your body. But eating good, wholesome foods is a way to take care of yourself – emotionally as well as physically.

Find ways to work through emotional problems by talking to a friend, joining a support group or writing a journal expressing your feelings. Start to love yourself enough to choose to eat healthily. Chapter 12 helps you build your self-esteem. Find even more ideas for feeling good about yourself in *Boosting Self-Esteem For Dummies* by Rhena Branch and Rob Willson.

Understanding the symbolism of food

The food you choose to buy, cook and eat symbolises your emotional state. If you treat yourself to something delicious you may be feeling happy in yourself. Or, you may be feeling down and be seeking comfort. If you can't be bothered to think about what you want to eat you're probably feeling low. The meal symbolises more than the food itself: it fulfils emotional, physical and psychological needs. The experience of eating combines emotions, sensory experience and atmosphere.

Consider what different foods mean to you. For example, meat and two veg tends to be associated with men; apple pie with mothers; chocolate with women; caviar with luxury. Our food choices as adults are coloured by the power of suggestion (often set up by advertisers). This knowledge may help you reflect on the wider significance of both the food and the context in which you're eating it.

Are you associating unhealthy food with comfort or pleasure? Is this association helpful to you? Can you identify a healthy food that you can link to a sense of reward? In your journal, create a table like Table 4-2 and record your emotional associations with specific foods.

Table 4-2	Nancy's Emotional Associations with Food		
Food	*Emotional association*	*Healthy or unhealthy connection?*	*Preferred choices now*
Cauliflower	Boring white mush. Reminds me of school.	This connection is unhealthy because cauliflower is nutritious	I can add turmeric to a cauliflower recipe. That way I connect health, flavour and colour with cauliflower.

Letting go of childhood conditioning

Eating habits are set up in childhood. With no understanding of the implications, young children follow the food choices and habits of their parents.

Reflect on whether your parents' food choices when you were a child help you to live a healthy life now. Your parents may have had to struggle with financial limitation or the unavailability of some of the foods that exist today. Their own emotional state may also have impacted their choices. Review the influence that your upbringing had on how you view food:

✔ What were the favourite foods of your parents or extended family? Which foods do you now particularly favour?

✔ How did your parents or extended family prepare food? Do you use the same methods?

✔ When were your mealtimes as a child? Do you eat at the same times now?

✔ How did your parents conduct meals? On trays in front of the TV? At the table? Did you have to finish all your dinner? Do you follow the same rules today as you did back then?

✔ Are you following your parents' lead or have you forged your own way with eating?

Notice whether, consciously or unconsciously, you've adopted your parents' habits. Does this approach feel good and work well for you as an adult? Have you chosen your own ways of preparing food, or are you compromising to fit in with a partner who, in turn, had her own childhood messages? Most importantly, now that you're an adult, how will you choose to nurture yourself and your family?

If you're a parent, you can set an example of healthy eating without being too rigid. If you're too strict, your children may rebel. Giving them some autonomy and encouraging a little bit of everything in moderation can lead children to develop good choices around food and avoid food battles or food fads.

If you decide that you want to make changes to your eating habits, you can re-programme your brain to enjoy new flavours. Perhaps you used to have sugar in your tea but now find the taste horribly sweet? Or you've given up smoking and find the thought of a cigarette disgusting? You can condition yourself to change.

In order to re-programme yourself successfully, you need to make sure that you reward your good choices. You can link pleasure to changing your habits and link pain to the old habits. For example, you can develop a positive picture that motivates you to change – an image of you feeling happy inside and out perhaps, and create a negative image of your old habits – perhaps linked to a feeling of being sluggish and unhappy. Each time you feel tempted to eat the foods that aren't good for you, think of the 'old you' picture and replace it with the 'new you' that chooses healthy ways to look after yourself. In this way, you're introducing negative and positive reinforcement through these images.

Having a healthy body image

Many people are unhappy with their body image. Women tend to worry about whether they're too fat, and men often worry about lack of muscularity.

If you're one of the many people who are unhappy in your own skin, here are some tips you can apply to help you value and appreciate your body:

- ✔ Avoid comparison with others.

- ✔ Give thanks for good health.

- ✔ When you look in a mirror, try not to think negative thoughts, but instead offer yourself love and appreciation.

- ✔ When you think that your self-esteem is low, work through the exercises in Chapters 12, 14 and 15

Remember that beauty starts on the inside. As Eleanor Roosevelt said, 'Nobody can make you feel inferior without your permission'!

People who have a negative body image can develop eating habits that are a danger to their health. They lose a realistic perspective of their image. The statements below are designed to help you decide whether you have a healthy attitude to food and check whether an eating disorder may be present. Read through the statements and consider how they apply to you:

- ✔ I sometimes make myself sick after a meal.

- ✔ I binge eat.

- ✔ I've put on weight recently.

- ✔ My friends say I'm thin, but I feel fat.

- ✔ I don't feel in control of my eating habits.

- ✔ Thinking and worrying about food is dominating my life.

- ✔ I've lost more than 6 kilograms (14 pounds) in weight over the last 3 months.

- ✔ I go on frequent diets, so my weight yo-yos.

- ✔ I'm fed up with not being able to lose weight.

- ✔ I worry that my body isn't sexually attractive.

If you've lost more than 6 kilograms in weight over the last 3 months, are making yourself sick after food, are worrying that you're not in control of what you eat or feel that eating concerns dominate your life, consult a professional, such as your GP. We also list resources for individuals dealing with eating disorders in the Appendix.

Weight extremes as avoidance

Madeleine was an extremely attractive woman who received endless attention from men. She found their interest embarrassing and difficult to deflect. She ended up having relationships that she didn't really want. Her subconscious strategy to stop the male attention was to put on a great deal of weight. As she became aware of this behaviour through coaching, she acquired assertiveness skills that enabled her to feel she could say 'no' to a man when she wanted to do so. As her self-esteem and sense of control returned, she lost weight.

If you're overweight or underweight, consider whether somewhere inside you're choosing to be that way. By working on the root cause of your eating problem, you can achieve a healthier body and a happier mind.

Adopting Healthy Eating Habits

Food is central to your health and survival and nurtures your sense of wellbeing. As we explore in the previous sections, your emotions play a big part in deciding what you eat. Therefore, you need to really think about what you eat and which foods offer your body the right ingredients for wellbeing, growth and good function.

Minimising unhealthy eating

As you build new eating habits, identify those foods you need to minimise. Unhealthy food choices include

- ✔ Refined sugars, such as some fruit juices and squashes
- ✔ Saturated fats, generally included in fatty meat, cream, butter and cheese
- ✔ Refined carbohydrates, such as white flour, white bread
- ✔ Sweets, biscuits, cakes, jams

We aren't suggesting that you have to avoid these foods altogether. Just be aware and carefully limit the quantities you eat.

Unhealthy eating patterns can occur suddenly. For example, if you suffer a bereavement, redundancy, divorce or depressive illness, you may unconsciously punish yourself by choosing the wrong foods. Your inner emotional state sabotages your ability to make good choices. The earlier section 'Having a healthy body image' helps you identify whether your unhealthy eating is straying into the realms of an eating disorder.

If you're over- or under-eating, become aware of the thoughts and feelings that influence you. This knowledge enables you to understand how your emotional moods manipulate your food choices. You're then in a better position to stop and reflect on how to approach food in a balanced way, taking care of both your physical and emotional needs.

Eating well for health and mood

Most people realise that home-prepared fresh foods constitute a healthy diet. Compare the food plate in Figure 4-1 (which is based on the Mediterranean diet) with your own typical daily intake and consider whether you need to make some changes. The plate breaks into recommended sections that need to be balanced for a healthy diet.

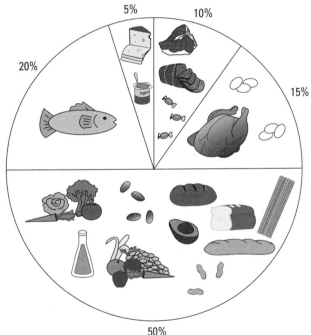

Figure 4-1: A healthy balance of food types.

Here are some healthy-eating pointers:

✔ Carbohydrate snacks, such as a sandwich before bed, help release serotonin for good sleep; warm milk adds extra calcium. Other snacks include peanuts, bananas, poultry, and wholemeal toast and crackers. These snacks contain tryptophan which is the building block for the feel-good hormone serotonin.

- ✔ Herbs such as St John's Wort can combat depression; valerian supports good sleep.

- ✔ Magnesium helps you to avoid tiredness, so tuck into magnesium-rich spinach, soya beans, sardines and prawns.

- ✔ Nuts such as *unsalted* pistachios and almonds are helpful in combating stress. Nuts contain stress-protecting B vitamins and vitamin E. Brazil nuts are good providers of selenium, an essential mineral.

- ✔ Oranges, strawberries and kiwi fruit contain vitamin C and reduce levels of stress hormones. Before a stressful event, you can safely take an extra vitamin C boost of as much as 3,000 milligrams to reduce stress chemicals and lower blood pressure.

- ✔ Protein builds muscle and is vital for growth. Try foods such as chicken, lean meat, fish, pulses such as hummus and kidney beans, eggs and low-fat cheeses in moderation.

- ✔ Tea is a source of antioxidants and evidence suggests that drinking green or herb tea four times a day reduces stress chemicals, whereas coffee increases them.

- ✔ Unsaturated fats are good for you because they lower cholesterol. You find this type of fat in non-dairy food such as oily fish, nuts, olive oil and seeds. Fish oil, in particular, is a brain booster. Aim to eat about 85 grams of oily fish (about the size of the palm of your hand) twice a week.

- ✔ Vitamins, minerals and antioxidants are found in higher quantity in organic food and in brightly coloured produce such as oranges, all varieties of dried fruits, bananas, carrots, red and green peppers and sweet potatoes. Many of these foods also provide potassium, which combats tiredness.

Connecting stress and fat

Stress affects appetite and alters your body chemistry to prepare you for fight or flight. This continuing state of alert demands extra energy, and so your body puts on fat to make sure that you have stores of energy to cope with the stress. In this way high levels of stress for a sustained period can lead to unhealthy weight gain.

Ideally, you need to avoid stress as much as possible (see Chapters 2, 12 and 13). But few people can find complete serenity and stress-free lives.

Work to protect yourself from the damaging effect that stress can have on your weight by keeping to a low-fat diet. However, buying low-fat foods isn't enough to keep you healthy because these foods often contain hidden sugars. As Figure 4-1 shows, you need some 'bad' or *saturated* fats in your diet, usually derived from dairy and animal sources, as well as more 'good' or unsaturated fats that come from fish, soya and olive oil.

Boosting your energy

Refined sugars cause the body to boost energy very quickly. They help you to feel good because they cause the brain to make serotonin – the feel-good hormone. But the high is short-lived. Sweets and sugary, fizzy drinks make your blood sugar soar, but then fall quickly – leaving you lacking in energy.

To keep energy levels up, eat complex carbohydrates regularly; don't go longer than 3.5 to 4 hours between food. Your body breaks down complex carbohydrates much more slowly, giving you stable blood sugar levels and steady energy release. Try wholegrain breakfast cereals, breads and pastas, porridge, cereal bars, beans, lentils, vegetables and fruits. Also, consuming good fats and protein at each meal extends the benefits of complex carbohydrates.

Minding what you eat

Many people eat without thinking about it. When eating becomes automatic, you get distracted and may eat more than you need. Negative emotions or stress can easily push you away from healthy eating, which can lead to a downward spiral where you get annoyed with yourself for not eating well – and then go on to eat more or eat something you know isn't good for you. And feel even worse!

The key is to stop and pay attention. Consider whether you give yourself time to eat with focus and enjoyment. What eating habits have you developed that are unhelpful to the concept of really thinking about what you eat? Here are a few eating habits to try to avoid:

- ✔ Eating at your laptop
- ✔ Eating with distractions such as the television or radio
- ✔ Picking from the fridge
- ✔ Snacking on the hoof or on the bus

One way to reconnect to your eating is to develop the practice of *mindfulness* – a way of paying attention to what you're doing. When you eat mindfully, you slow down your eating and think wholeheartedly about the process of your meal. You pay attention to each mouthful, which brings you more fully into the experience of the flavours, textures and colours of what you're eating. You become directly aware of the moment-to-moment sensory feedback of your meal. You're not judging; you're observing. Over time this method enhances your enjoyment of eating and can help you make more careful food choices. Eating mindfully for just a few mouthfuls each meal is a step in the right direction.

With practice the experience of mindful eating becomes one of purpose and pleasure. As you pay attention to what you're doing with clear thinking and without distraction, you tune into your body's natural signals that you've had enough food.

Give mindful eating a go. Place a small handful of raisins in a small bowl. (This activity is more fun with two or more people, so try it with a friend.) Select one raisin from the bowl and move it into the palm of your hand. Look at it as if you were seeing it for the first time. Notice its colour and texture. Bring it slowly to your nose and sniff gently to notice its aroma. Place it on your tongue and observe the response in your mouth as the saliva releases and you become aware of the taste. Move the raisin around your mouth and notice the sensations without chewing. As you bite into the raisin, detect how the taste changes. Chew the raisin thoroughly, following its progress as you swallow it and feel it go down your throat, your food pipe and into the stomach.

With practice, you can try dedicating a whole meal to mindful eating. Prepare to sit down at a table and eat a meal without any other activity – no newspaper, book, TV, talking or music. You can light a candle and make the table look attractive. Start the meal and pay complete attention to what you're eating, like your experience with the raisin noticing the experience with raisin.

This slowing down of an everyday activity can make you more aware of how you're approaching food. You tune in to your five senses – what you see, hear, smell, taste and touch. You notice your feelings.

Certain foods may connect you with long gone associations. If old childhood habits cause you to have difficulty eating particular foods, you may find that slowing eating down in this way allows a fresh experience of the food. This technique may allow you to introduce a food that was previously difficult to eat with enjoyment.

Try mindfulness next time you go shopping so that you consciously notice the colours, smells and textures of the food. Be focused and analytical but without judging yourself, and you may find that this method helps you to make good choices.

Creating a Healthy-Living Plan

Changing your eating habits doesn't happen unless you make it happen. To improve your relationship with food and the way you eat, you need to get in the right frame of mind, realistically appraise your weight, set goals for the future and then plan to achieve them.

Getting in the right mindset

Motivation is key to your success. Believe that you can change, and then take action to do so in order to achieve your goal of health and happiness.

You need to get rid of anything inside that's holding you back. Take a look at Table 4-3 and use it to notice those thoughts and feelings that help or hinder you.

Table 4-3	Seeing How Your Mindset Can Help and Hinder
Unhelpful Mindset	**Helpful Mindset**
Thoughts: 'I'm inferior', 'I'm unlovable', 'I'm a loser', 'I'll never be the weight I want to be'	**Thoughts:** 'I'll have a go', 'I can succeed', 'I'll feel great when I take good care of myself and my eating habits'
Feelings: Guilt, anger, shame, fear, jealousy, despair	**Feelings:** Calmness, enthusiasm, confidence

Notice when unhelpful thoughts and feelings arise, and allow them to pass through as clouds in a landscape, or challenge them and see how realistic they are (or aren't). Choose thoughts that encourage and motivate you to integrate your new habits into your life.

Aiming for a healthy weight

All humans vary in size and structure. You need to identify the foods that help you feel good on every level – mentally, physically and emotionally. For you, the right approach may or may not involve dieting. Feeling happy in yourself is the most important factor.

In order to devise a plan of action, gauging your actual weight against what doctors consider to be healthy is helpful. Calculating your *body mass index* (BMI) assists in planning your next move. Follow these three steps to find your BMI:

1. **Work out your height in metres and square it (multiply the figure by itself).**

2. **Find your weight in kilograms.**

3. **Divide your weight by your height squared (the figure you reached in step 1).**

For example, if you're 1.6 metres tall and weigh 65 kilograms, the calculations are as follows: 1.6 ÷ 1.6 = 2.56; and then 65 ÷ 2.56 = a BMI of 25.39.

For good health, you need to aim for a BMI of between 18.5 and 25.

As well as BMI, check how much fat you're carrying around your midriff. A waist circumference greater than 80 centimetres for women and 94 centimetres for men may put you at risk of developing heart disease and diabetes.

When you have a realistic picture of your weight, you can see what your healthy-eating plan needs to accomplish – weight loss, weight gain or maintenance of a healthy weight.

Setting your goals

Consider the eating pattern that's right for you and your lifestyle. Before you begin to look at your present habits, visualise the emotional state you want to achieve. What state of health would you like to be in? Think about your preferred level of fitness, shape and size.

Imagine yourself waking up in the morning having achieved a healthy way of eating and with a body image that feels good. Take yourself on an imaginary journey with the new 'you' in place and ask yourself the following questions:

- ✔ When I wake up in the morning, what's going to be different about the new me compared to what has been in the past?

- ✔ What will it be like to get up and walk into the bathroom and greet myself knowing that my eating patterns have changed and resulted in the healthy body change that I see?

- ✔ Who's going to notice the changes and what difference will this make to my life?

Make a list of all those advantages that follow from choosing to eat healthily.

Creating this positive outcome is key to motivating you towards successfully achieving your future vision. Start acting 'as if' you've already achieved this goal: how do you walk, talk and act? Don't postpone feeling good until you achieve your final goal: imagine success now and you're more likely to reach the result you seek.

Making a self-care plan

Break down your goal into manageable chunks and plan a campaign of change. Your plan needs to be workable and within your resources.

Simple things can make a difference, so try any and all the following:

✔ **Choose a sensible eating plan:** Follow a plan that's supported by nutritional practitioners and research, such as the Mediterranean Diet or the Low GI Diet (see Figure 4-1).

✔ **De-stress:** Consider discovering and practising a technique such as meditation or self-hypnosis. (The Appendix has details of some organisations you can contact).

✔ **Get active:** Regular exercise is essential but doesn't have to be laborious. Do something that you find fun: walk, run, dance, skip, walk up and down stairs rather than take a lift. Exercise releases endorphins, which boost you both physically and emotionally. Chapter 6 has more information on the benefits of physical activity.

✔ **Keep your body ticking over:** Have a healthy snack such as fruit, raisins, nuts, or oat bars approximately every 90 minutes and don't wait until you're so hungry that you eat too much.

✔ **Make eating an enjoyable experience:** Light a candle, lay a tablecloth and share a delicious meal with your partner or family to make eating special.

✔ **Rethink your shopping habits:** Make a list and stick to it – unless you choose something healthy. Change your shopping habits to deliberately visit shops that offer you healthy foods. Don't go shopping when you're hungry; you may buy too much.

✔ **Stock up on good stuff.** Give away food that isn't good for you and fill your cupboard with healthier choices.

✔ **Watch your mood:** Try to access a good emotional state before you shop, cook or eat.

Choosing healthy food feeds not only your body but also your sense of self-esteem. You find that taking control of your eating enables you to feel happier and more energised as you take good care of yourself. You no longer need to punish yourself by eating food that doesn't promote your general wellbeing. You really are what you eat: what you choose either boosts your emotions or depletes them.

Food and feeling good

Jenny was in her mid-40s and found herself alone after her husband of 20 years walked out of their marriage. After the initial shock, she began to enjoy her own company and spending time with her friends. She was a good cook and started to indulge her friends and family with elaborate meals. She felt lonely at times and ate chocolate bars between meals. She often drank half a bottle of wine before bed.

She was definitely enjoying her new life, but she was shocked when her doctor told her that she was obese with a body mass index of 32. Her waist had increased to 33 inches. Her doctor further said that her health would be affected if she didn't change her weight.

Jenny decided to review her life and define what was important for her. She didn't want to stop entertaining, and so decided to ask her friends for support. She did a charity fun run with one of them. Together they planned an exercise regime. She read about healthy eating and included healthy meals each day and substituted fruit, nuts and seeds instead of unhealthy snacks. A year later her BMI was down to 24 – and she was dating the organiser of the fun run.

Watch out for all or nothing thinking with your plan. So many people start a diet on a Monday and then if they break it on Tuesday they postpone starting again until the next week. If you over-eat at lunchtime remember that you don't have to over-eat at supper! Similarly, don't postpone going to the gym until you're able to stay for two hours at a time. Thirty minutes (or even ten) is better than nothing. Try dividing your day into three segments and make a diet and exercise plan for morning, afternoon and evening. Doing so allows you to approach each segment of your day with fresh thinking. Be compassionate with yourself if, to begin with, you have difficulty making change happen. Don't give up: you're looking for long-term gain from short-term pain! Accept that you're human and at times you're going to take two steps forward and one back.

Ask for the support of family and friends. This support, coupled with optimism and a positive attitude, helps you to succeed. And reward yourself for progress. A night out or a new pair of shoes can really give you a lift.

Chapter 5

Tackling Tiredness: Following Your Body Rhythms

In This Chapter

▶ Tuning in to your body's needs

▶ Recognising day, night and seasonal rhythms

▶ Dealing with sleep problems

▶ Making time to stop and relax

*B*ody rhythms are essential to your sense of physical and emotional well-being. Worries seem far worse when you're tired. Your mind revs up into a hyper-alert state and your body feels fatigued. Thinking clearly is difficult because the supply of oxygen to your brain alters when your body is out of balance. Everything seems harder to cope with and becoming negative and pessimistic is all too easy. Emotions can hijack reason when you don't listen to the needs and rhythms of your body.

The good news is that you can train your brain to notice when you're becoming unbalanced, and so take action at an early stage to protect yourself. In this chapter we suggest ways for you to listen to the inner rhythms that guide you to wellbeing. These signals exist to help you make the right decisions for yourself, so that you can maintain emotional and physical health.

Letting Your Body Follow Nature's Way

Plants and trees have a cycle of growth and rest. They have essential needs for air, warmth, water and nourishment. Fields need to lie fallow and seeds require a certain period to grow, while the soil nourishes their roots. When you next walk in the country or in your local park, notice how the natural world obeys nature's law.

As a human being you also have natural laws to follow. Unlike plants, however, you also have higher and spiritual needs that require you to respond consciously rather than automatically to your surroundings. To gain inner balance you need to meet these basic needs.

Today's complex and technological world of computers, 24 hours-a-day Internet access and air-conditioned offices can detach you from your natural rhythms. You can become part of the machinery. For example, people often work in inner-city office blocks that have no natural daylight. Even your computer needs electricity to function, and yet many people forget to eat or drink properly during a busy day.

You can easily and inadvertently tune out of your natural needs for day and night rhythms and activity/rest cycles. Your *limbic system* is the regulator of your body rhythms, prompting the balance of sleep or activity. This system is also the centre of your emotions, temperature control and immune defences, supporting digestion, energy levels, growth and sexuality. So when you ignore your body's call to follow its natural rhythms, you affect many other aspects of your body's functioning.

Everyone needs to take time out. Even in an urban environment you can connect to the natural world around you. People feel less stressed when they walk in the countryside or sit in a park or by a river at lunchtime. Nature is a great healer: substantial evidence suggests that patients who have a view of nature through a window, posters of art or a natural scene, and music require fewer painkillers and heal more quickly. Studies show that these environments reduce stress, enhancing heart rate and lowering blood pressure.

You need to make a date with yourself to listen in to how your mind and body are feeling so that you can respond to an inner call for fresh air, rest, daylight, food or water.

Tuning In to the Rhythms of the Day

Getting in touch with your body – its needs and abilities, demands and preferences – makes all the difference in getting through the day. When you listen to your body and work with its natural rhythms during the day, you get into bed calmer and less exhausted at night.

Knowing when you work best

Are you an owl or a lark? Become aware of which time of day you feel most alert. Several studies indicate that most people have a preference as to whether they feel more productive and alert in the morning or the evening.

About a third of people are *larks* who hit the sack early and bounce out of bed ready to work, and another third are *owls* who like to go to bed late and wake up late. The final third have no specific preference. (Interestingly, teenagers – especially boys – are mostly owls, and some evidence from neuroscientist Professor Russell Foster suggests that they are more productive at school when the school day is altered to allow later starts.)

Pushing yourself to perform at a time of day that's not in tune with your own rhythm can be mentally, physically and emotionally draining. Where practical, adjust your day/night schedule to fit in with your own peak performance period.

Managing your time around your rhythms isn't always easy. Much of modern life demands that you respond to time pressures that aren't of your making, because people respond to a global marketplace. For example, you may have to get up early or stay up late in order to make a conference call with someone in another time zone. Try to take short breaks at other times of the day, if possible, to help your body balance itself and maintain energy. Whenever possible during these breaks, get outside into daylight. Sunlight activates your body's production of melatonin, which reinforces natural day/night sleep patterns.

Balancing rest and activity

As well as your day/night sleep rhythm, your body also has another essential rhythm: the *ultradian rhythm* of activity/rest. The ultradian rhythm is built into your physiology to prevent overload. This rhythm cycles about every 90 minutes, prompting you to rest briefly in order to switch the brain and body into a rest and recovery mode and recoup energy after a period of concentration.

Figure 5-1 shows you how the ultradian rhythm works. Performance begins to run down after 45 minutes of sustained activity, leading to the need for rest and recovery for 20 minutes after the 90-minute interval.

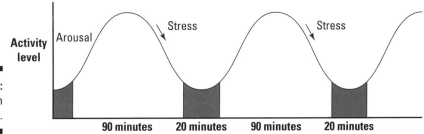

Figure 5-1:
Ultradian
rhythms.

Health and safety executives recognise the ultradian rhythm and understand that overworking can lead to accidents. Policies are in place that prescribe fixed hours for people who operate machinery or drive long-distance vehicles. Unfortunately, office and professional life seems to have conveniently forgotten that the brain and body can operate at peak performance only for certain periods of the day! Pushing people beyond their natural rhythms impacts both the individual and businesses. The consequences include bad decision-making, frayed nerves, irritable communication and absence due to illness.

The increasing pace of modern life often causes people to ignore these rhythms. But your body needs you to respond to the ultradian rhythm. It tells you when to take your mid-morning or mid-afternoon tea break and when to enjoy one of the healthy snacks we describe in Chapter 4.

The following simple self-observation exercise shows you that your body changes every 90 minutes, coinciding with your ultradian rhythm:

1. **Block first one nostril and then the other.**

   Notice which nostril allows more air into the nose.

2. **Repeat in about two hours.**

   You probably notice that the flow of air has switched so that in the first period one nostril lets in more air, and in the next period the other nostril does. This switch is linked to your ultradian rhythm.

As well as breathing, your body automatically switches the blood supply between the left and right brain along with your ultradian rhythm. Using both sides of the brain is part of your natural survival instinct, ensuring that you can focus on the task at hand with your left brain and also keep the situation in a broader context with your right brain. Whenever you take a break, you're supporting this natural process.

Many people sit at their computers all day with barely a break. When you do so, you put your physical and emotional wellbeing at risk. Check this out for yourself by asking yourself the following questions. In a typical working day:

- ✔ Am I getting adequate water and liquid for my physical needs?

- ✔ Do I have a pattern for the day where I'm on the go without a break? (This can be described as a 'doing' pattern.)

- ✔ How often do I take exercise, and of what kind?

- ✔ What are the natural cues that I notice when I need to stop what I'm doing and take a break? Do I respond to them?

- ✔ What breaks do I take in the day?

- ✔ When do I eat and do I give myself a real break to enjoy my food?

Taking care of your physical needs enables you to manage emotional challenges more effectively. When you're exhausted, you break more easily and everything can seem overwhelming. This stress can impact relationships at work and at home, as well as your ability to perform tasks effectively.

Identify now whether you need to make any changes in your routine, such as scheduling breaks, making sure that you have water to sip during the day and having a walk in your lunch period.

Re-energising through breath

Your breathing changes rhythm when you're emotionally upset. You're more likely to experience a feeling of tension when you haven't listened to your own inner rhythms – for example, when you have a late night or work all day without a break.

You can listen to the way your breath flows in and out. When you're tense, the rhythm of your breath becomes shallower, and the inhalation and exhalation tend to equalise, with breathing usually moving into your upper chest. When you're calm you breathe using your lower chest, or diaphragm, and the out-breath is longer.

You can create a state of physical and emotional equilibrium by practising this simple breathing exercise:

1. **Wherever you are, stop and bring the focus of your attention into your body.**

   Feel your feet on the ground. Calm your mind.

2. **Take three breaths, breathing in on a count of 4 and out on a count of 6.**

   As you breathe in, draw in a remembered sense of a time and place where you felt peaceful and loving to yourself. As you breathe out, imagine the breath flowing through your body. Visualise this breath carrying oxygen back through all the tissues of your body.

You don't have to shut your eyes or go anywhere special to do this exercise: you can practise this breathing exercise sitting at your desk and no one will notice. Whatever the time of day, you can re-energise and calm yourself by gently breathing in this way for three or more breaths.

See Chapters 2 and 13 for more information on breath techniques and emotions.

Considering Seasonal Rhythms

Seasonal Affective Disorder (SAD) occurs when the brain has low levels of *serotonin* (the chemical that helps you combat depression). This decrease in serotonin happens when you have less exposure to sunlight. In the UK, SAD is therefore a problem for people during winter months; in the darker, northern countries, the disorder is much more prevalent.

Another hormone, *melatonin,* switches on with darkness. This hormone slows down your body clock. With SAD the reduced light in winter causes your body to release more melatonin, accompanied by cortisol, and the mixture of these chemicals can cause anxiety and depression.

You may be one of those people who get low in winter months. Often this feeling is mild and called the 'winter blues'. But for others, feeling a bit down can change into depression if you don't take action to help yourself. Check whether you experience some of these symptoms:

- ✔ You have tiredness that persists throughout the day.

- ✔ Your mood remains low with unexplained anxiety.

- ✔ You need more sleep than usual.

- ✔ You're eating more than usual.

- ✔ You're snappy with friends and family.

Experiencing some of these symptoms is natural in the months of long dark days and less sunshine. In days gone by, before electricity, you would have heeded these external influences and slept more in winter. In winter you often feel like you want to hibernate, just like some animals do. More effort and energy is needed to push the body to continue to be active during these dark months.

Here are some self-help tips for when you have the winter blues:

- ✔ Eat serotonin-releasing foods, such as complex carbohydrates (see Chapter 4 for more on a healthy diet).

- ✔ Find time to exercise.

- ✔ Lighten your home with bright colours and decorations.

- ✔ Practise one of the stress-reduction techniques in Chapters 2 or 3.

- ✔ Be discerning about what tasks and responsibilities you take on today and what you may be able to put off until the summer months (if possible), so that you don't overload your system.

- ✔ Sit near a window when indoors.

- ✔ Spend time outside, particularly in the middle of the day.

If you find that simple measures don't make any difference to the winter blues, consider buying a high-intensity natural daylight artificial light source. You can set this machine to come on in the morning to provide a gradual and natural-type light on awakening.

Recharging Your Body: Getting a Good Night's Sleep

Sleep recharges your body, mind and spirit. Tiredness clouds the mind and makes the glass seem half empty. But everything looks brighter after a good night's sleep. Responding to your body's sleep rhythm is therefore essential for emotional healing.

Understanding why your body needs good sleep

Good sleep is essential to physical and emotional wellbeing. The body regenerates at night, and sleep allows it to boost your immune function.

Sleep deprivation impedes the brain's natural processes for regeneration. The result can make you more anxious because your body chemistry doesn't have the opportunity to rebalance itself. You may experience nervous energy on those days when you haven't slept well: you may notice a different taste in your mouth and feel jangly and on high alert. Eventually, without sleep you become paranoid, which is why military forces use sleep deprivation as a method of torture.

Lack of sleep also impacts your health physically. Night shifts reverse the pattern of the normal working day and impact the brain's natural tendency to sleep during the hours of darkness and be active when it is light. In a global environment an increasing number of people are working night shifts, and yet research studies demonstrate that these disturbances of natural rhythms can cause illness. Research studies into the health of air crews in Norway, Denmark, Iceland and Finland show that flight attendants experience added health stress because their natural rhythms are disturbed by flying through time zones. Their natural sleeping patterns are interrupted, and their stress levels increase. Other studies show marked increases in incidents of breast cancer in women who have to work night shifts. In fact, the Danish government has paid out compensation to 40 female night workers.

If you work at night, ensure that you get adequate rest when you can. You may want to review the risks associated with long-term night working and see whether you can rotate shifts.

As well as boosting your immune function, sleep helps you process thoughts and emotions. Your brain works 24 hours a day and at night it 'sorts' your experiences.

Keep a Dream Diary for a month to track the way your brain picks up one event and links it to another in your dreams. The process is rather like the defragmenting process on your computer – storing, sorting and sifting the information that the brain has taken in. Therefore, sleep helps your emotional healing.

Knowing how much sleep you need

Most people need an average of seven to eight hours sleep. People do vary, and some average six hours and others average nine. Less than seven hours can lead to sleep deprivation, which directly affects the immune system (see the preceding section).

You experience several cycles during sleeping hours. During the first deep sleep, your body focuses on immunity, producing essential antibodies to defend against infection. As you continue to sleep your brain goes into different cycles and rhythms, including *Rapid Eye Movement* (REM) sleep. REM occurs every 90 minutes and is the period of sleep during which your brain processes the day's experience. You're most likely to experience dreams during REM sleep. A good night's sleep occurs when you experience several cycles of REM and non-REM without interruption.

Developing healthy sleep patterns

Sleep is so important for your emotional wellbeing that you need to plan how to ensure that you get enough of it. Going to sleep requires you to switch from an active mode, in which the brain is geared for action to solve problems, to one in which the body and mind relax. This change signifies a switch when the sympathetic nervous system, which is linked to drive and activity, winds down and the parasympathetic nervous system switches on to reduce the body's alertness, bringing about relaxation. You need to develop a process whereby you create the right environment to switch out of your thinking brain and into relaxation.

Sleeping patterns and problems vary. Some people have difficulty getting off to sleep; others wake in the night or very early in the morning and are unable to get back to sleep.

Ongoing disturbed sleep can be a symptom of depression or anxiety. You may also have a lasting low mood, or daytime sleepiness. If you have these added problems we suggest that you consult a health professional (the Appendix contains some contact details).

Make a determined effort to create the right habits and environment to support good sleep. Identify what helps or hinders you sleeping well. For example, we find that our clients report going to sleep later than they intend because they:

✔ Drink more alcohol than is good for them

✔ Get comfortable on the sofa and fall asleep without undressing

✔ Go out too often during the week

✔ Lose track of time while surfing the Internet

✔ Watch too much television in the bedroom and don't wind down

If you've fallen into bad habits, you need to work at restoring a healthy pattern. Here are some suggestions:

✔ **Avoiding nicotine, caffeine and alcohol:** All these substances can be stimulants and therefore make sleep more difficult. Caffeine in the afternoon reduces the quality of sleep at night. Alcohol may help you get to sleep but is likely to lead to early waking.

✔ **Creating a good ambience in your bedroom:** See the place you sleep as a room for rest and sleep; make it comforting. Don't work or argue in there, and avoid noise. Make sure that you cut out unnecessary artificial light so that you're more aware of the natural transition from night to daylight.

✔ **Filling your stomach:** Try a warm milky drink and a complex carbohydrate snack, such as a banana or fruit smoothie before bed.

✔ **Getting physical:** Exercise in the morning or early afternoon releases any tension that may have built up in your body.

✔ **Letting go of anxiety:** Notice worrying thoughts before bedtime and talk them through, or write them out before you go to bed so that you can put them aside. If you wake up in the night, don't listen to thoughts and concerns floating about your head like an internal radio. Think about something else or clear your mind with some meditation (see Chapter 13).

✔ **Relaxing from the bottom up:** Do a body scan exercise in which you move your attention from your feet up through the parts of your body. See Chapter 2 for details.

✔ **Slowing your thinking:** Find a ritual that slows your brain and narrows your attention. Some people find that reading an absorbing book is helpful because doing so allows the mind to lose concentration gradually. Choose something that doesn't frighten you or make you think too hard.

✔ **Soothing with a lullaby:** Listen to some tranquil or meditative music, which calms your brain.

✔ **Sticking to a routine:** Set a sleep pattern with a regular 'wake up' and 'light out' time. This routine allows your physiology to gear you up to expect sleep.

If sleep still eludes you, try this Sleep Switch exercise.

1. **Calm your mind.**

   Tell yourself that you're going to fall asleep but reassure yourself that if anything untoward happens, you'll wake up. Imagine your thoughts are like waves on a choppy sea that gradually stills and becomes calm.

2. **Focus on your breathing.**

   Slow your breathing and allow it to fill the abdomen on the in-breath and release the breath gently with a longer out-breath. The upper chest becomes still. Mentally say the word 'sleep' to yourself on the out-breath until you begin to relax.

3. **Close your eyes and identify a calming image and sensation that helps you to focus on feeling sleepy.**

   Some people imagine that they are lying on a lilo on a gentle sea, lapping up and down and relaxing; others may see themselves in a quiet woodland glade. Create an image that's right for you and combine it with the memory of how you feel physically when you're falling asleep. If any worries, hurts, emotions or concerns of the day come back into your mind, switch your attention away from them and back to the image and the sensation of sleep.

4. **Gradually relax all parts of your body.**

   Say to yourself, 'My feet are feeling sleepy, my legs are feeling sleepy, my body is feeling sleepy, my jaw is relaxing, my eyes are softening and feeling sleepy, my forehead is relaxing and feeling sleepy, my mind is feeling sleepy as I drift off into sleep. Every part of me is feeling relaxed and sleepy and warm.'

5. **Focus your mind on counting down slowly from 55 to 1.**

   If you're still awake when you reach 1, just repeat the word 'sleep' on every out-breath.

Feel comforted that, even if you aren't totally asleep, this state of relaxation is healing you and setting you up for the next day. Whilst being asleep is preferable, being in a relaxed and meditative state still allows your body and mind to quieten, lowering your stress chemicals.

Avoiding Fatigue

Fatigue takes its toll on your emotional and physical health. You can't address emotional issues or manage life efficiently while feeling exhausted.

Work is a particular culprit for inducing meltdown. The long hours and target-driven culture of most workplaces push people into fear-based behaviours.

Instead of looking after themselves, they tap away frantically at their computers, trying to look productive so that they aren't considered next in line for redundancy. This behaviour can mean that you don't stop or take sufficient breaks during the day to reflect the natural rhythms and needs of your body.

Recognising the symptoms of profound tiredness

Feeling tired at the end of a busy day is natural, but if you frequently wake in the morning feeling exhausted, overwhelmed or as if you can't cope, you need to take urgent action to address your needs. Prevention is better than a medicine, and so picking up the early signs of fatigue and developing strategies to avoid overload allows you to stay calmly in control.

Become alert to warning signals of profound tiredness. A body in a state of permanent overdrive can result in a variety of physical symptoms, including:

- ✔ Bowel disturbance
- ✔ Chest pain
- ✔ Clammy hands and feet
- ✔ Extra heartbeats
- ✔ Feeling 'revved up'
- ✔ Feelings of exhaustion on waking in the morning
- ✔ Grinding teeth at night
- ✔ Headaches
- ✔ Muscle stiffness
- ✔ Physical tension, particularly in the neck and shoulders
- ✔ Poor concentration and anxiety
- ✔ Sighing/yawning
- ✔ Tight jaw or throat
- ✔ Visual disturbance, dizziness and light-headedness

Your body and mind alert you to the danger of burnout. Take the preceding signs and symptoms seriously. If persistent, consult a professional. And as you do so, take time to really think about your life situation and whether your profound tiredness has more to do with environmental and emotional pressure that take you beyond your limit of tolerance and anxiety.

Identifying what's wearing you out

Pay attention to the situations you're in or what you've been experiencing throughout the day. Many things may put pressure on you. For example, you may find the following exhausting:

- Communicating by phone or face to face
- Doing household chores or concerns
- Dealing with the parenting demands of a baby, toddler or truculent teenager
- Driving or commuting
- Exercising – guilt over a lack of it or from overdoing it
- Living up to sexual and intimacy expectations
- Managing queues and crowds
- Work pressures of targets, meetings and interviews

Although you can't eliminate many of the preceding factors from your life, you can take time out and examine why certain activities stress you out. You can choose to change your mental response to the situation and develop the ability to remain calm on the inside even in the midst of chaos on the outside. You can also re-introduce activities that recharge you to help make you better prepared to respond to life's more challenging aspects.

Steering clear of burnout and dis-ease

Chronic stress means that your body and mind are in a state of continuous alert, and this pressure eventually wears you down. Preparing for important exams, struggling with long-term marital unhappiness, losing a loved one, or coping with work stress can drain your body's reserves.

Notice and avoid states of prolonged distress. They can happen to anyone, so don't deny them. Trying to be Superman or Wonder Woman doesn't work. Unfortunately, when you're in a distressed state, you're likely to feel trapped in the sheer need to keep going. Healing emotional pain (whether old or new) is hard because your mind is hyper-alert and doesn't have access to the quiet reason that you need to manage emotions effectively.

Avoiding burnout is about awareness of your inner state. You need to notice your inner rhythm and switch off when you sense that you're in overdrive. (See Chapter 12 for some strategies to develop the ability to step back and regain perspective.) As an adult, you have to take responsibility for remind-ing yourself to rest when you need to do so. You're no use to family or work when you're bad-tempered, unhappy or sick. And forcing yourself to keep going can actually lead you to escalating fatigue or even illness.

Caring for yourself as well as others

Many people invest a lot of their energy in caring for loved ones. From bringing up an autistic child to caring for a spouse who has dementia – caring is hard work. And research shows that caring really does wear you down.

A study by Professor Stafford Lightman at Bristol University examined how susceptible carers are to illness. The study found that instead of creating an effective immune response in the face of infection or after an influenza vaccine, more than half of participants didn't make the antibodies necessary for self-protection.

So when you're expending lots of time and effort caring for someone, you need to make sure that you take some time out to look after yourself too. Otherwise you may become ill, and that's no good for you or the person you care for.

Keep the following in mind to help reduce your feelings of fatigue:

- **Find a happy place:** Focus on positive feelings, imagining an inner smile as you think of a special occasion or something or somebody you love or who makes you laugh. Tune in to the things that revitalise you.

- **Listen to your emotions:** Don't try to deny how you're feeling. Acknowledge feelings and take action to address your emotional needs. You may need a chat with someone, or if you're feeling sad or low you may need more rest than usual.

- **Practise the three As:** Avoid doing anything that's not essential; alter your response to a stress-causing situation; and accept what you can't change. For example,

  - *Avoid* surfing online late into the night for information or entertainment that you really don't need.

  - *Alter* the way you think about a problem so that you focus on what is working rather than what is not working. (If your teenager wakes you up coming in late, don't feel irritable; remind yourself that he is safe and well.)

  - *Accept* the fact that you're likely to get caught up in a traffic jam from time to time and can choose to remain calm.

- **Respond to your body's needs:** Drink when you're thirsty, eat when you're hungry, exercise when you need a stretch, and go to the toilet when you need to do so.

- **Slow down:** Modern life has speeded up. Travel is more stressful as the roads and trains become busier. Walking speeds in London have increased by 10 per cent in ten years according to a study by the British Council. This pressure when travelling can lead to outbursts such as road rage, where anger and frustration hijack the emotional brain. Try to slow down: take gentle breaths, move calmly and stay in control.

✔ **Take a break:** When you become aware of an aching body or a sense of fatigue, stop. Even a 5–10-minute break can revitalise you. Sit in your chair and do something different, or take a power nap. Schedule your day with breaks and a proper time out for lunch. Set your mobile phone or computer to remind you every 45 minutes to take 5 minutes out.

✔ **Take a 'duvet day':** Take some time out and stay in bed all day. This approach can work wonders for healing.

Physician heal thyself

A GP colleague of the authors found that he was getting exhausted by the demands of his patient group. He took a week out to recuperate his strength and energy. After that time he always set a period of 20 minutes aside each day when he locked his surgery door, set his alarm clock, lay down on his patients' bed and went to sleep. He reported that this nap made an enormous difference to his ability to manage the emotional demands of his work and recommended that his patients do the same.

Chapter 6

Actively Engaging in Your Emotional Healing

In This Chapter

▶ Incorporating exercise into your busy life

▶ Appreciating the present through mindfulness

▶ Healing painful memories through movement

▶ Finding your voice through song

You feel emotions in your body, and your body can also hold on to emotions, often with negative consequences. Retaining emotions such as fear, anger, sadness or guilt for weeks, months or even years can block your ability to heal. In this chapter we introduce you to active solutions that can release the emotional pain that may be locked into your body.

This chapter guides you through a variety of active techniques that use your body, mind, breath and voice to experience physical release of pent-up emotions. You're likely to discover that the active approaches in this chapter go beyond emotional release and help you create a positive mood and regain perspective, which leads you to feel empowered in making good life choices as you move forward.

Before you explore the emotion-releasing approaches in this chapter, you may want to identify where your body is holding tension and why. Turn to Chapter 2 for more information.

Exercising for the Good of Your Body and Mind

A good workout provides many physical and emotional benefits. In addition to helping you avoid obesity, ongoing research indicates that:

✔ A healthy body enhances your sense of self-esteem and develops your personal resilience to challenge.

✔ Exercise building muscular strength improves health and elevates survival rates following illness.

✔ The amount of walking that you do in the day relates directly to the difference between living well and dying early. Just 30 minutes a day – which can include walking in your home, climbing stairs and doing housework – can help you stay healthy.

✔ Exercise significantly improves long-standing back pain. Remember that any exercise programme – especially if you suffer from back pain – needs to be individually designed and include activities for both stretching and strengthening.

✔ Exercise protects you from diseases such as diabetes, coronary artery disease and depression.

✔ Regular exercise reduces your risk of dementia and Alzheimer's disease. Research suggests that older adults who exercise three or more times a week for 15 minutes reduce the risk of dementia by nearly 40 per cent. Exercise even benefits participants who're frail and have low initial levels of physical fitness. The slogan 'use it even if you've started to lose it' makes sense!

The following section explores some of the emotional benefits of getting up from your chair and getting active.

Re-balancing your chemistry

When you're stressed, your body produces chemicals that rev you up but also limit your complex thinking. Recurring anxious or depressive thoughts can cause additional stress and cause you to lose sight of the positive. (See Chapter 2 for more details.)

Fortunately, exercising helps you switch off the stress response and re-balance your system. When you exercise, your body creates 'feel-good' chemicals called *endorphins*, as well as other chemicals such as adrenaline, serotonin and dopamine, which naturally elevate your mood.

As the various feel-good chemicals associated with exercise affect your mood, you can decide to let go of negative feelings that you may consciously or unconsciously be holding within your body (see the following section 'Releasing emotions during exercise'). Just by going to the gym, walking, dancing or stretching, you have the opportunity to change your emotional state and focus on the positives – positive energy, positive thoughts and positive emotions. Instead of ruminating on the negative aspects of your life, you can encourage your brain and body to function normally again.

> # Getting unstuck
>
> Your body holds on to memories associated with previous episodes of threat. Your muscles and joints automatically tense up when you go into situations that have been difficult in the past.
>
> To help you understand such reactions in your own life, identify times when:
>
> ✔ Your jaw tightens or locks.
>
> ✔ Your throat constricts.
>
> ✔ Your neck and shoulders tense.
>
> ✔ Your eyes twitch
>
> ✔ Your stomach cramps or churns.
>
> ✔ Your back throbs.
>
> The preceding are all 'stuck' responses that deliberate movement. Fortunately, you can replace them with healthier responses and then further open new doors of emotional experience by choosing to release old emotional pain while you exercise. You literally shake or move the pain out of your system, as we discuss in the section 'Releasing emotions during exercise'.

Regular vigorous exercise also reduces detrimental *over-breathing* (see Chapter 2) and restores healthy breathing, which in turn reduces your anger and depression.

Releasing emotions during exercise

When you start an emotional healing exercise programme, you're likely to become more aware of your emotions. This awareness is a good sign; it shows that you're bringing feelings to the surface for healing. However, the experience can also feel uncomfortable.

Acknowledge whatever arises as you exercise. If feelings of hurt or anger come up, don't try to push them down or reject them. Doing so only encourages your body to hold them longer.

Instead, try any or all the following techniques:

✔ Visualise your emotional pain taking on a physical form. See it being released from your muscles and sliding out of your body as you stretch or move.

✔ Focus on easing tension in your jaw, neck, shoulder and joints (see the sidebar 'Getting unstuck' for some other common tension spots).

✔ Repeat an affirming thought such as 'I'm releasing old tension and allowing my body to feel free' as you exercise.

✔ Pay attention to the specific emotions that you feel and the body parts that seem to hold blocked energy. Freely move your body in response to the emotion and 'act out' the feeling in order to release it.

For example, moving your arms or legs with a slow drawing back and then a rapid release movement mimics the acting out of anger. A punching or kicking movement releases pent-up feelings without damaging others.

✔ If you feel sad or anxious, hold yourself in a hug with arms crossed for a minute or two. Acknowledge your feelings by saying 'Yes, I feel sad' or 'I do feel fearful'. Then gradually release your arms and lift them to the sky to draw in new feelings of positivity, courage, connection and strength.

Choosing the right exercise for you

When establishing your exercise plan, consider the following points:

✔ **The forms of exercise you prefer.** You know the types of exercise you've enjoyed in the past and those you haven't. Focusing on activities you enjoy means that you're more likely to stick with your exercise regime. And remember that exercise can include activities beyond traditional sport and fitness activities. (That's why we cover a variety of strategies in this chapter, including dance and body therapies such as yoga.)

Many people were put off exercise after being forced to play a game they didn't enjoy at school. Although you may feel an initial resistance, remind yourself that you're in a new situation and that you can decide to enjoy what's now a fresh experience.

✔ **The type and amount of exercise that's realistic for your busy life.** Choose an exercise that you can conveniently do, otherwise you may find ways to avoid it! Make a list of exercises that can fit into your everyday activities and set some realistic goals. Remember: you don't have to do hours upon hours of strenuous activity; just 30 minutes of walking can make a difference.

✔ **The type and amount of exercise that's going to make the most difference for your situation.** For example, research shows that intense aerobic exercise for at least 30 minutes a session three times a week is as effective as medication for treating mild to moderate depression. Exercise referral on prescription is now available from the NHS for individuals suffering from diseases like Parkinson's and from injuries. Consult your doctor, who will most likely refer to you to a physiologist.

As in many things, variety is the spice of life. Combining stretch with continuous aerobic exercise (such as walking, running, swimming, cycling or tap dancing) typically offers the most benefit for your body and mind.

TIP

In good company

Choosing a friendly, supportive person or group to work out with or participate in other physical activities we describe in this chapter adds to your emotional release. Research shows that when you surround yourself with positive people and positive experiences, greater well-being follows.

When you engage in physical activities alongside another person, you give and receive moral support. By sharing an experience with someone else, you satisfy an essential, social aspect of your human needs. And having an exercise buddy or group can provide opportunities to relax with others when the physical exertion stops.

You can easily add activity, exercise and enjoyment into your daily life in a variety of ways:

- ✔ Start your day with a favourite piece of lively music. Stretch, move or dance along with it to get your body moving. Focus on raising energy, releasing tension and breaking up habitual physical and emotional patterns.

- ✔ Use the stairs in your house and create a step up and step down regime. Lead with one foot, stepping up one step and then back down. After 50 steps, change the lead. The pace and speed of your movements regulates the exercise load.

- ✔ Walk the stairs to the top of the building where you work, if possible.

- ✔ Beat boredom and get adventurous by trying one new activity every month. Ever wanted to try canoeing, snorkelling, karate or trampolining?

- ✔ Sign up for a class. A yoga, martial arts, Pilates or aerobics class is a great way to meet new people and get some exercise in the process.

- ✔ Join a sporting club, such as for tennis, cricket, netball, football, rugby or golf, where you can combine activity with team spirit and a sense of belonging. Go biking with your family or walk your kids to school.

REMEMBER

Exercise isn't an all-or-nothing affair. If you don't get to exercise as planned, that's okay. Just get back on track tomorrow.

Paying Attention

Taking note of what's really going on in your immediate world and in your own mind may not seem particularly active at first. But trust us, deliberately paying attention to a movement activity does, in fact, take both effort and energy.

Walk this way

Everyday walking has many benefits. You work your muscles, reduce stress, interact with people and get outside in the fresh air – all with a very low risk of injury. Your bones also become denser, which is particularly valuable if you're at risk for bone thinning, or *osteoporosis*.

A national scheme is now in place, with links in your local area, called Walking the Way to Health. Find details on the web or through your local Primary Care Trust. You can obtain a free pedometer on loan for three months that helps you set goals for walking. This encourages you to reach a target of 10,000 steps per day.

This section offers several ways to increase your awareness and heal emotional wounds.

Walking mindfully

Mindful walking is different from fitness walking. When you walk mindfully, you pay full attention to the activity of walking and notice every detail of what you're doing. Mindful walking can relieve you of negative thoughts and emotions for a period of time. When you focus on only your movement, negative feelings and stressful events take a back seat.

Choose a place – indoors or outdoors – wherever you feel confident and can walk comfortably and safely. Choose an area that offers a specific route or path that you can repeat without interruption. You can walk inside your home, in your garden or in a park. We don't recommend that you walk in your street or anywhere that you may be disturbed. You can walk with or without shoes.

1. **Stand still and pay attention to your breathing.**

   If your breath is in your upper chest, move the breath down to your diaphragm and abdomen. You can shift your breath just by becoming aware of its placement. See Chapter 2 for more on breathing. Do this for at least three minutes and begin to move when you feel that your breath is relaxed.

2. **Start to walk very slowly and continue to focus on your breathing.**

   Focusing on breathing as you move helps further calm your thoughts. Count the number of steps you take as you inhale and exhale. Try to take four steps on the inhale and six on the exhale.

3. **Notice with full attention the experience of walking throughout your body.**

   Feel your feet touch the ground, your clothes on your back, the way your arms move as you move your legs. Take note of how you place each step. Notice your senses of sight, sound and smell. Allow yourself to become absorbed in the experience of being present.

4. **Repeat a simple phrase in your mind to keep negative emotions at bay.**

   Try a simple statement such as 'I free myself from old difficulties', 'I'm calm and at peace' or 'And this too will pass'.

5. **Re-focus your whole attention on the act of walking if distractions such as stressful thoughts or bodily discomforts come into your mind.**

   When you come to the end of your path, just turn around and go back to the beginning so that you're walking back and forth.

6. **Continue to walk mindfully for any period of time between 5 and 45 minutes.**

   Stop at a moment that feels right to you.

Don't judge your experience. No right or wrong way exists when walking mindfully. Just be present in the moment. Breath by breath, stay present for your own experience – not allowing the past or future to colour the moment.

For more activities involving mindfulness, turn to Chapter 13.

Journeying through nature

Being in nature can revive and refresh you. A timeless quality exists when you're surrounded by birdsong, trees, plants and flowers. After spending some time out in nature, many people report a sense of connection to something greater than their emotional problems and find the process healing. Try to make getting out into nature – even sitting on a park bench for ten minutes during lunch – part of your regular routine.

In a journal or notebook, make a list of the places – walks, parks, beaches and other locations – in which you remember experiencing a sense of peace and ease. For example:

- ✔ What specific places hold happy childhood memories?
- ✔ Where is your favourite quiet place in your garden or local park?
- ✔ What specific flowers or trees help you to feel happy?
- ✔ Which certain colours or scents resonate with you?

When you feel upset, allow your imagination to drift to one of these special spots. Let your breath settle and bring back the feeling of contentment and pleasure that you experienced in this place. This location becomes your inner place of safety, one that you can return to anytime.

Hang a few pictures from books or magazines around your home or office to remind you of your special imagined spot and make it seem real. Whenever you look at these pictures, return to feeling the positive emotions you associate with these locations. To make sure these images stay fresh in your mind, move the position of the pictures from time to time.

Recalling favourite stories

As a child, much of your education probably came through stories – many of which contain animals undergoing adventures in memorable settings. *Winnie the Pooh* and *The Wind in the Willows* come to mind for us. Like a special spot in the real world (see the earlier section 'Journeying through nature'), the setting of a beloved story can serve as a refreshing place to take a mental holiday for a few minutes.

Take a few moments to remember stories from your childhood that you enjoyed – and recall stories that you read to your children or grandchildren. Jot down the names of a few positive stories in a journal or notebook and then describe:

- ✔ **The setting.** What was the world of the story like?

- ✔ **Those involved.** Was someone reading to you, or were you reading on your own? Were you reading the story to someone else?

- ✔ **The feelings.** How did you feel while you listened to or read the story? Safe? Happy? Secure? Inspired?

If you can't recall a children's story, read the following sidebar 'The lone flower.' See whether this little tale helps you develop feelings of contentment, resilience, refreshment, courage or strength.

Slowing your pace

If you find that the daily pace of life is increasing, you're not imagining things:

- ✔ Walking speeds in London have increased by 10 per cent in the last ten years according to a British Council survey.

- ✔ Studies suggest that 30 per cent of people are tired all the time.

Getting caught up in too much activity leads to you losing perspective, so try to find a balance between rest and activity. Often this balance means slowing down when your body gives you signals such as fatigue or tension. Tiredness signals that you're at the limit of tolerance and you need to recover. Tension indicates that too much is going on and may suggest strong emotions about the situation. (Tiredness can also indicate lack of fluid or food, associated with reduced blood sugar levels; see Chapter 4).

The lone flower

A once-beautiful flower, struggling with its health and energy, found that holding its head up and finding the rays of the sun was becoming difficult. So its petals drooped and its head came forward. It stopped trying to push roots deep into the soil for more food and moisture. Without a renewal of its life force, it felt as if its life was ebbing away.

But then, the flower began to slowly relax its tissues and gently let in the nutrients from the soil. It felt the healing warmth of the sun on its petals. As it did so, the slumped stem began to straighten and its downward gaze began to lift.

One day the flower stretched with all its might and was able to hold its bloom fully upright once again. To its delight when it looked up and around, the flower realised that it wasn't alone – but part of a beautiful garden with other flowers and plants at different stages of growth.

At that moment the numbness left the contracted roots and the once-withering flower stood tall. It savoured the sensations of its roots intertwining with other nearby plants. It basked in the warmth of the sun and realised that it was not isolated but deeply connected to all the other living things in the garden.

Thus a blessing was given to the flower. It had the courage to open up and give life a second chance in order to rediscover its own special place in the garden of life.

You're a human _being_ as well as a human _doing_. Listen to your body and reflect on what creates imbalance. What thoughts are driving any mismatch between activity and rest? Are you telling yourself things like 'I must achieve' or 'I should do or finish this' or 'I feel guilty if I take time out'?

Feeling good when you're fatigued is difficult, and so slow the pace and rest if you find yourself constantly tired. It's likely that you're not taking care of your physical or emotional needs in some way, so your body is signalling to you to stop and review what you need to do.

Find ways to stop and just be. Identify what helps you to slow the pace, wind down and recover perspective. Some calming activities include:

- Listening to music or reading a pleasurable book or magazine.
- Going for a walk or sitting in natural surroundings.
- Getting out holiday or travel pictures that bring back good feelings.
- Stroking your pet, which fosters a loving connection and, according to many studies, boosts your immunity.
- Soaking in a warm bath, refreshing in a shower or taking a swim.

Shifting Old Emotions through Bodywork

You can release memories of old emotional injury from your body through a variety of physically engaging activities, including movement, dance and martial arts. *Bodywork* is fully engaging your body in movement with the deliberate intention to clear emotions that may still be held in the body. Bodywork can be *passive* and involve a hands-on practitioner, or *active* and include you engaging in yoga or a martial art.

In the following sections, we examine body-focused approaches to healing yourself.

Adjusting your posture and releasing defensive body armour

You can change your emotional state by altering your body position. You may have developed a defensive or rigid body posture as a result of holding on to negative emotions such as depression, anxiety or anger.

Pay attention to your physiology in different situations, such as sitting at your computer, accepting feedback from your boss, feeling criticised by your partner or parent, or coming home after work. Signs of defensive or rigid posture include:

- Looking towards the ground rather than straight ahead.
- Drooping shoulders.
- Crossing your arms and possibly your legs.
- Tensing the joints in your jaw, shoulders, arms and back.
- Moving your head and neck with tight or restricted motion.
- Slouching or twisting your body, instead of holding it in a balanced, upright posture. (In an upright posture, a line dropped through the centre of your head falls into the middle of your pelvis.)

Fortunately, you can re-educate your body to relax and release tension and pain. Just standing up straighter, with your shoulders back and your head straight, can help you feel stronger both physically and emotionally. Take a look at yourself in the mirror to notice the difference and watch yourself as you first deliberately adopt a defensive position and secondly adopt a confident, open and strong posture. You may need to practise this latter posture frequently if you've developed habits of how you stand as a result of past stress, fear, depression or anger.

Quietening your body and mind through movement

Focused physical exercise – practices such as The Alexander Technique, Pilates, Tai-Chi and yoga – improve your core stability, which relates to the muscular connection between your abdominal wall, diaphragm, pelvis and lower back. Core stability enables freedom of movement, balance and co-ordination. These specific exercises are relevant to emotional release because they integrate a series of movements that reduce tension and require co-ordinated control of mind and body. They also enable you to shut out negative thoughts and feelings for the period of the activity. Within purposeful physical exercise, you can focus your attention on the movement itself and be wholeheartedly within the experience. This focus creates a setting for the release of difficult emotions.

You can generally find teachers and classes by going to classified ads, looking in your health directories, or researching on the web. You're likely to find options for one-to-one coaching or group work. You can also consider purchasing a DVD on any of these techniques or refer to *Pilates For Dummies* by Ellie Herma, *Tai Chi For Dummies* by Therese Iknoian or *Yoga For Dummies* by Lilias Folan, Georg Feuerstein and Larry Payne

Freeing your spirit through dance

Dance is practised throughout the world as a form of emotional expression, whether it's formal or informal. Some forms of dance are vigorous and bring about aerobic levels of exercise, including:

- Latin American and salsa
- Some ballroom dancing, such as quickstep and foxtrot
- Scottish and barn-dancing
- Tap dancing
- Jive and Lindy Hop
- Free dance to music that you choose (even if you don't know the right steps, you can still dance)

Other forms of dance encourage a release of emotions through free movement. Some dances are meditative and spiritual, freeing the mind by moving the body:

- **5Rhythm**, developed by Gabrielle Roth in the 1960s, is a dance form based on five rhythms: flowing, staccato, chaos, lyrical and stillness. Groups continue to gather and practise 5Rhythm today.

- **Some Indian and Sufi practices** follow a process in which you allow your body to loosen and express itself. The practice concludes with a quiet meditative stillness.

- **Qi Qong** is an energy-based practice and includes movement that shakes out negative emotional energy.

You don't have to go to a dance class to enjoy the emotionally healing benefits of dance. Select a CD from your collection that moves you; wild rock or a gently swaying lullaby – whatever stirs you. Turn down the lights and relax into the music. Allow your body to move in whatever way feels right to you. Let your emotional spirit conduct your movement. You may encounter both pain and joy. Feel free: no right or wrong way exists to this exercise. Let your emotions out as if you're a child again.

Breathing the Breath of Life through Song

Singing is the oral expression of emotion. Around the globe, people express themselves through song.

You get loads of benefits from singing:

- Singing is fun – and fun is good for you.

- Singing regulates good diaphragmatic breathing and brings about relaxation.

- Singing in a community or church choir brings you together with others in a shared endeavour. You don't always need to read music; you can even find choirs for 'non-singers'!

- Singing requires and creates energy, which allows you to move away from everyday preoccupations.

- Singing helps you find your voice, strengthen it and develop the confidence to speak up – all useful skills when you're healing emotions.

Start to sing in the shower or the car today. Sing as noisily and joyfully as you can. Don't judge yourself – just go for it! A little vocalising everyday can re-engage you with positive emotion.

Conducting your breathing rhythms for singing

Central to all singing is the ability to use your diaphragm, breathing in so that the abdomen rises. Then the ability to slow the out-breath allows you to control your breath and sustain your singing through the phrase. Chapter 2 covers the fundamentals of breathing and the pitfalls of over-breathing.

You can regulate your breathing rhythm yourself, rather like a conductor of an orchestra. When singing you want the breath in your diaphragm, which lies like a parachute between your lungs and the contents of your abdomen. For strong, healthy singing, your diaphragm acts like a bellows, expanding your lower ribs and pushing your abdomen out. The movement of the upper chest is minimal and your shoulders stay still.

The magic of music

As part of a dancing or singing experience, music triggers emotions and can transform negative emotional states into positive ones. Whether you're listening or performing, music can lift a persistent negative mood and reconnect you to harmony in your mind and body. The power of music can elevate feelings of courage and motivate people into battle. Football teams use specific themes to pump up their spirits before a match. Peaceful music can reduce anger and restore love. The right tune can soothe a crying baby to sleep – or make you want to jump up and dance.

You can consciously use music to tap into different emotional states. Find a quiet time to review your music collection and then pick music that suits your emotional goal. For example:

✔ If you're feeling pent-up sadness, choose a sad song to release your tears.

✔ If you want to feel energised, listen to some rock, South American salsa or bossa nova.

✔ If you want to re-create the mood of your teenage years, pick a song from the past and dance like you did back then.

✔ If you need courage or want to feel joyous, find something that lifts your spirits. Many songs can do this – remember 'I whistle a happy tune' from *The King and I?*

Following are some specific examples that work for us, but you're sure to have your individual preferences:

✔ To energise yourself, try Beethoven's piano concertos 1, 3, 4 and 5 or 'Pomp and Circumstance' No 1 by Elgar.

✔ To create joy, listen to Schubert's piano quintet in A Major, 'The Trout'; 'The Four Seasons' by Vivaldi; or choral works such as the *Gloria* by Vivaldi, *St Matthew Passion* by Bach and *The Messiah* by Handel.

✔ To inspire love: curl up with Tchaikovsky's piano concerto No 1 or the cello concerto, op 85, by Elgar.

Mary moves on – musically

Mary and her mother had always been close. At times Mary had felt her mother was not only a parent but also a friend. They went to concerts and theatre together, enjoying meals before these events. When her mother died suddenly of a heart attack, Mary felt trapped in sadness and self-pity. She had had little time to say good-bye or tell her mother how much she loved her.

After going on a retreat, Mary remembered times where their love and connection had been particularly strong. Recalling a particular concert they'd enjoyed, Mary decided to listen to the music quietly on her own. As she listened she started sobbing uncontrollably. She didn't try and stop herself but continued crying until she felt as if a well of sadness had been released.

Eventually, Mary became calm and was able to remember all the positive experiences that she had shared with her mother and imagine what her mother would want for her now. Mary eventually decided to create a music scholarship in her mother's name at her local college of music.

As you release air from your lungs, your vocal chords resonate. You can feel this vibration by creating a humming sound and placing your fingers around your upper neck. (When you're stressed and breathe in the upper chest, you restrict your voice and the pitch becomes high and constricted. You literally lose your voice.)

For some people singing comes naturally, but if you struggle, feel anxious or find that your throat hurts after singing, consider finding a singing coach. Just one session and a few tips can make quite a difference. Also, music therapists are professionals who are able to choose and develop music to resolve health or emotional issues.

Singing to restore positive emotions

Some specialist singing methods available use vibration as a form of healing. These include:

- **Chanting.** You use harmony and repetition with different small groups within a choir singing in sequence, as a 'round'. You may have sung in this way at school.

- **Toning.** You create different pitches of sound and observe how they vibrate within your body. You may exhale singing 'Oh' or 'Ah' or 'Ee' and allow that sound to continue for the whole of the out-breath.

To release emotions as you perform or listen to music, carry out the following:

- ✔ **Be open.** Acknowledge and examine all the feelings that arise.

- ✔ **Get the details.** Notice the mental, emotional and physical reactions you're experiencing while you're singing or listening to the music.

- ✔ **Name it and claim it.** Name the old injury and then express the connected feelings appropriately. You find more information in Chapters 8 and 9.

- ✔ **Return to love.** Reconnect to a sense of love, self-care and compassion.

- ✔ **Change perspective.** Replace the unhelpful emotions with a positive emotional state. See Chapters 3, 10 and 12 for ways to switch emotions.

Part III
Emotional Healing
for Real Life

In this part . . .

You need to think about how your emotions are directing your life – often without you realising it. The questions and activities is this part help you review your past and find ways to lessen emotional pain. Identify actions to defuse anger in yourself and others and find ways to express your feelings in an assertive (rather than an aggressive) way.

As you consider the key changes in your life's journey, you may need to overcome your fears, work through grief and prepare for continuous change.

Chapter 7

Putting Your Emotions in Context

*Y*our emotions are influenced by the *context*, both physical and emotional, in which you live and have lived. Whether or not you live in a home you like, work in job you enjoy and feel supported by other people, all determine the way you feel on a daily basis.

How you respond to situations in your home, work and personal life is influenced by the expectations of your parents. The voices of your ancestors echo down through the generations to your parents and to you, often providing sets of spoken and unspoken rules of behaviour that may no longer be relevant to the world in which you live today.

No 'one-and-right' way exists on how to feel about a situation, whatever parental norms you may have experienced. You can now break out of past habits and find new ways of living that allow you greater happiness. Two children brought up in the same environment with the same parents may have vastly different experiences. One child conforms and is 'the good child', but feels repressed and unable to express himself. The other rebels and moves away to lead a completely different life, breaking with convention. Same situation, different response; neither one is right or wrong.

This chapter helps you review your own influences – past and present – and check whether the expectations of family, peers and environment have narrowed your perspective. You're a unique personality and the responsibility is on you to identify and create the environment that best meets your own emotional needs.

Researching Your Family History

Your past has inevitably shaped you. Gaining insight about these influences is the key to developing wisdom about how to manage yourself, your life and your emotions now and in the future. To ensure that habitual behaviours you picked up from others or experienced at an earlier stage aren't dogging your current behaviour, spend some time reviewing the following information:

- **Where you come from (your social and cultural context).** Where were you brought up? What was your community like? How has it influenced you?

- **What expectations others had of you.** What were the beliefs and behavioural messages you were given as a child?

- **What emotional backdrop applied to your upbringing.** Were you aware of your parents' emotions? Were you encouraged to share your own feelings? Was affection physically offered, with touches, hugs or kisses?

- **Where you fit – or don't fit – within your family environment.** What birth order are you? Was the attention you were given 'good enough'? How did your placing affect your development?

Emotions are infectious. If you had a parent or close family member who was prone to depression, alcoholism or some other debilitating condition, you may have picked up some similar behaviours. Alternatively you may have become a *caretaker,* someone who always tries to heal or protect the other person. This caretaking behaviour can follow you into adult life and although it can have positive aspects, it may no longer be appropriate and can even seem controlling to others. Indeed, over-caring can lead to *co-dependency,* in which one person is or is perceived as needy and the other sees himself as rescuer. This dynamic results in both people losing their senses of identity and neither being fully self-sufficient until the pattern is broken.

Take a piece of paper and draw your family tree. Start with yourself as the trunk of the tree and list your parents as the main branches. Draw limbs off your parents' branches for your siblings. Add your grandparents and all your aunts and uncles. Go back two or three generations, if possible. After you've sketched out the tree, look over the various limbs and branches and gather information about

- **Family rules.** Do strong messages exist about what you *should* do or be? What about things that you should absolutely not do or be?

- **Myths, family stories and labels.** Who are the heroes? Who are the villains? Who are the 'black sheep' or the 'prodigal' children? Also, who don't you speak of or appears to be forgotten?

- **Notable patterns.** Do you share a similar occupation, lifestyle, illness, location or behaviour to anyone in your tree?

✔ **Types of people surrounding you.** Who are they? What do they care about?

✔ **Ways in which people act or go through life.** What are some predispositions that you may have inherited – or imagined you inherited? For example, are you pessimistic and was this influenced by a family member?

Many people find that unconscious scripts and stories are playing out within families. Research shows that girls who become teenage mothers often have a mother who was also a teenage mother. You may discover that your choice of career or study or hobbies reflects a talent that existed earlier in your family history. This new information may allow you to connect in a conscious way to family patterns that you now recognise have influenced your life choices.

After you've drawn your family tree, take another look and consider which members you're close to. In the centre of another sheet of paper, draw a small circle with your name in it. Work out from the centre and list those individuals who you feel closest to, followed by those you feel more distant from. What draws you to the people you listed as closest to you? What pushes the more distant people away? Do you have a problem with certain people? What are the emotional issues outstanding and how may you resolve them? (See the later section 'Resolving Old Family Issues' for more.) Allow yourself time for these activities; you may want to come back to your drawing several times or talk with family members to gain more information.

Understanding family patterns enables you to make choices to release old responses and heal yourself in the future. Decide which aspects of your family you admire and which aspects don't now fit the person you are. Make peace with the past; even if it has been painful, you've developed strengths. Realise that you have the power to choose how your family influences the life you want to lead as you move forward.

Resolving Old Family Issues

The ideal family of 2.2 children where everyone is happy all the time is a fairy tale. In reality each family has some resentment, rivalry, unwanted discipline or unrealistic expectations. No perfect way exists to love someone or bring up a child, and so mismatches of needs for emotional warmth, encouragement or sufficient attention inevitably arise. Luckily most families manage to find real moments of shared enjoyment despite the challenges.

Emotional healing is necessary if you recognise that the pain you're feeling – whether anger, resentment, guilt or sadness – is upsetting your daily experience of life. Sometimes healing happens naturally and you gradually find yourself letting go of an issue that used to upset you. But you may need to allocate some time to addressing a problem consciously in order to heal it.

To go or not to go to university

Mary was born in 1935, growing up in a time when few women went to university. However, she was bright and, with encouragement from her teachers, she won a place to read English. At the end of her first year, her mother decided that she was becoming too intellectual to attract a husband and insisted that she leave. Mary meekly agreed but regretted this decision all her life. She married young and had children but felt unfulfilled intellectually and suffered ill health and depression. For all her life, she was unable to participate actively in work and felt that she hadn't taken the opportunity to contribute all she felt she had to give. For her lifetime she berated herself for following her parents' agenda and asked herself, 'Why didn't I speak up for what I really wanted to do?'

The following sections take you through the process of identifying, exploring, accepting and forgiving family-related emotional wounds.

Examining expectations

Many factors shape your vision of what you want from your life, but the influence of your family on these expectations can be particularly powerful.

By reviewing the following expectations, check whether your life today and your vision of life in the future reflects who you are and want to be – or whether it reflects the expectations of others:

- ✔ What is your view or definition of 'success'?

- ✔ When you were growing up, did you feel that you were capable of success?

- ✔ As you grew up, in what ways did you follow family expectations? In what ways did you rebel? How did your siblings respond?

- ✔ Are you still marching to someone else's tune even though you may now be well into your adult years?

Being a parent isn't easy. Finding the balance between positive encouragement and the realities of life is particularly challenging. Subtle differences in parental messages matter. For example, recent research demonstrates that praising a child for 'working really hard' is more effective than praising him for 'being so clever'. The latter statement is finite whereas 'working really hard' gives the message that the child has the capacity to succeed through his own efforts.

Your parents' own experiences shaped the way they managed expectations of you. For example, if they were successful in a specific field, they may expect the same of you; however, if they never fulfilled their dreams, they may resent you for having achieved more than they did.

Parental put-downs often come from a parent's need to release some of his or her own pent-up frustration. Comments such as the following can cause long-lasting wounds and limit your sense of personal potential:

- ✔ You're a complete idiot – how could you be so stupid?
- ✔ You'll never amount to anything.
- ✔ What makes you think anyone would want to marry you anyway?

Parents can also layer their own expectations on children based on their own disappointments and experiences rather than the current reality. For example

- ✔ When I was your age. . .
- ✔ I never would have wasted an opportunity like you did. . .

Being placed on a pedestal by your parents can also be a burden. Trying to live up to their hopes and dreams can be a huge pressure. Parents who practically worship their children aren't loving their children for being themselves but rather for who the parents want the children to be. All humans long for love and acceptance. Overly praised and protected children can become paralysed; they adapt to parental expectations and don't dare to be honest about what they really think and want for themselves. This dynamic can exhaust children's energy, blur their identities and lead to adaptive behaviours where they're acting out the parents' needs rather than their own. Loss of identity and suppression of emotional needs can lead to a variety of behaviours, including addictions such as alcohol or cannabis misuse.

Defining yourself

Your past may contain horrible incidents with your family, but you can decide to take charge of your own self-perception and be honest with yourself. The following activity helps you set aside the past and create a vision of yourself in the future. Take ten minutes of quiet time and do the following:

1. **Think back to your childhood and listen for any remarks that may have limited your ability to make good decisions for yourself.**

What were these comments? See the preceding section 'Examining expectations' for these types of limiting parental statements.

2. **Envision those limiting words and phrases written on a blackboard and consider how they impact your life.**

   How did these words affect your life growing up? Do you still heed them today? What emotions do they inspire in you?

3. **Imagine that you have a large, powerful eraser and can rub out your limiting statements.**

   As you erase the words, bring in a sense of compassion towards the people who said them (see Chapter 13 for more on introducing positive emotions). Recognise that these individuals may have experienced similar treatment themselves and knew no different.

4. **Imagine writing empowering statements on your now clean blackboard.**

   Choose words and phrases that help you feel liberated from the pain of the past. Some examples include 'I am strong and talented', 'I can be the person I want to be' and 'I am confident of my abilities and can achieve my goals.'

If you're a parent, stop and consider what expectations you may be unconsciously placing on your own children or attempting to live out through them. Reflect on whether you need to accept your child as a unique being who came through you to live his own life rather than a person you created to live as a mirror of your expectations. Turn to Chapter 18 for more information about children's healing.

Realising that no one has a perfect childhood

Parenthood is complex and demanding. Each child brings a unique personality to a family and alters its dynamics. People – including parents – are fallible and make mistakes. Being too judgemental of your parents is counterproductive and achieves nothing. Most people feel neglected, frustrated, criticised or underestimated by their parents at some stage, but this feeling doesn't have to cast a shadow over the rest of their lives.

The majority of parents do the best they can with the resources they have available and in the circumstances they face. Parents rarely set out with the wilful intention of harming or abusing their children. Your parents may well have been doing the best that they could. A key difference exists between unintended hurt and wilful neglect. (Of course, if you've experienced or partaken in past abuse, you can benefit from expert support. See Chapters 8 and 9, and the Appendix for contact details on professional help.)

Acknowledging that things weren't exactly as you would have liked them to be, and considering the emotion that this fact raises in you, helps you to achieve emotional healing. You must then go a step further and consider what strengths you gained through your experiences and work to become thankful for them. Healing occurs when you come to terms with what has happened, accept it and then put it to one side and build on it.

Releasing old traumas through words and action

If you experienced a trauma or any type of abuse in your family, you may have powerful locked-in feelings. Allowing these emotions to come out with real force and strong words can be very helpful.

Find a safe space where you can express words and action:

- ✔ **Release your harshest words.** Include swear words at this point, if you're okay with them. Direct these words at a substitute for the person or event – for example a chair or a photo.

- ✔ **Act out your feelings.** Let the emotions find a physical release. For example, if you feel anger, hit a pillow again and again with real force, without damaging yourself. Or try twisting a towel as hard as you can, shouting and yelling if this comes naturally. When you finish, you may want to slowly focus on the process of untwisting the towel and further releasing your feelings.

Don't hold back. If you've been hurt, accept that this is the case and name the injury, allow the feelings and accept that they are your own. This allows you to let go of the suppressed emotions. This activity is the first stage of releasing old trauma. By acting out in word and action, you allow the emotions to move out of your body.

You may find that sadness and crying follow your emotional release. Your body is responding naturally to relieving itself of stress chemicals and tension. Allow the sadness and crying to continue; it will stop.

You may feel a little tired after this activity, so if you have a demanding day ahead try to reschedule appointments. Be gentle with yourself. Nourish yourself in mind and body, including eating healthy food. See Chapters 4 and 14 for more information on self-care.

Choosing to share your feelings

As you examine your past, you may discover that you associate great emotional pain with a specific person. You may feel compelled to express your pain in words to someone who has upset you. Before you do so, stop and consider:

- ✔ Why you want to discuss your injury with the other person.
- ✔ What you want to gain by having the conversation.
- ✔ Whether you're seeking revenge on, or trying to affix blame to, the other person.
- ✔ Whether the conversation is likely truly to help your relationship or whether you simply need to get the situation off your chest.

After considering the preceding aspects of your situation, you may want to proceed with sharing your feelings. Consider trying the following techniques:

- ✔ **Write out your emotions.** You may experience very strong emotions and have difficulty in seeing the person face to face. Write out your feelings and explain what happened. Describe what you need for the future.

  You may choose to never share this writing. Instead, you may create a ritual where you destroy it or burn it, imagining the past injury being released. See the sidebar 'Letter-writing to release pain'.

- ✔ **Find a neutral person to facilitate a meeting.** Consider inviting an objective referee who can mediate and establish a safe environment in which both parties feel able to talk. Involving a family member as facilitator may or may not be appropriate, but do plan to meet in a neutral, yet private place without emotional colour or attachment for either of you.

Finding forgiveness

To *forgive* means that you accept, acknowledge and let go of the injury to your feelings. Forgiving doesn't mean that you have to trust that person, and it doesn't make what happened right.

Forgiving isn't forgetting. Your past is your own; you always have it with you. But you can benefit from letting go of negative emotions connected with the past. These emotions can hurt you more than they hurt the other person.

Letter-writing to release pain

Neil was abandoned by his mother when he was nine years old. She told him to wait on the pavement where, without explanation, he was taken into social services care, which his mother had previously arranged. He locked away his bewilderment, anger and sadness inside him for years.

As part of counselling as an adult, Neil decided he wanted to express his feelings to his mother, even though she was now dead. He chose to write a letter that explained his feelings and explored questions he knew would never be answered.

Eventually, he read the letter out to her gravestone, releasing years of tears and pain. Through the process of writing and reading the letter, he came to understand how desperate his mother must have been so many years ago. He then burnt the letter in a ritual, an experience that left him feeling both exhausted and relieved.

Unexpressed emotions can turn inwards (see Chapter 2). Holding hostility can lead to raised blood pressure and greater risk of heart attacks because with no outlet for expression, your body functions as if you constantly need to take life-saving action. Forgiveness allows your body and mind to regain balance again.

Jean developed total hair loss soon after discovering that her first husband had abused their daughter. Although she was happily re-married and the abuse had happened more than ten years earlier, she was unable to forgive herself. When she allowed herself to work through the strong emotions of guilt and rage that she held in her body, her hair started to re-grow.

You may not be able to forgive, but you can still seek ways to be at peace with yourself. Express your emotions using the following process:

- **Name all the feelings.** You may have a mixture of sadness, hurt, anger and hate, combined with complex emotions such as guilt and self-blame. Figure out all the emotions you're experiencing by writing in a journal or talking with a friend or counsellor. Chapter 3 can help you identify and name specific feelings.

- **Name the injury and its effects.** Write in a diary or speak to a friend or counsellor about specific damage and subsequent effects.

If you find yourself getting caught into a negative cycle of self-blame, anger or recrimination, step back, accept your experience and encourage compassion towards yourself and others. Try to rise above and see yourself now and in the future clear of these difficulties.

Forgiveness comes as you move through anger and hurt to acceptance and self-belief. This process doesn't mean that you have to let the perceived wrong-doer back into your life; it means that you're ready to believe in your own right to wellbeing.

Identifying Your Support Network

A good network of loving, supportive individuals benefits your health, happiness and longevity. Everyone's support network is different, but most include:

- ✔ A person with whom to share your joys and on whom to offload your worries and problems.
- ✔ A group within which you feel accepted as you are, quirks and all.
- ✔ A group displaying a degree of unconditional love.

Making one-on-one connections

Sharing your problems can hasten healing. Take steps to find someone with whom to talk and encourage others to do so.

Making friends later in life requires effort and commitment but gives huge rewards. Often people are busy with work and family and yet will welcome the opportunity to share on an adult level. Identify your own interests and seek out clubs or groups locally in your community or on the web where you're likely to meet similarly minded people. Social networking sites can enable you to reach out to new friends and also contact old ones. Contact details of specific support groups are in the Appendix.

Girls often build friendship bonds by sharing vulnerabilities, but owing to biology and social conditioning, some boys and young men have difficulty sharing their emotional concerns and experiences. When an emotional trauma hits a young man he may just internalise his grief and mask his problems through bravado and activity. However, most men agree that talking helps.

Tim was sent to boarding school aged 10. He felt bereft. His mother seldom wrote to him. This neglect chipped away at his self-esteem and sense of being lovable. He was bullied by the other boys throughout his school years and became increasingly isolated, but he always suffered in silence. When he suffered a mild heart attack at the age of 40, he finally decided to seek help and work through his experiences. He realised that his heart was signalling that he was still in pain. Before this event he had felt that a man was weak if he talked about problems or had therapy.

Denying or repressing emotional pain can lead to illness, alcoholism, drug-taking, loneliness and even suicide. The occurrence of suicide in young people, particularly young men, has been rising in recent years; so be proactive and help the young people in your life to share their feelings.

Sharing an activity can break down old reserves and give young people permission to talk about their worries. The activities don't have to be spectacular adventures, simply take time out to:

- ✔ Cook a meal together
- ✔ Play a game
- ✔ Take a walk

Martin took his 24-year-old son Simon on a camping trip, because he had been working very hard and not devoted enough individual time to Simon. They enjoyed sharing the physical activity. On the very last night of the trip, Simon suddenly shared with his father his feelings about his parents' divorce ten years earlier. When they got home Martin received a text from Simon saying: 'I feel as if a weight has lifted from my shoulders. Thanks.'

Going for groups

Some people attract a group of friends to them more easily than others. If you're shy, you may find social events awkward. Feel the fear and attend them anyway, because even one good friend is worth having. Identify hobbies or events that draw you towards like-minded people because this gives you a common topic to discuss or share.

Your current group of friends may not have personally experienced the events you've been through, which can result in them just not being able to empathise with your feelings. Divorce is a common occurrence these days and so people are generally able to find someone with whom to share their experiences. However, abuse or the death, illness or disability of yourself, a parent, partner, sibling, child or friend are less common, and many people struggle with what to say.

For example, discovering that your child is disabled or has a debilitating disease can be traumatic. Expectations of parenthood and family life are shattered; you're in mourning for the life you would have had. You have to create a new picture of life within the parameters of this changed world. Parents report that talking with others in a similar situation eases the pain and mitigates the difficulties of everyday life.

Plenty of support groups are available for most life situations. If you can't build a network within those people you already know, take steps to develop a group in your local area – or by phone or on the Internet. Extending yourself takes determination and courage, but if you're feeling the need for support, taking the plunge is worthwhile.

Balancing Your Life: Choosing Priorities

Leading a balanced life underpins your emotional stability. Being out of balance generates a sense of dissatisfaction. You can be in an excellent job, earning a large income, living in a big house and sharing your life with a lovely partner, but if you feel that you're neglecting one area of your life, you may feel deprived. This topic isn't a 'soft' one; it's your life.

Spending your time well is fundamental to your emotional wellbeing. In the following sections, we look at one critical part of your current environment of which you can take considerable control: the balance between the time you spend working, enjoying others and exploring your interests.

Masking your emotions with over-activity

Imbalance can creep up on you. You may find that you focus on one area of your life for a specific period and then get stuck in that groove out of habit. For example, you may suddenly realise that you're neglecting your children by focusing on DIY or because you have a major project on at work; or that you're neglecting your partner because you've become so focused on your children.

Spreading yourself too thinly dissipates your energy. Loved ones may resent your lack of attention. Additionally, you may be avoiding potentially more challenging situations. Your 'busyness' can become an excuse to keep people at bay or fulfil some deep need:

✔ You may be driven to overwork because you're trying to:

- Prove yourself.

- Achieve some goal.

- Avoid going home to a difficult relationship.

✔ You may find yourself focusing on your children in order to:

- Avoid being with your partner.

- Justify your role within the home.

- Feel that you're a 'good' parent or 'caring' partner.

✔ You may get wrapped in specific hobbies or interests such as

- The tennis or golf club

- Football, cricket, rugby

- Sailing every weekend

- Evenings out with your friends

Your current behaviour may relate to your past. Sheila lost her sister when they were both in their teens and thereafter focused all her energy on excelling at work, eventually becoming a workaholic. After a period of sickness, her manager suggested counselling. Sheila realised that she was trying to live her dead sister's life as well as her own. She discovered techniques to give herself permission to stop, be herself, slow down, delegate and enjoy life – all while not feeling guilty for being the 'one left'.

Gauging your work-life balance

Achieving your ideal work-life balance requires that you stop and take an overview of your life. Everyone's work-life balance is different, and so you must figure out what matters most to you. Thorough evaluation then enables you to give your time to the priorities that you really care about.

You can examine your work-life balance in various ways:

✔ Imagine that you're at the end of your life and looking back. What would you like to feel that you achieved and spent your time on? How would you like to be remembered by those you care about? What do you want to be said or written about you in an obituary?

✔ Imagine that you ask your family, your partner (if you have one), a friend and a work colleague to make a short speech of comment about you right now, what may each say? What would you like each of them to say? Is there a gap? Other people sometimes see your work-life balance very differently from how you do. Ask for feedback so you try to find ways to compromise where appropriate and possible.

✔ Imagine that you have a year free from financial or family obligations and are able to focus on what matters most to you. What would you do?

✔ List the ten things that matter most at work and the ten people who matter most to you. Reflect on whether you're giving these activities and people a sufficient amount of your time.

✔ Identify what you most like to do with those you love and list those things in your diary. Identify what you need to focus on at work and list them in your diary. Formulate a plan to do each of these things in the next six months.

✔ What can you alter or avoid in order to focus on what matters most?

Online overkill?

Being busy on the Internet or your mobile phone at all hours of the day or night can detract from balance and from your personal relationships. Many people get drawn into surfing the net at night when they can be spending time with their partners. The Internet offers a 'surrogate' support network where people talk to strangers via social websites. Some people get seduced by pornographic sites with the promise of excitement or comfort.

The result can be fantasy lives that include virtual 'adulterous' affairs, competitive games, gambling, uncontrolled spending and supposed friendships with people you never meet. All these behaviours can be addictive; they're also at the expense of being with those who are a real part of your actual life. Support groups for Internet addiction are available; see the Appendix.

Managing the ups and downs of life

Work life can be fulfilling but also stressful and challenging. Sometimes it can be all-consuming, leading you to neglect those you most care about. You can get caught up in the fear factor generated by recent trends of redundancy, restructures and changing management programmes. You may have to face a variety of work-related fears, leading to *what-if thinking,* such as:

- ✔ What if I get made redundant?
- ✔ What if I get passed over for promotion?
- ✔ What if I have to re-apply for my job?
- ✔ What if I get a new boss I don't get on with?

Also, what-ifs can extend beyond the workplace:

- ✔ What if my partner leaves me because he gets fed up with being neglected?
- ✔ What if my children grow up before I've spent enough time with them?
- ✔ What if my parents get old and I haven't been there for them?

Little advantage is gained in worrying about things that may never happen. Make plans but live in the moment of 'what is' rather than 'what if'. This shift in your thinking helps you value what's going well and gives you greater perspective when making decisions about the options you face.

Every action you take has a consequence, and so consider all aspects of your life. But remember that everything changes and what constitutes balance today may not do so tomorrow!

Gender bending – housework needs doing

The workplace was originally created by men for men with wives at home. This situation is no longer the case, and yet most organisations still run with an unspoken assumption that somebody is available to pick up the domestic chores. When both parties are working and having to share child care, shopping and housework, things can quickly become stressful.

These tensions can interrupt good relationships and lead to conflict. Many couples report arguing about who's 'too tired' to do the cooking or washing up, each vying to be the worse off. This behaviour isn't healthy and doesn't promote happiness and ease in a relationship.

Few people are living the traditional roles any more. In most cases, running home and family are now shared responsibilities. Men can be househusbands (or at least provide direct care with children several hours every week), and women can be the chief breadwinner (or at least provide a necessary percentage of the total household income).

Relationships today require new agreements about who does what in the household:

- **Review with your partner, the various requirements needed to run your home and family.** Discuss household management issues with your partner as early as possible, before disagreement or resentment build up. Allocate tasks and take turns to cover emergencies.

- **Set aside time alone for just you and your partner.** The *quality* of the relationship itself becomes more important now that relationships are more equal. Create quality time for each other as adults. Find a few minutes each day and at least an hour-long block each week for you and your partner to do something together, just the two of you – no children, no work, no outside responsibilities. This may be a romantic dinner at the kitchen table, a walk or a visit to a gallery. The key is that you enjoy uninterrupted adult time for the two of you.

- **Plan for leisure time.** Scheduling downtime may seem odd at first, but you may have to block out fun time each week until you get the hang of it. And leisure doesn't need to be elaborate; it can be anything that refreshes you and your loved ones – walking after dinner, taking a short bike ride or playing a card game.

✔ **Eat together.** Factor in space and time for meals as a couple or family. When you're both tired, you and your partner may be tempted to pick up a takeaway and eat it in front of the television, but real conversation requires nurturing. Cooking and eating a meal together at a table (without the television on) nourishes not only your body but also your relationships.

Travelling Along Life's Emotional Journey

Memories of past events can revisit you unexpectedly. Something that happens in the present triggers off an automatic response, putting your mind and body in a state of arousal. Your brain connects your current situation to a past threat and you think alarming things such as:

✔ Oh no, it's happening all over again!

✔ I didn't handle it then, so how can I possibly handle it now?

Become aware of how your brain seeks to associate a word, a sound or an event with emotions. For example the word 'marriage' may create warm feelings in one person but a sense of disappointment or hurt in another.

When you become familiar with your brain's automatic process of linking a word with an emotion, you can engage your thinking brain to analyse what's happening and acknowledge when old memories are being activated.

Developing this skill enables you to make more considered choices that relate to the current scenario rather than to the past one – a process we explore in greater detail in the following sections.

Matching emotions to events

Powerful memories may cause you to react inappropriately.

Suzie was excited about going on holiday with her new partner but found herself anxious when she didn't hear from him for four days before they were due to fly. She realised she was connecting this situation to a time when her ex-husband had been out of contact for several days when she was due to deliver their first child. Suzie was currently in a different situation and whilst it was natural for her to be a little anxious because she hadn't heard, her brain had become emotionally aroused because of the old memories and she wasn't thinking clearly (see Chapter 2). After identifying her emotionally heightened response, she was able to assess her current situation on its own merit. She was happy to discover that her new partner was away on business and had left his phone charger behind and was unable to call.

Appreciating the nature of needs

Your brain stores memories of when your needs aren't met. Small events such as your parent being late to collect you from school or your boss forgetting your appraisal meeting get filed into your emotional memory bank.

Everyone makes mistakes, but the emotional part of your brain keeps an unconscious 'bank account', totting up how often a specific person lets you down. At some stage you may unexpectedly lose your temper with that person or burst into tears. You may not consciously have noticed the gradual build-up of emotional intensity, but your emotional brain is warning you to protect yourself in future.

Monitor the emotional bank accounts between you and others. Life is about give and take and isn't an exact science, so a bit more give than take is acceptable. But if a relationship becomes a one-way debit – for example friends who accept your invitations for supper but never invite you back – you drain the goodwill that exists between you and the other person. You may need to take action to restore the emotional credit account, moving from the red to the black.

Switching the messages

You can alter the memory messages that your brain signals to you in order to break out of a destructive behavioural pattern. For example, you may be in the habit of arguing with your mother about a specific aspect of your life, or perhaps you and your partner have always argued about his mother calling up on a Sunday morning when you want to relax.

When habits build up, your brain sends an automatic response before you have a chance to stop and think, triggering the same behaviour. Fortunately, you can replace the old messages with the new ones by rewiring your brain. (Otherwise, before you know it, your mother-in-law rings again and you find the same old words tumbling out of your mouth.) Here's how:

1. **Identify the trigger and your usual response to it.**

   For example, the phone ringing while you're still in bed may be the sound that sets you off on Sunday mornings.

2. **Decide what you would like to happen differently in future and have a replacement thought ready.**

   Identify a specific thought that will lead you into a different and more helpful response for your own emotional state. Also consider what you need to say to anyone involved.

Instead of thinking 'Oh, there she goes again. How irritating', decide ahead of time that you're going to think 'Ah, there's your mother ringing again to find out how we all are.'

3. **Take a gentle breath and focus on a calming thought or image.**

Plan a breath with a slow out-breath (see Chapter 2 for all about the importance of healthy breathing). Your calming image can be anything – perhaps you picture yourself on a nice sunny beach.

4. **Say your replacement thought to yourself – or aloud.**

You need to repeat your replacement phrase several times to re-programme your brain. You may need to rehearse saying what you want to say to the other person. For example, 'It's great to hear from you, but our Sunday mornings are rather special. Would you ring after 11am next time?'

Build your new response into your life step by step. You may feel awkward the first time you do something differently, but continuity and repetition will create a consistent new response.

Chapter 8

Facing Up to Emotional Challenges

. . . .

In This Chapter

▶ Spotting avoidance behaviours

▶ Noticing hidden messages in actions

▶ Sharing feelings

▶ Working through traumatic events and disappointments

. . . .

*U*nresolved emotional issues that you haven't worked through have the capacity to interrupt your quality of life. Subtle and not-so-subtle defence mechanisms can stop you being fully aware of what you're doing, feeling or saying, which prevents you thinking clearly and in your own best interests.

Awareness of your emotions gives you the ability to make better choices. You benefit from addressing unresolved emotional challenges and responding to them in conscious ways.

Consider the story of the woman walking down a road. A deep ditch had been dug since she last travelled the path, and she fell in. The next time she walked along the road, she forgot about the hole and again fell in. On the third occasion, she remembered her past experiences, changed her behaviour and stayed clear of danger.

You're going to face unexpected life hazards along your path, and you need to have a sense of physical or emotional threat. Emotions are your survival mechanism. They signal danger, which is why, whether a situation is new or old, you need to keep tuned into these signals and analyse what they're about. This ability to stop and think enables you to interpret whether a threat is real or imagined and what you need to do about it. If you remain on automatic pilot, you may inadvertently fall back into unconscious ways of responding.

In this chapter we help you identify ways in which you may be avoiding difficult feelings and then show you how to move on from the threatening situations associated with these emotions.

Working Through Denial

Denial is a psychological defence mechanism that acts as a barrier to expressing emotions honestly. You may unconsciously erect a barrier to avoid looking at particularly painful feelings or situations where your family or cultural values don't permit free expression of certain feelings.

Denial signifies that you're not addressing disturbing issues. As we examine more closely in the following section 'Avoiding emotions', you may be avoiding something important. Denial of your own feelings can also result in you attributing your feelings to others, as we discuss in the later section 'Projecting Your Feelings on Others'.

Denial, avoidance and projection often occur when you're too frightened to speak up. You may insist that you're 'fine', even when you obviously aren't, because you're fearful of expressing your problem.

Avoiding emotions

Denying your emotions can lead to *avoidance behaviours*, which can be both conscious and unconscious things you do to get away from a problem or act as if it doesn't exist. Whether conscious or unconscious, avoidance behaviours mean that you're dodging the truth.

Avoidance behaviours take many forms. For example, you may avoid a conversation with your partner that you know may result in a confrontation about a difficult situation. An alcoholic may hide alcohol in an innocent looking bottle. Partners of alcoholics may unconsciously collude in their behaviour by pretending not to notice, and yet gain a sense of being needed in the process. A partner may avoid confessing to an affair even though challenged. These behaviours are confusing for all concerned. You sense secrets and lies, but you can't resolve the problem without openness and honesty.

Investigate where you may be denying the expression of emotions. Consider the effect in your own life and for those around you. To unearth denied emotions, ask yourself the following questions:

✔ How do I feel physically when holding in strong emotions?

✔ Do I ever sulk? What are the circumstances?

✔ Do I divert my actions or change the topic in order to avoid an honest discussion?

✔ From whom in particular do I feel like I need to conceal my feelings?

✔ Do I feel that someone else is in denial about some aspect of his or her emotional life?

✔ Do I use busyness, addictions, excessive alcohol, drugs, smoking, sport or hobbies as ways of avoiding facing emotional issues?

If you discover that you're using denial in some way, ask yourself how that may be affecting your behaviour.

Rosemary was brought up in an emotional hothouse. Her parents were constantly at odds, but over time, her father ended up suppressing his anger because intense outbursts didn't lead to his needs being met. For example, her father often returned from work expecting supper but found that his wife was out.

Instead of expressing his anger, her father gradually gave up responding, became depressed and took early retirement. From his example, Rosemary discovered that anger isn't a useful emotion, and in her own marriage she suppressed her response when her needs weren't met. Like her father, Rosemary became depressed and repeated the family pattern – until she found out how to address her underlying emotions and bring them to the surface (without resorting to anger; see the later section 'Defusing anger' for more on handling this complex emotion).

Opening up

Holding in emotions has a cost for yourself and other people involved. Others can't possibly address issues that you don't inform them about, and vice versa. Therefore, recognise that you have a responsibility to involve and share feelings with others so that you can work together to turn emotions into positive action.

In order to bring denial into the open and express emotions with others in healthy ways, try the following:

✔ Name the emotions you're denying and identify ways to address your needs in the future. See Chapters 3 and 7.

✔ Rehearse what you want to say and how you're going to manage your feelings during the discussion, particularly when you need to involve another person in expressing or addressing your needs. See Chapters 9 and 14.

✔ Practise techniques to reduce emotional reaction and arousal. See Chapters 2 and 13.

✔ Explain what you want in the future in terms of your own feelings and needs, rather than blaming others. See Chapters 3 and 14.

✔ Focus on the benefit of speaking your own truth even when your expressed feelings are met with denial. If the other person doesn't accept or understand your position, you're still valuing yourself enough to articulate your feelings.

Your ability to heal emotionally depends on being honest with yourself about your feelings. Involving others isn't always essential, but evidence indicates that emotional suppression leads to a range of problems such as alcoholism, isolation and emotional distancing. You can't experience true intimacy when dishonesty or disguise exists – even if that dishonesty is only with yourself.

Projecting Your Feelings onto Others

Projection occurs when you experience feelings that you don't allow in yourself and you attribute those feelings to, or blame them on, another person. For example, you feel angry about an upcoming dinner with the in-laws, but you accuse your partner of being hostile about the situation. Or you blame a co-worker for being unreliable and not showing up at a client meeting when in fact you hadn't showed up for the previous meeting and were feeling guilty.

Projection is a mind defence mechanism. You project in order to avoid feeling the discomfort of owning your emotions and reactions directly.

When you project thoughts and feelings onto another person, you're often assuming that you know how the other person is going to behave or respond. For example, when you think, 'There's no point raising this issue with Joanne because she never listens anyway' or 'If I say no, I'll lose my job' without any evidence, you're projecting. These assumptions are your own about how others *may* behave, filtered through your mind. You're not giving other people the information they need to deal with something directly.

To avoid projection, you must develop the ability to monitor and accept your emotional reactions to life events. When you find yourself shutting down after an emotional situation, ask yourself – what are my feelings? Am I in pain? Find a way to acknowledge and express your feelings. Projection is a defence mechanism, an effort to protect your own emotional vulnerability. Facing up to the fact that you projected your feelings onto someone else is courageous.

Turning denial into positive action

Noticing emotions rather than denying feelings frees you to be authentic. *Authenticity* involves expressing to yourself and others what is truly happening inside you, honestly reflecting your emotional state. In order to recognise denial in yourself:

✓ **Monitor your self-talk.** Take time out when you sense that you may be suppressing your feelings. Quieten your body and mind and allow yourself to return to the situation to identify what emotions you may be holding in (see Chapters 2 and 12). Notice more complex, secondary emotions such as feeling guilty about feeling upset or feeling angry about feeling hurt. Transform your inner dialogue to acknowledge the emotions you're experiencing. Remind yourself, 'It's fine to feel upset', and then identify whether you need to take action.

✓ **Explore irrational beliefs.** Challenge thoughts such as 'if I express my emotions, I'll lose control' or 'I'm just a hot-headed angry person'. Similarly, question yourself whenever you mind-read or make assumptions about another person. Work only with facts and honesty. (See Chapter 12.)

✓ **Consider what you need to do now.** The past is the past. Right now, you can do things that are productive and forward-thinking. For example, if you've been denying suppressed anger, review the circumstances of the denial and transform the energy associated with anger into positive action that shifts the situation in a fresh and constructive way.

If others distance themselves from you or you sense them directing emotions or actions towards you that seem out of context, ask yourself – are they projecting?

If you suspect that someone is projecting an emotion or action onto you, you're likely to sense a mismatch between your interpretation of the situation and theirs. Gather facts so that when you discuss the problem you're able to seek agreement on what happened, without emotional colouring. Focusing on facts rather than emotions enables you to explore the confusion between your interpretations and disentangle the projection from the reality. You may gain a deeper understanding of why the other person was projecting onto you, such as lack of self-esteem, fear of your response or a sense of powerlessness. The best outcome is to enable the other person to have the confidence to express herself honestly in future.

Expressing emotions – with a vengeance!

Actions can signify revenge: people destroy their partners' possessions in a fit of anger. A wife cuts up her ex-husband's expensive suits and smashes his vintage wine collection in fury when he leaves her for another woman.

Brian and his wife Ingrid agreed that their marriage was over. They talked co-operatively about selling their home, splitting their assets and dividing the care of their children. Shortly after Brian moved out, he and Ingrid had a disagreement on the phone relating to access to their son. Suddenly the relationship turned sour. Ingrid punished Brian for their divorce by turning his children against him and refusing him access. She reneged on their agreement and denied him further contact with his children. The bitter actions of revenge wounded him and his family.

Expressing Emotions Appropriately

Expressing your feelings is often essential to healing and living healthfully; and yet expressing your feelings appropriately requires care.

Talking with your body

The messages you send people extend beyond your words. Body language represents the majority of the messages you communicate. You discern how someone feels through eye contact, touch, a smile or a sneer. A subtle look over the dinner table can silence what you're going to say. Whether people's eyes are smiling along with their mouths tells you whether they're sincere. Your inner state is written all over your face and expressed through a frown, tension in your neck and shoulders, and crossing your arms.

Remember that you also communicate through your actions and behaviours. You convey messages by, for example, 'forgetting' to do what you said you were going to do, cooking a meal you know your partner doesn't enjoy, or attending to an 'urgent meeting' rather than taking your partner out for a birthday dinner.

In such situations, also try and analyse what others may be saying to you through both spoken and unspoken communication. Identify what the situation would be like if you resolved it with different actions and behaviour, and work towards achieving that aim. Plan carefully how to discuss problems in a more open, direct and consensual way. The following sections provide some great starting points for this process.

Using words

Words both praise and destroy. Verbal abuse leaves wounds every bit as painful as physical punches. Every word that people utter has emotional connotations, and each person develops unique associations to language. Just think about the word 'work'. For some it may mean fulfilment and achievement, for others it may mean boredom and drudgery.

You can use words to:

- ✔ **Criticise and diminish another person:** 'You don't have an intelligent thought in your head. You're so stupid.'

- ✔ **Punish someone for what you feel has been done to you:** 'How could you forget Valentine's Day? You're thoughtless!'

- ✔ **Make someone feel guilty:** 'If you loved me, you'd come and visit me more often, like a good daughter.'

- ✔ **Blackmail someone emotionally into doing something:** 'I work all day to feed you and the family, so the least you can do is make love to me when I want you to.'

- ✔ **Be sarcastic:** 'Oh so you've just done a great job of taking care of me when I don't even have a shirt to wear for work today?'

Some people are articulate and can make their point clearly and quickly. In contrast, other people need time to reflect on what's happened before being able to express feelings. In order to use words to build understanding rather than confusion, try the following approaches:

- ✔ **Allow time and space for other people to express themselves.** Don't interrupt, finish sentences or assume that you know what the other person is going to say.

- ✔ **Listen, empathise and try to understand other people's perspective.** Paraphrase what you hear by saying something like, 'You seem to be saying that I criticise you too much and that you're feeling very upset about this.'

- ✔ **Seek to express yourself in a way that respects other people's opinions, even if you don't agree on the subject.** You can respectfully disagree by saying something like, 'I don't agree with everything you say, but you do have a point to make.'

- ✔ **Own your own feelings and express them in the first person.** Instead of saying 'You hurt me' or 'You make me feel angry' or 'You're selfish', say 'I feel hurt when you do such and such' or 'I feel angry when you say that'.

✔ **Generate solutions to the situation.** Make a specific request, such as, 'I'd appreciate it if you can do such and such.' Ask the others for their solutions too so that you make sure you don't tell them what you think should be done. If you have a disagreement about a subject, seek areas of agreement within the topic. Write down these unifying aspects in order to emphasise your common ground.

✔ **Don't send mixed messages.** Avoid contradicting yourself a sentence later or saying one thing and doing another. Be clear.

✔ **Be specific and avoid generalities.** Don't express opinions as facts with statements such as, 'Everyone knows this is the case.' Instead say, 'In my opinion, I believe this is the case.'

See Chapter 14 for more ideas on successfully communicating your feelings.

Defusing anger

Anger is a natural emotion, but it can be uncomfortable for yourself and others to experience:

✔ Some people feel guilty about feeling angry and seek to suppress it; this suppression can turn inwards and result in depression.

✔ Some people express anger easily, which can be frightening for those around them.

Managing your own anger

Anger is often experienced when expectations of yourself or others aren't met. Words to watch for include *should*, *must* and *ought to.* For example, you can be angry:

✔ **With yourself** when you don't come up to your own standards: 'I really ought to have been able to be at my child's school concert. I should have said no to making the presentation to my team.'

✔ **With others** when they don't do what you want them to do: 'He should have picked up the laundry on his way home.'

✔ **With life situations,** such as traffic, trains or computers: 'Trains must run on time, otherwise I can't stand it.'

Women and men

Many emotional challenges surface within relationships between men and women. Although one can't generalise, our clients report some patterns that may help you enhance your cross-gender understanding:

✔ **Men often complain that women aren't clear enough about what they want.** That instead of asking and expressing their needs, women assume that 'men should know what women want'. Men don't always 'read' emotions easily. (For example, a man may clearly see that a woman's upset, but he doesn't necessary realise that she's angry about criticisms received at work earlier that day.) To improve these situations, women can explain the situation and give men the option to do something specific in response to help them.

✔ **Women often complain that men stonewall them, refusing to talk about problems.** Additionally, many women feel that men avoid issues until they become major difficulties, at which time they explode. One of the reasons for this behaviour is that the male cardiovascular system takes longer to recover than a woman's. Women are better able to calm themselves down after a stressful discussion, whereas a man's response tends to be angrier and more defensive. To improve these situations, men can tune in more frequently to emotional problems and have the courage to listen and discuss differences before negative emotions build up to boiling point.

Feeling anger can be a sign of a threat to your physical or emotional security and so you need to acknowledge it without letting it overwhelm you. Replace words such as *should*, *must* and *ought to* with *I would prefer*. For example:

> ✔ 'I would prefer to come up to my own standards, but I can accept myself if I don't always do so.'

> ✔ 'I would prefer that others did what I wanted, but I can manage when they don't.'

> ✔ 'I would prefer that life situations were the way I like them to be, but I can survive when they aren't.'

The important message you're giving yourself is that you *can* manage events even if they don't go perfectly.

Managing others' anger

Responding to other people's anger requires that you stay calm and not become frightened. Being compassionate is easier when you recognise that pain and hurt lie beneath the anger. The other person's needs haven't been met and so, just like a small child, she's drawing attention to this fact.

To help manage conflict in a non-violent way, try the following approaches:

✔ **Praise and acknowledge what you do value about the person or relationship:** Find something that you appreciate about the person and express this simply: 'I appreciate it when you do *xyz*'.

✔ **Don't assume that you know what the other person is going to do next:** Rather than saying something like, 'I know you're not going to listen,' try something like, 'I appreciate this time to sit and talk. I'm glad we can chat through our disagreement about Katie coming in late last night.'

✔ **Treat the other person as if the relationship is going well:** As Goethe said, 'How you treat people is what they become.' When you interact with others as if they were frightening, stupid or inconsiderate, you're likely to reinforce this behaviour.

✔ **Take time to consider how the other person may be feeling:** Actively listen not only to the words but also to the emotions that underlie the words. Someone may be acting aggressively and yet feel really hurt and upset underneath.

✔ **Accept and acknowledge correct statements:** Don't get defensive and pretend you're right if, in fact, you aren't. For example, just say, 'Yes, I can see that I was inconsiderate when I didn't pass on that message,' rather than counter-defending it with a statement such as, 'You never pass my messages on to me!'.

✔ **Gently probe for more information:** The other person may have many other pressures that have built up and the anger may not be really aimed at you or be your fault. Perhaps something else went wrong but you're the nearest person to express frustration at.

✔ **Ask a question that's relevant but not directly related to the problem:** For example, cabin staff are advised to ask an irate airline passenger a related but lateral question such as, 'And are you travelling with anyone else today?' This type of question diverts focus and can defuse the anger.

Reducing the Impact of Traumatic Events

People seldom expect to experience traumatic events. But you may have found yourself saying, 'This is something that just doesn't happen to me.' The reality is that most people either go through some kind of shocking event themselves or know someone close to them who does.

A *crisis* is a situation in which none of your normal coping strategies applies. It radically changes your life in some way, upsetting the normal order. You really can't prepare for such an event. And indeed anticipating something that may never happen (or if it does, takes a completely different form to what you imagine) is pointless. However, you can help yourself after the event has happened – to prevent the consequences disturbing you for longer than necessary.

Asking for help

Despite certain situations being too difficult for you to manage on your own, you may insist on maintaining a 'stiff upper lip' tendency, imagining that admitting your emotional vulnerability is a weakness.

Many people battle on through trauma and tragedy on their own until sadly they experience breakdowns. Talking to another person can help you to make sense of a situation, as well as provide the healing qualities of sympathy, empathy and support that enable you to get through.

Jahmal was in his first term at university when his best friend was killed in an accident. They had been together since primary school, and he was devastated. But university was supposed to be 'fun' and all Jahmal's mates were going out every night, so he felt he should join in. None of his friends had experienced the death of a friend themselves, and so although they tried to be supportive they just didn't know how to empathise or what to say.

Jahmal soldiered on but towards the middle of the next term he started to experience insomnia, fatigue and depression. He tried to ignore his symptoms but after a while he realised that he needed help. He went to the university counselling service and soon found that talking to a professional about his friend and his feelings offloaded some of the emotions he was experiencing. After a few months he began to feel that some of the burden of grief and depression was lifting.

Managing post-traumatic stress

Post-traumatic stress can occur when you experience or witness a sudden, shocking and unexpected life-changing event. Your brain responds by storing trauma memories in a sensory manner. Thus, you're likely to be able to conjure up the place, the scene, the feelings and the people you were with, almost as if the event were happening now. Memories associated with traumatic events can return to plague you with 'flashbacks' for many months – if not years, triggering your fight, flight or freeze survival response (which we describe in Chapter 2).

Trauma can constitute many different situations:

- ✔ Accident
- ✔ Discovery of a suicide
- ✔ Mugging, burglary, rape or violent attack
- ✔ Natural disaster such as earthquake, flooding, fire or tsunami
- ✔ Sudden and unexpected ending of an intimate relationship
- ✔ Sudden death of a loved one
- ✔ War, disability or sudden illness such as stroke or heart attack

Responding to trauma

The immediate response to traumatic events is that you go into survival mode, and initially your brain may numb your emotional responses. You may experience a sense of unreality. You may act on automatic pilot. Those who suddenly lose a limb, for example, may not immediately notice that they've done so. Often people can't cry immediately after a bereavement. You're in shut-down survival mode, able only to think about what needs to be done, not necessarily to 'feel' the emotional impact of it. Some people may accuse you of being 'uncaring', but this behaviour is just a natural response to shock.

Following trauma, you may notice various physical symptoms (if these continue for a prolonged period, we suggest you seek professional help from a GP):

- ✔ Diarrhoea
- ✔ Fainting, trembling or weak limbs
- ✔ Flashbacks of the event
- ✔ Inability to think clearly or remember facts
- ✔ Insomnia
- ✔ Irritability or crying
- ✔ Loss of appetite
- ✔ Panic attacks about the event (see the later sidebar 'How to react to a panic attack' for more details)

After a while, you become aware of reality and acknowledge the sadness and shock of what's occurred, allowing yourself to express whatever emotions rise to the surface. These feelings can be uncomfortable, but don't suppress them; suppressed emotions only bubble up later in some way. Many servicemen returning from Iraq and Afghanistan find that they can 'carry on' until they're out of immediate danger. Then the emotion hits them. So find someone with whom you can safely share your experience and the feelings that arise from it, so that you can adjust to the reality of what's happened.

How to react to a panic attack

Flashbacks and sustained anxiety can trigger panic attacks, which can be frightening. During a panic attack, you may feel as if you're having a heart attack: you become short of breath and your heart may flutter. Here are some actions you can take:

✔ Stop, gain control of your mind and breathe in for the count of 4 and out for the count of 6. Repeat for a period of time, until you feel your body calming down. See Chapter 2 for more on the power of breathing.

✔ If you feel that you're hyperventilating, take a paper bag and breathe into it, or cup your hands over your nose and mouth and breathe into those. Doing so restores the balance of carbon dioxide that allows your body to distribute oxygen to tissues and your thinking brain to function.

✔ Tell yourself: 'This is just a panic attack. I'm okay. I can think calmly, take control and feel safe. This will fade away.'

✔ Try the AWARE technique. **A**sk yourself what has activated the attack and scale the severity on 0–10 (with 10 being high). **W**atch yourself slow the **A**rousal response by slowing your **R**espiration. Bring in a calming image associated with **E**njoyment.

Certain music, journeys, places and people can remind you of the traumatic event. Be discerning about what helps or hinders your emotional stability. Avoid painful reminders for a period of time while you adjust. Then gradually plan how you're going to re-introduce people and places back into your life in a controlled way that doesn't upset you. The assistance of a coach or counsellor can be particularly helpful when re-introducing elements you associate with a traumatic event.

Dealing with flashbacks

If you experience flashbacks of a traumatic event, you may need to take more direct action to overcome trauma.

The following Memory Changer Process helps you take control of flashbacks by *re-framing* your memory of the event to focus on feelings of safety and dissociate yourself from the disturbing memories of the incident:

1. **Identify the specific memory that disturbs you.**

   Notice the anxious feelings that arise in you when you recall the memory. These feelings are symptoms or *triggers*, which you can use in future to signal you to stop and take action to manage them.

2. **When you experience one of your trigger emotions, practise slowing your breath.**

Visualise yourself in a safe place where you feel calm and relaxed. Notice the mental and physical feelings of calm and safety. Try the six-breaths-a-minute exercise in Chapter 2.

3. **Gain control of your thoughts.**

Replace panic-inducing thoughts such as 'I can't stand it' with calming thoughts such as, 'The event is over. I've survived. I can manage.'

4. **Take control of your memories.**

Imagine that you have a television screen in front of you. A remote control is in your hand and you're in control of how you think about the event. You can run the scene before you in whatever way you choose, moving from a time before the event when you were comfortable and safe, through to the moment after the event when you knew that you had survived and were safe, even if you'd experienced a loss or shock.

5. **Focus on the feeling of safety and imagine yourself as a calm observer.**

Imagine your calm observing self floating nearby but to a place where you don't see the television screen. Your calm self is there to give you emotional grip, help you to feel safe and detach from the disturbing images and feelings you previously experienced about the event. See Chapter 13 for more on finding your calm observing self.

6. **With the remote control in your hand, switch on the film and identify images of you before the incident, when you were safe and comfortable.**

Use the remote to decide how you want to watch the event: you can fast-forward it, make it smaller, make the scene black and white or take control of the images and sounds as you choose.

Let your calm observing self remind you that you're okay and in a safe place.

7. **See yourself watching the film as the observer.**

Fast-forward the film, starting from before the event, and go through to the end, noticing every detail.

Move your attention forward and back using the fast forward and then the rewind until you're able to watch the whole sequence without anxiety or disturbing feelings.

8. **Replay the entire event, focusing on your ability to remain calm and dissociated.**

Repeat the process until you're able to experience feelings of safety while watching all the images and memories.

After you've successfully watched the film of your traumatic event several times, you may want visualise taking out the DVD or tape and filing it away or destroying it entirely. Visualise yourself doing this – perhaps even imagining yourself shredding your DVD.

Delayed trauma

Bob was a policeman who attended a horrific pile-up on a motorway. Amid the carnage, he witnessed a man being burnt to death. Bob carried on working but often woke suddenly at night with images of the fire.

Two years later he was called to another crash but was unable to go to the scene. He sat paralysed in his patrol car, and told a colleague, 'I just can't go there'. His unexpressed emotions had finally surfaced.

Bob ended up taking a period of leave, during which he underwent stress counselling. He decided to return to work, but in a job that didn't involve traffic duty.

If you struggle with flashbacks, you may also benefit from *Eye Movement Desensitisation and Reprocessing* (EMDR). This technique encourages you reprocess the traumatic events with both your left brain and your right brain, formulating the events as a continuous narrative rather than a series of fragmented memories. This process enables you to release yourself from locked-in physiological arousal associated with the traumatic memory. See the Appendix for details on finding an EMDR therapist.

Re-parenting yourself

Various events in your adult life can remove your sense of autonomy, returning you to dependency, including after a hospital admission, a period of incapacity, imprisonment or service in the armed forces. You can also experience a parent-child dynamic within a controlling relationship where you give up your power of self-determination to another person.

When you return to normal life, you have to make decisions again – about your self-care, routine, daily life actions and behaviours. You're effectively having to *re-parent* yourself outside of the institution, situation or relationship.

Your attitudes about your own parents can influence your re-parenting process. Here are some examples of how your parents may have behaved and the possible effect on you:

- ✔ **Acting coldly and ignoring appropriate feelings:** You may be a cold person, uncomfortable with hugs and other expressions of warmth.

- ✔ **Judging your performances and praising you only for your achievements and not your efforts:** You may have low self-esteem and be reluctant to accept achievement for its own sake – you're continually aware that someone else exists with 'better' success.

✔ **Over-indulging you and ignoring bad behaviour:** You may struggle to say no as an adult, take on too much or have an attitude of self-importance.

✔ **Over-protecting you:** You may have difficulty taking risks.

✔ **Punishing you for behaviour they deemed unacceptable:** You may have a sense of toughness and a need to treat others in a controlling and over-disciplining way.

To understand that your parental experiences may be affecting your current responses and actions, ask yourself the following questions:

✔ What kind of parenting did I experience as a child?

✔ Does the way I was parented have an effect on my attitudes now?

✔ When I think of an ideal parent, what qualities does this person have?

✔ How may these qualities now be applied to my life in the areas of work, relationship, friends/family and time for myself?

After examining the effects of old parental or institutional experiences, you can take conscious control of how you look after your own needs. Create a sense of your ideal parent within your current life situation. Is your ideal parent a mother or a father – or an amalgamation of both? Think about those qualities you associate with this ideal parent and draw them into your own inner world. How can this inner parent advise you to manage the daily disciplines and needs of your current life? What kind of inner voice can you create that's recognisably your own and also compassionate, caring and encouraging? This approach can help you to arrange your work and time, as well as ensuring that you care for your emotional needs in order to make good life decisions (see Chapter 9 for more information).

Developing emotional resilience

Resilience is the ability to believe that you can manage situations without them overwhelming you. Resilience builds through both unconscious and conscious processes.

You develop resilience as a child every day in the playground, gaining the skills to manage the rough and tumble demands of school work, friends and enemies. As you grow up you become more aware that certain events and situations challenge you more than others. You can develop resilience through both *experience* (for example, successfully transferring to a new job) and *planning* (for instance, organising strategies to respond to the imminent death of a terminally ill parent).

Difficulty responding to emotionally challenging situations typically falls into two paradoxical categories:

- ✔ **Arrogance:** You believe that you can manage anything and don't need any specific strategy or help. Arrogance often hints at an insecurity to admit that you're human and is problematic because no one manages everything. As a result, you may not plan sufficiently or ask for help.

- ✔ **Lack of confidence:** You believe that you're helpless and can't manage anything, which renders you powerless to cope. You may also fear being found out for not being 'good enough' or assume others are far more qualified to make decisions than you. You end up paralysing your ability to take action.

Your lack of action in response to a situation may be based on an underlying fear – perhaps one you haven't even identified or expressed. The Downward Arrow Technique is useful for identifying underlying fears.

Denise was fed up with her boss. She resented the fact that he gave her routine assignments even though she was a qualified MBA. She felt her skills were being underused. However, she didn't want to raise the issue with him and in early coaching sessions pretended that she didn't mind too much. Therefore, to explore why she was unwilling to address this issue we took her through the Downward Arrow Technique.

The key to the Downward Arrow Technique is to keep asking yourself the question: 'And what would be so awful about that?'. You can apply the Downward Arrow Technique yourself, but you may find a facilitator, coach or counsellor helpful. This other person can press you to move through the sequence until you have insight about what's really holding you back.

In Denise's case, we asked her why she didn't raise her concerns with her boss:

> *Denise:* He may tell me I'm being demanding.
>
> *Helen and David:* And what would be so awful about that?
>
> *Denise:* He may think that I'm being 'Miss Clever Two Shoes'.
>
> *Helen and David:* And what would be so awful about being clever?
>
> *Denise:* He'd tease me for being too smart about everything.
>
> *Helen and David:* And what would be so awful about that?
>
> *Denise:* My Dad said that no one likes smart people and I would be ostracised and lonely.

Deep inside, Denise's mind was associating loneliness with being clever. When she realised this fact, she developed a logical strategy to challenge this belief (see Chapter 12), which gave her the resilience necessary to address her problem and eventually request a promotion.

Action is the key to developing resilience. Do any or all from the following menu of ideas:

- **Prepare:** Be clear about the problem, identify your desired outcome and prepare how you're going to manage the task. What do you need to do? What do you want to say? Consider your worst fears and plan how you can manage if the worst happens.

- **Plan:** Divide your goal into easily manageable steps.

- **Reassure:** Build yourself up with self-talk. Tell yourself, 'I can make a plan to help me manage this situation' or 'It's natural to worry, but I trust my ability to manage the situation.'

- **Manage the situation:** Take actions to resolve the problem and achieve your objectives.

- **Breathe:** Control your stress response and practise the four-breaths-in six-breaths-out technique we cover in Chapter 2. Don't forget to stand tall.

- **Listen and then speak up:** Don't jump to conclusions or make assumptions. Stick to the facts you're dealing with.

- **Visualise:** Create a *circle of safety* around you. Imagine an invisible pod that surrounds you and protects you in difficult situations. When you feel threatened, see this bubble protecting you – verbal threats hit the bubble and bounce away like arrows. They can't pierce your shield.

- **Focus:** Look at the present. Ask yourself, 'What do I have to do here? What do I need to say right now?'.

- **Review:** Figure out what worked well, as well as what you may have done differently. Take time to reward yourself for your efforts.

Coming to Terms with Disappointment

Traumas (see the earlier section 'Reducing the Impact of Traumatic Events') shake your world; disappointments are more likely to just pile up and weigh you down. Like trauma, disappointment is inevitable from time to time. Life is difficult – full of challenges, peaks, troughs, ups and downs, routine, boredom and change.

If you demand perfection, you may be setting yourself up for disappointment:

- ✔ **You disappoint yourself by not meeting your own standards.** When you're not the 'super-person' you think you should be, you lose faith in yourself.

- ✔ **Others disappoint you or let you down in some way.** You become cynical and start to believe other people can't be trusted.

- ✔ **Life disappoints you.** You don't receive the security, wealth and certainty that you expect or believe you need in order to be happy.

Focusing on disappointment drains your energy and can lead to sighing, cynicism and world-weariness. Accept that life is the way it is – but that this difficulty is not a let-down but simply a reality. Save your energy to work out how you're going to manage these inevitable ups and downs. Transfer your focus from disappointment to what has gone right in your life and what you can be grateful for. Instead of looking at the gutter, look at the stars.

Forgiving yourself and others

Other people are almost certain to hurt you at some time, but holding on to negative feelings harms you physically and emotionally. Hostility causes a variety of effects, including raised blood pressure, raised heart rates, anxiety, depression, isolation, poor relationship with others and reduced mental health. When you choose to forgive yourself or those you feel have caused you hurt, you help yourself heal and improve your immunity and wellbeing.

Any of the following signs indicate that you may be holding on to negative emotions and may need to forgive someone (perhaps yourself) for some past action:

- ✔ Avoiding friends or family

- ✔ Consuming alcohol or drugs in excess

- ✔ Dwelling on an event that hurt you

- ✔ Engaging in addictive behaviour

- ✔ Experiencing mental health problems

- ✔ Having difficulty enjoying the present

- ✔ Hearing that others think you have a 'chip on your shoulder'

- ✔ Losing a sense that life holds good things for you in the future

- ✔ Planning revenge or punishment

- ✔ Ruminating on a past injury

- ✔ Showing outbursts of anger

When you choose forgiveness, you replace the negative with positive feelings of enjoyment of the present and hope for the future. The forgiveness process starts with recognising that you must:

- **Name the injury:** List the areas of your life that have been affected.

- **Claim the injury:** Allow the pain. Don't go into avoidance or denial. See the earlier section 'Avoiding emotions'.

- **Assess responsibility:** Blame may be part of your response to injury, but it can leave you stuck in a victim mentality. Although certain incidents have an obvious perpetrator, sometimes *you* must take responsibility for your own response. For example, one child may feel damaged by her parents whereas another sibling doesn't; one husband whose wife leaves him may acknowledge that he wasn't totally attentive, whereas another may blame her totally. Analyse your situation and figure out responsibility – but don't waste too much time and energy on assigning blame.

- **Rebalance the scales**: Actively restore belief in yourself so that your sense of self-worth overrides your sense of injury.

- **Choose to forgive.** Let go and regain the sense that you're worthy of receiving love.

Don't be too hard on yourself. You're human and therefore fallible! Admit your actions and express regret sincerely, asking for forgiveness if appropriate. To gain the feeling and intention to forgive, try starting and ending the day by offering loving kindness first to yourself, and then to significant others such as friends or those you revere, and finally extend loving kindness to those you dislike or who have harmed you. See Chapter 13 for more details on loving-kindness activities.

Finding your personal mantra

The focus of your thoughts shapes your emotions and the quality of your experience – in the face of great disappointments. Become familiar with any negative thoughts that arise when you contemplate challenging situations, but then realise that you can switch to feelings of inner calm by finding a personal mantra that helps you manage.

Creating a *mantra* means practising a phrase, word or sound that you continuously repeat to help create a state of inner peace. An example of a phrase can be 'all will be well'; a word can be 'calm'; and a sound can be 'ohm', sung to a particular note. Your mantra may:

✔ **Be the universal prayer, which comes from a Sanskrit Mantra:** May good befall all. May there be peace for all. May all be fit for perfection. May all experience be that which is auspicious.

✔ **Relate to a personal spiritual goal.** For example, in the midst of difficult emotions, you may need to switch state by reminding yourself, 'Despite my anger with XYZ, I now offer myself love and appreciation' or 'When in the middle of depressive thoughts and feelings, I know that this too will pass.'

Your mantra cuts off your automatic negative thought or feeling (see Chapter 12) so that you can replace it with a thought that provokes a positive state of mind.

Sometimes your mantra is linked to a behavioural change and a sequence of movements such as in the *Emotional Freedom Technique* (EFT). In EFT, you physically tap a particular sequence of energy points, acknowledge your problem and use a phrase such as: 'Despite my anger, I now completely love and accept myself.' See *Emotional Freedom Technique For Dummies* by Helena Fone.

Jill was 38 when she came to coaching convinced that her life would never be a success. Throughout her early life, her mother had been depressed and in and out of mental hospitals. Jill became the mother to her younger brother and saw him achieve success. Her coach encouraged her to find a personal mantra that she repeated whenever she found her mind moving to regret and self-pity. She recorded and played the mantra 'I release old pain and embrace joy in my life' to herself everyday as a self-healing practice.

Building on your past

Successful change comes through decisions and actions. However difficult your past, you can begin to build on the strengths that you develop by coping with the challenges life throws at you. Take control of how you respond and be clear about your goals with yourself and others. Others can help you only if you tell them what you seek and what you need help with.

Associate pleasure and reward with change and associate pain with staying the same. In order to achieve this aim, become more aware every day of what actions you're taking and whether they're moving you forward or keeping you stuck in the pain of the past. Notice whether the statements you're making are clear about where you're going or whether you're speaking in self-defeating or mixed messages. Congratulate and reward yourself for your progress.

Chapter 9

Managing Relationships

. . . .

. . . .

*R*elationships are part of life. Humans need connection and a sense of belonging. You're a social creature; without love and company you wither, just like a flower without water.

Conflicts generally arise when people's views and needs differ. Other people don't always behave as you ideally want them to, which can be hurtful and disappointing. Some people mean to hurt you, but others are totally unaware that they've done so.

You must take responsibility for your part in relationships. Doing so takes focus and consideration, which in turn can involve hard work and reward. You have to realise that external relationships are a reflection of your internal state. Accepting your own fallibility helps you not only to forgive yourself, but also to let go of judging others. No one is perfect. Everybody muddles along to the best of his ability and everyone makes mistakes. Emotional healing occurs when you let go of the power that any individual or experience has to upset your equilibrium. Discussing problems without blame allows each person to share feelings and solutions.

This chapter helps you develop healthy relationships, whether with a parent, a friend, a partner or a colleague. You can adapt the methods and processes to the situations that need healing in your own life.

Bonding with Others: No One Is an Island

Humans across the globe form social groups. People constantly talk, text, email and participate in social networking sites to connect with one another. Accepting this need to bond with other people is an essential ingredient of emotional health. A baby who doesn't receive a loving touch fails to thrive, loses weight and becomes developmentally delayed. People who commit acts of violence are often described afterwards as 'loners'. And recent research shows that loneliness is a greater indicator of ill health than genes or nutrition.

Loving yourself so you can love others

Your relationship with others is only as good as the quality of your relationship with yourself. Catering for your own emotional needs is an essential first step. You're like a battery: if your emotional reserve is empty you have nothing to give away to others.

Do you find loving yourself difficult? Perhaps you

 ✔ Criticise yourself for mistakes.

 ✔ Feel unlovable: don't like or love who you are.

 ✔ Don't acknowledge achievements.

 ✔ Don't forgive yourself for some misdemeanour in your past.

The key to emotional health is to accept yourself *and* your imperfections. Every human being deserves love. Let go of inner anger, self-hatred or frustration; they only make you unhappy. Self-criticism makes living with yourself difficult and can make living with you hard for others too, because you're likely to criticise them.

Challenge thoughts such as:

 ✔ 'How could I have said something so stupid?'

 ✔ 'What on earth made me do that?'

 ✔ 'Why didn't I do. . . ?'

Tell yourself that what's done is done. Regret only serves a purpose when identifying what you can do differently another time. Self-love is essential to healthy relationships.

Valuing uniqueness

The philosopher Nietzsche wrote:

At bottom, every man knows well enough that he is a unique human being, only once on this earth; and by no extraordinary chance will such a marvellously picturesque piece of diversity in unity as he is ever be put together a second time.

Comparison diminishes you and serves no great purpose. You can lose energy by focusing on what isn't right instead of what *is* right within you. Whilst you may gain knowledge from acknowledging how you differ to another person, you gain more from valuing the totally unique person that you are yourself.

Take some paper and write down the following:

- ✔ How you feel when you're at your best emotionally.

- ✔ One way in which you're going to show yourself love today.

- ✔ Two actions you'd prefer not to have done, and for which you forgive yourself. (Considering how you'd forgive someone you love for similar behaviour may help you forgive yourself.)

- ✔ What you appreciate about yourself.

- ✔ What you can be proud of.

Loving yourself transforms your relationships because they are a mirror of your inner state. Value the unique person that you are (see the sidebar 'Valuing uniqueness'). No one like you has ever lived in the past and never will again. Embrace your vulnerabilities; they are also your strengths. (See Chapter 7 for more information on forgiveness.)

Knowing where to look for love

The idea that the only type of love you can receive outside your family is that between two adults in a loving relationship is a myth. People receive love from many different sources, including:

- ✔ Extended family
- ✔ Network of friends
- ✔ Pets
- ✔ Social groups, such as adult classes or hobbies

✔ Spiritual sources represented by your God, spiritual leaders or religion

✔ A sense of loving connection through nature

✔ Strangers who offer a smile or a kind word

✔ Work colleagues and clients

✔ Members of the caring professions

Spending time with people who make you feel good

The people around you have a big impact on how you feel. By analysing all the relationships you have, you get a clear picture of who you like spending time with, and who you may prefer to pull back from.

The following Relationship Mapping Exercise provides you with a model to review your social groups:

1. **On a big piece of paper, draw a spider diagram to map out the people in your life.**

   Put yourself at the centre of the diagram and add branches for family, friends, work and other social groups. Use pencil so you can adjust your diagram.

2. **As you write down each person, notice how each name makes you feel.**

   How close or distant do you feel to significant others?

   • **For strong relationships,** draw over the pencil with a solid line in a felt tip pen. You may want to use different colours for different people.

   • **For weaker relationships,** draw over the pencil with a dotted line in felt tip.

   This can help you, visually, see where action may be needed. It may be fine for some relationships to be more distant or, indeed, to let go of some.

3. **Based on your discoveries in Step 2, consider what action you want to take.**

   Do you need to take action to heal any of the relationships you identify? List the people you want to spend more time with, and those you feel you need to drop.

Figure 9-1 gives an example of a Relationship Mapping Exercise in action.

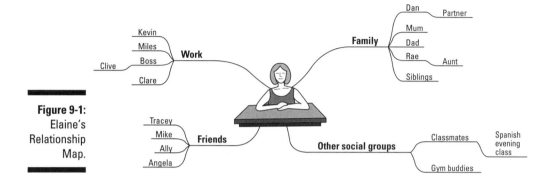

Figure 9-1:
Elaine's
Relationship
Map.

Your social groups can limit or encourage your success. As you change and grow, you may find that your friends change too. Identify the social scene that works best for you now. You need to show courage and action to research and develop the social life and contacts that meet your needs today.

You can also adapt this exercise to explore your feelings about relationships you had in the past. You can think about your family during childhood, ex-partners or old friends. This exercise helps you identify which type of people boost your sense of belonging, and which have a detrimental effect on your wellbeing.

Relating to the Opposite Sex: Me Tarzan You Jane!

Many emotional misunderstandings occur between men and women. Both biology and cultural norms may help to explain some of the underlying reasons for this conflict. Men and women are driven by different hormones, physiology, genes and chromosomes. This diversity shapes distinct emotional responses in family, loving and working relationships. These influences play a part when considering emotional healing.

We aren't aiming for stereotypes here. Sex and gender are complex topics, worthy of multiple *For Dummies* books! As you read through the following, consider how your own gender – as well as others' genders – align or are in contrast to traditional gender-based reactions.

Looking at emotions during puberty

Boys and girls experience huge and diverse physical changes during puberty that impact behaviour. The brain alters and adjusts itself, pruning neural networks that are redundant and accelerating growth in the areas related to thinking.

- ✔ Boys experience a massive rise in the hormone testosterone which leads to a rapid increase in muscular strength and a drive to be physical and take risks. Increased testosterone accounts for the greater likelihood of boys forming action groups and gangs and a general decrease in verbal expression of emotions, which can lead some teenage boys to feel isolated and unable to express their fears about life.

- ✔ Girls experience a rise in the hormones oestrogen and oxytocin, which encourage bonding. These hormonal changes cause a natural tendency to build strong social groups and receive support within them. As a result, girls are more likely than boys to express emotion and share vulnerabilities, feelings and worries.

The family environment is particularly important at the time of puberty. As a parent you can provide support during the transition between the child belonging within a family network and taking a place in the outer world. Allowing teenagers the time and space to express emotions provides them with skills that they take into adult life. When emotions aren't released, they remain bottled up. As a result, boys often externalise their distress, which can lead to antisocial behaviour and crime, and girls frequently internalise, which can lead to problems such as eating disorders and self-harming.

The puberty of a child is a difficult time for you as a parent. You have to juggle your own needs with the demands of your children. Accept that you can't always get it right because no parent can. Also take care of your own stress and your needs for privacy and time out. If you're being lambasted by irritable teenagers, make sure that you get support elsewhere. Don't worry, this period does come to an end! See Chapter 18 for more ideas on parenting teenagers.

Seeing how biological difference impacts feelings

Researchers have found biological reasons for the different emotional behaviour of men and women. Recent research indicates that more men are *systematisers* and more women are *empathisers*. The *corpus callosum,* or web of nerves that connects the two sides of the brain, is thicker and more dense in women, suggesting that their ability to multitask is biological. (Men, by contrast, tend to focus on one task at a time.) This biological difference may also explain why women are able to connect emotional signals to language and express emotions in words more easily than men.

Sensory sharpness and high serotonin levels in women help make them generally quicker to intuit feelings, more alert to danger and less prone to take risks. Higher levels of testosterone in men encourage greater risk-taking, increased aggressive behaviour and a tendency to compete to be the dominant male in a group.

Cultural norms and social conventions compound biology, leading men to get angry more frequently and women to cry when their emotional needs aren't met. Each can find the emotional responses of the other somewhat confusing and upsetting.

Understanding how men and women differ biologically can help you understand members of the other sex. For example, after making love, a man's level of oxytocin, the bonding hormone, peaks and then drops significantly, whereas a woman's remains high. While his oxytocin is high, he's in bonding mode. As soon as it drops, however, he's ready to get up and go, while she's still in the mood for cuddles. This biological difference can lead to misunderstanding and pain. Discussing how biological differences drive behaviours can help you acknowledge diverse needs and create a compromise.

Neither biology nor culture is a reason to feel 'boxed' into behaving a particular way. Both genders continually adapt to social and economic circumstances. Instinctive behaviour may drive your brain, but you still choose to respond to situations and other people. No single way is better than another. Enjoying difference promotes healthy relationships.

Coping When You Feel Let Down

One of the hardest lessons in life is discovering how to manage the emotional ups and downs surrounding hopes and dreams, and the disappointments that other people's behaviour causes. Healing takes place when you can review the situation and feel able to let go of the emotional attachment to pain.

Identifying your needs

Emotions are most frequently stirred when other people don't do what you want them to do. You may have to accept other people's right to behave the way they do even when you don't like it. From your own perspective your needs matter most; from their perspective, theirs do!

Sometimes you need to compromise and other times you need to hold firm in order to protect yourself and what you care about. You don't know how to distinguish between these situations unless you identify your needs and how they differ from another person's. Start by deliberately thinking about what you personally value and consider acceptable behaviours. When you're in a relationship you can use these identified values as guidelines for yourself and a discussion point with your partner to foster understanding and compromise.

Discussing values with your partner is particularly useful in the early stages of a relationship when you're getting to know one another. You're in a better position to be alert to behavioural mismatches and decide the reasonable course of action. People can end up in an abusive or unhappy relationship because they didn't clarify their own values and expectations before entering into the relationship. Raising potential relationship problems early tests the potential strength of the partnership to resolve differences.

Create a chart like Table 9-1 in your journal to work out what you need from a relationship.

Table 9-1	Relationship Needs Assessment	
My Ideal Relationship Needs	*Behaviour That Is Acceptable to Me*	*Behaviour That Is Not Acceptable to Me*
Being able to be me; being heard and valued	Adapting my needs to my partner	Being treated with disrespect

Considering your expectations

Expectations drive emotions and can take you up or down, sending you on a roller coaster of hopes and fears. Your social group often shapes what you expect of people. Other people involved may not have a clue what you expect or need from them, particularly if they've been raised in a different environment. For example:

- ✔ You expect your friend to call to check that you're recovered after flu.
- ✔ You expect your new date to call, text or email immediately after just seeing him.
- ✔ You expect your spouse to buy you flowers on Valentine's Day.

You're going to be disappointed when people don't meet your expectations. Consider carefully what you expect of the other people with whom you have relationships. You need to balance optimism with realism. Sometimes you ask too much of others, and at other times you may expect too little and give too much away.

Expectations are key to successful relationships. Take time not only to reflect on your expectations but also to share them with a coach, counsellor or someone you trust who knows you well. Sharing your expectations provides a more objective sounding board for you to work out some of the following questions before you share the expectations with your partner:

- ✔ Can I honestly call this expectation reasonable?

- ✔ Can I honestly call this expectation realistic?

- ✔ Can I honestly say that everybody has the same expectation of this situation as I do? If not, how may other people's perspectives differ?

- ✔ Can I honestly say that if other people had this expectation of me, I would come up to their standard; or may I disappoint them?

- ✔ Can I develop an expectation that's optimistic but doesn't lead me to expect so much that I'm disappointed?

Relationships are about give and take. Observe the strength of your positive emotions and the body signals you experience when you're around the other person. Ask yourself how you feel when you're with him. Do you feel energised and enlivened – or tired and diminished? Does your relationship have a balanced ebb and flow that brings out the best in you both?

Your own happiness doesn't have to depend on the behaviour of others. Indeed, this assumption gives others the power to upset you. If you're feeling disappointed, you may not be able to change the other person's behaviour, but you can focus on feeling good despite it, unless it impacts on your core values and needs. And if your core values are being affected, you really need to review the situation and relationship thoroughly.

Releasing blame

The phrase 'it wasn't me; it was them' starts in the playground when something goes wrong and the teacher looks for the culprit. Perhaps you can remember feeling upset when unjustly accused? Blame is relevant where someone is the innocent victim of a violent or illegal event. Generally, though, it takes two to tango and holding on to blame stops you healing.

Jennifer was someone who held on to her anger after her husband walked out 15 years before. Only when she came to coaching with severe headaches and stress did she begin to examine her own part and eventually stop blaming him. She had thought that she was a good wife taking care of house and home but her husband had felt deprived of affection. Their needs differed. She discovered that blaming herself or him was pointless: they had done what they could with the skills they had available at the time. Gradually she released the emotional pain and rebuilt her own life.

If you're experiencing pain about another person ask yourself these questions:

- ✔ What is the true cause of my pain? What has upset me?
- ✔ How am I blaming someone else for my pain? How does this help me?
- ✔ Would other people I respect see things the way I do? If not, how may they see this situation?
- ✔ What other approach may help me to let go and adapt to the situation?

Some people feel so angry at the hurt that another person causes that they commit acts of revenge. Retaliation is a no-win situation, because the act ultimately harms the perpetrator as much as the intended victim. If you harbour vengeful feelings, you need to stop and calm yourself using a breathing or relaxation technique (see Chapters 2 and 13). Accept what you're feeling and restore a rational response to address the situation in a way that doesn't harm you or anyone else. You may benefit from talking to someone. We include contact details of support organisations in the Appendix.

Moving on from 'if only he would change' or 'this should never have happened', and letting go of blame, frees emotional energy that you can focus in more constructive ways. We aren't suggesting that the pain you experienced isn't real, but becoming absorbed in blame ultimately hurts you. In contrast, healing allows you to

- ✔ Accept the situation and release it to focus on the present and future.
- ✔ Ask whether the other person can blame you for part of the problem.
- ✔ Identify your own emotional needs and take action to meet them.
- ✔ Review your own behaviour and take lessons from it.

Blame can be a rational response to a situation, for example where justice is demanded. On other occasions, however, holding on to blame weakens and victimises you, which ultimately does you more harm than good.

Keeping things real

In Chapter 12, we warn you against perfectionism – that killer of joy. People can build unrealistic ideals about how relationships should be, setting themselves up for an emotional roller coaster of conflict and disappointment.

Here's how you may put unnecessary pressure on your relationship:

- ✔ **You expect a person to follow your rigid rules.** For example, you want your partner to behave in a particular way that suits your needs and you get upset if he doesn't.

- ✔ **You expect relationships to be continually harmonious, which is impossible.** Therefore, all you achieve is you and the other person burying any problems to avoid conflict rather than dealing with them.

Perfectionist demands lead to criticism and can disrupt your relationships. People are fallible and make mistakes. Although maintaining certain standards is important, the ability to be flexible can help you balance your emotions when things go wrong.

Dealing with Anger

Aristotle said, 'Anybody can become angry – that is easy, but to be angry with the right person and to the right degree and at the right time and for the right purpose, and in the right way – that is not easy.'

Anger is a natural response to personal challenge, but it can also be a major social problem when not managed. A Mental Health Foundation report published in March 2008 indicates that 1 in 4 people worry about how angry they feel, and 1 in 5 end relationships because of how the other person behaves when angry.

Some people express anger easily. Occasionally, an angry outburst clears the air, but often it damages relationships, resulting in fear or resentment. Successfully managing your anger so that you express it in controlled, healthy ways is therefore essential for happy, lasting relationships.

Thinking about where you direct your anger

Many people tell us that they end up shouting at their partner or children when their anger is really the result of pressure from a variety of causes elsewhere.

Here are some things that can test your emotional resilience:

- A cancelled train
- A deal falling through at work
- A failure of the computer system
- A dressing-down from your boss or a client

Unable to outwardly express your emotion in these situations, you hold in the feelings until you can release them – frequently at home. And so the unsuspecting teenager who hasn't cleared up breakfast, or the dog that trips you up as you get home is often on the receiving end of several hours of built-up emotion!

Zenna, a fitness instructor, blew her fuse at the wrong person one day. She shouted at a client who had taken a mobile phone call during a session. When the client walked away, Zenna burst into tears and apologised, explaining that she was upset about a row with her husband. The client wasn't the cause of her emotion but an excuse to release it – inappropriately.

Emotions expressed strongly in words may cause others to respond with similarly strong emotional reactions. This situation is likely when the other person feels attacked. Consider carefully the best way to discuss a problem. Plan the time and setting to create a sense of caring rapport (see Chapter 16).

Become more conscious of what your real problem is:

- What or who is upsetting you?
- What would you like to say or change?
- Would expressing your feelings in this situation be possible? If so, how best can you do so? If not, try writing down your feelings or talking through them with someone.

A breathing space exists between a situation that causes you emotion and the way you respond to it. Use this time to identify the options available to you. Your emotional brain reacts very quickly. Become alert to the trigger signals that warn you that you're about to lose it, such as tension in your body, flushing or an 'adrenaline' rush. With practice you can pick up the warning signs and create a breathing space, in which you can analyse the underlying cause of your reaction. This ability to recognise and reduce your arousal state is essential, allowing you to make choices ensuring that you express your feelings in words safely, in the right way, to the right person. (See Chapters 2 and 13 for more on breathing and physiology.)

Use your homeward journey to process your work day so that you arrive home prepared for the evening, ready to express yourself in a healthy way. As you're leaving your desk, make a note of what you need to do the next day and then begin to let go of your working day. With each step towards your home, think of leaving the concerns of work behind you before you re-enter. You're tuning out of work mode and tuning into your home and personal life.

Measuring your internal pressure cooker

Emotions build up. Whether that emotion is anger, jealousy or anxiety, unless managed and released it will at some point 'blow' just like the steam from a pressure cooker.

Stop occasionally during the day and ask yourself how you're feeling. Monitor your body regularly, becoming aware of physical sensations such as tight jaw, tense shoulders, clenched fist or shallow breathing. These sensations result from the build-up of chemical responses in your body preparing you for fight, flight or freeze (see Chapter 2). They signal your emotional state.

One useful technique for releasing some pressure is the Internal Tap technique:

1. **Imagine that you're sitting in a peaceful place.**

   Notice what that feels like. Suddenly someone rushes in and says your kitchen is on fire. Your body is immediately primed for action. A tap is nearby, and you intend to put water on the fire. You have control of the tap. Imagine how strongly you need to twist it in order to fill a bucket of water to put out the fire. You're likely to twist it all the way.

2. **Imagine that you have a emotional tap that responds to your emotions.**

   Recall a recent time when you felt strong emotion. Your body tap was probably on full flow.

   Now imagine that you have the power to control this flow. See and sense yourself being able to turn down the tap to an appropriate level. You may even perform a physical movement as if turning the tap. Notice how this sensation feels in your body and mind.

Use this Internal Tap technique to turn down your emotional responses in real situations. Realise that you're in control.

Don't judge your feelings: tell yourself that they simply exist. They alert you to something that isn't working for you. As you become more aware of your emotional pressure gauge, you gain control of how you express your feelings.

Taking time out to control anger

Anger triggers your body for physical activity or for the release of your emotional tension. For example, your breath speeds up, which opens up your brain's emotional centres, moving blood away from your thinking brain. (See Chapter 2 for more detail.)

Here are three techniques you can use to help you stop and think clearly:

- **Change your breathing:** Notice when you're breathing in your upper chest. Focus your thoughts on moving your breath down towards your stomach area. As you breathe, let your abdomen expand outwards. With every in-breath think 'I am breathing in calm' and with every out-breath sigh and think 'I am breathing out disturbing emotions'. (See Chapter 2 for more breathing techniques.)

- **Change your thoughts:** Thoughts impact both your feelings and breathing. Thinking 'I can't cope' or 'I can't stand it' makes you more anxious and disrupts your breathing and ability to think clearly. Take time to think calm thoughts such as: 'I can manage this situation and work out what I need to say and how best to say it.'

- **Change your posture:** Remember how your body feels when you're calm and confident. Let go of tension in your jaw, shoulders, hands and wrists. Straighten your spine, allowing space in the belly for your calming breath.

You aren't suppressing your emotions, just discovering how to acknowledge, manage and express them in a constructive way.

How your body gives the game away

Emotions drive physiological changes that show in your body language even when you believe that you're disguising them. Have you ever sensed that someone is fed up even if he says he isn't? Unresolved emotions may leak out in a sigh, a subtle facial expression, a shrug of the shoulders or twitch of the head. You may think that you're managing to contain your emotions, but others are probably aware of them, which is another good reason to acknowledge trapped feelings and release them.

Dealing with abuse

Sometimes anger can cause people to lash out and be abusive. The cause of abuse can go back generations. Although this fact doesn't excuse the behaviour, it can help you to understand it. Abusive behaviours are seldom conscious. Children watch the behaviour of their parents, and an abused child may perceive abuse as normal even though it caused pain.

A violent parent can become the mental model for an adult relationship. People can become imprisoned in this conditioned behaviour, until they understand how past experience is influencing them. But the past doesn't have to be a determinant of your future. You can build new ways of responding.

Any kind of abuse – emotional, physical or sexual – damages self-worth. You're likely to feel a sense of betrayal and your trust diminishes. If you're the victim, you may even sometimes think that the abuse is your fault.

If you're in an abusive situation, you need to review what's happening as objectively as possible:

- **The abuser:** If you're aware that you're bullying or harassing someone, you probably realise that you aren't behaving well. You may sometimes hate yourself for what you say or do. Review your personal history. Are you following a pattern set by a parent or authority figure? Are you feeling isolated or misunderstood? What are your own emotional needs now and how can you express them in a constructive and co-operative way? Get help. Taking care of your own needs enables you to give love and care to others.

- **The victim:** If you feel victimised, consider what advice you may give to a loved one who was in this situation. Is the behaviour of the other person reasonable? How can you set boundaries of what is and what isn't acceptable? You need to state your needs and ask for what you want (see the earlier section 'Identifying your needs' for more on this aspect of emotional health). No one deserves abuse and as an adult you can take responsibility for your own self-care (see Chapter 11).

Recovery from severe abuse is difficult without expert support. Whether you're the abuser or the victim, please seek help. You can find useful contact details for counsellors and supportive help lines in the Appendix.

Healing Your Relationships

No relationship is plain sailing: whether at work, at home, in love or in friendship, you're bound to encounter occasional difficulties when relating to others. The good news is that we have some sound advice on how you can work through problems and build strong, stable, happy relationships.

Letting go of past hurt

Many people hold on to grievances for years. They almost wear their suffering like a badge of honour even though doing so only ensures that they continue to experience pain each day. They experience obsessive loops of negative thoughts, such as:

- ✔ 'How dare he do that to me.'
- ✔ 'This is so unfair.'
- ✔ 'I'll never get over this.'

And people caught in this way of thinking never do get over it, because they mull over the events continuously, reliving the hurt or indignation rather than choosing to focus on something new.

Simon was an only child. His parents both had to work to pay the bills and so he spent much of his childhood alone. He felt alone and frightened during his childhood and was resentful that his mother wasn't there for him. He was 62 years old when he came for coaching, but his mother still featured large in his life. Not only had she 'ruined' his childhood, but also well after her death he still allowed her to ruin his adult years and interfere with his relationships. Through coaching, Simon came to understand that focusing on his grievance was interrupting his pleasure of life. Step by step he replaced his negative thoughts with memories of the childhood experiences that he did enjoy. He started to focus on the positive, and his anger at his mother faded.

When someone says or does something that really hurts you, the event can become engraved on your mind and hard to forget. Here are some examples of harsh statements that some of our clients had embedded in their minds:

- ✔ 'My mother said that she hated me.'
- ✔ 'My father said that I was to blame for my sister's death.'
- ✔ 'My partner said that I was ugly and stupid and no one would love me.'
- ✔ 'My sister said that my fiancé finds her more attractive than me.'

Each statement held immense pain for the person concerned.

You may have suffered a similar hurtful experience. One way to help to ease this event is to try to put yourself within the context of the life of the person who hurt you. The following Timeline Exercise helps you reflect on the situation. You may want to do this exercise with a friend or counsellor who can give you support.

1. **Imagine your life as an invisible line in the room.**

   This can be from left to right of you or sometimes the line goes from back to front, through you.

2. **Stand in the area that feels like today.**

   Feel yourself present now at the age you are and with the maturity and experience you have to date.

3. **Decide where your past is and face towards it. Gradually walk down your invisible time line, back through your life.**

   Notice what this feels like and whether certain events or experiences come to mind.

4. **Go back to the time when the person made the statement that so upset you.**

   Stop there and reflect on the following:

   - What was the person going through at that time? Try to think whether the person was happy or under pressure (and if so, from what).

   - What events were occurring that may have put stress on the person?

   - What was your own position within this situation? Did you personally do everything possible to ease whatever problems existed?

   - When you think back, do you think that the person really meant to hurt you so much?

   - Can you find any way that you can now put the statement into the context of what was happening and, if not forgive, choose to let go of its power to continue to upset you?

5. **Walk back to the area of the timeline that represents the present moment.**

   With the knowledge and insight you've gained, consider what thoughts, emotions and behaviours may now help you to manage your memories in a way that allows you to enjoy life.

Be compassionate to yourself and to the other person as you do this exercise. He may be totally unaware of how much he hurt you. He may not even remember making the statement. Put the moment in context and realise that he can't have been happy himself to have said these things. For example, the father who blamed his child for his daughter's death was clearly suffering from trauma. You're not excusing the behaviour, but finding some empathy for the person's pain.

Remove the power of words to upset you but don't beat yourself up if you find yourself unable to do so. Just revisit this exercise from time to time and see whether a moment arises in the future when you feel more able to let the pain go.

The French dramatist Molière advised that 'One should examine oneself for a very long time before thinking of condemning others.' Pointing fingers at others is easy. But doing so deflects attention into past wrongs rather than focusing on affirmative action in the present.

Talking through problems

Conversation can be the most effective way to work through pain and problems. Sadly, when people are upset, very often they suppress their feelings. This suppression denies the other person the necessary information to change or compromise. You can't expect someone to know the shape of a problem unless you describe it.

The way you approach a conversation about your relationship makes a big difference. Focus on feeling compassionate towards yourself and the other person. If you're volatile, blaming and emotional, the conversation is likely to go wrong. The other person is less likely to listen to your problems or respond well to your needs.

Here are some tips to help you discuss issues:

- ✔ **Starting out positive:** Come to the meeting with a good intention to resolve the problem in a mutually beneficial way.

- ✔ **Being comfortable:** Decide on a time and place that helps you both feel at ease. Create a positive and safe place in which to talk. You may choose to light a candle or have some music playing so that you both feel relaxed, with uninterrupted time for each other. Taking a walk together is another option.

- ✔ **Following a process:** Start with a positive statement; express the problem in a way that takes personal responsibility for your own response – 'When you did that I found it difficult and was upset.' Then suggest a new way of managing the situation or behaving in future. Check whether the other person finds this idea fair and acceptable.

- ✔ **Staying calm:** Whatever you say, you make more impact if you keep your cool. Practise the self-calming techniques in Chapter 2.

- ✔ **Listening:** Be willing to listen to the other person's perspective. The person has a right to respond, even if you find hearing it difficult.

> ✔ **Accepting your mistakes:** If feedback is justified accept it, saying: 'Yes, I can see that I did do that.' Make a suggestion about how you can behave differently in future.
>
> ✔ **Ending the chat as friends:** Finish with a summary of what you did and didn't agree. Set some actions for change if appropriate. Try to keep the warmth of mutual intention fundamental and central to your conversation. Consider finishing with a shared meal or drink.

Check the state of your relationship with a partner quite frequently – for example, once a month. Regular chats ensure that pain doesn't build up over a period of time, creating an inaccessible void between the two of you.

Thinking about how you relate to others

By carefully considering your approach when relating to people, you can build happier, healthier relationships and minimise conflict and misunderstanding.

Developing emotional intelligence

Emotional intelligence is the ability to be aware of your emotions and to manage them. It also encompasses the ability to empathise with others and manage their emotions so that you create mutually fulfilling relationships.

To start, you focus on yourself:

> ✔ You understand your feelings and know where they come from.
>
> ✔ You acknowledge your emotions and know how to manage them and develop resilience to life's challenges.
>
> ✔ You know how to motivate yourself to do difficult tasks.

Then you think about how your actions affect others' feelings:

> ✔ You recognise and manage the emotions of other people and develop empathy.
>
> ✔ You motivate others.
>
> ✔ You express feelings appropriately and develop good relationships.

Take as an example two managers, Dave and Rose. Both have the same qualifications and length of service. Both their companies are in crisis and they need to cut back bonus payments and make redundancies.

Rose doesn't feel comfortable sharing bad news. She quickly grows emotionally weary listening to the concerns of her staff. She composes an email informing them that bonuses are being cut and that with redundancies on the cards, they must prove their value and relevance to the business. Three resignations are tendered immediately. Those who remain are frozen in fear. Morale is at rock bottom.

Dave is in the same position of having to cut staff and costs. He prepares himself personally, recognising that the conversation is sure to be difficult and that he needs to listen to concerns. He takes the time to come out of his office and speak personally to each group. He explains that business conditions are challenging and that he values their hard work but that bonuses can't be justified. He assures people that his door is open for questions and he will reward them again as soon as he can. He explains that staff cutbacks may happen, but he will do his best to relocate people within the company and work with them to find solutions. Morale is high.

Rose lacks emotional intelligence and so is unable to manage the emotional impact of the situation. But Dave has developed the resilience and empathy required to manage both his own emotions and the emotions of his staff. He is emotionally intelligent.

Becoming the emotional strategist

Emotions can play havoc with your quality of life when you don't recognise and deal with them. We aren't recommending that you become a robot; emotions are an integral part of being human. What we are suggesting is that you can achieve greater quality of life when you:

- ✔ Consider how other people may feel and respond.
- ✔ Define the situations that cause you difficulty.
- ✔ Devise strategies to manage both yourself and those situations.
- ✔ Understand your own emotional tendencies.

The Three-Position Exercise can help you formulate a strategy that helps you deal with your feelings and consider those of other people. Imagine that you have to explain to your partner that you have got into debt. You may be nervous of confronting him about this problem. You may feel ashamed of yourself for not managing your money better and worry about your partner's response. The Three-Position Exercise can help you plan the conversation:

1. **Think about yourself.**

   You spend the majority of your time within your own thoughts, emotions, concerns, experiences and needs, looking out at other people and the world. If you stay in this situation, empathising with how other people may feel or anticipating how they may react can be difficult.

Imagine the discussion you're about to have and decide what thoughts, emotions and behaviours help you to manage your own feelings. For example, you may acknowledge your anxiety and guilt about the situation you have to share with your partner. Prepare yourself to listen to some difficult comments and consider how you're going to manage your own feelings within the situation.

2. **Think about the other person.**

   Standing in another person's shoes gives you insight into his potential concerns and needs. Imagine what's happening in your partner's life, his character and personality and how he may respond to the situation.

   Consider how he may feel. For example, your partner may be both angry and also fearful for his security. How can you share the information in a way that helps your partner to feel less anxious?

3. **Imagine you're a third party.**

   Position yourself as an imaginary wise third party who's looking in on the conversation you're about to have. This position removes your own emotional needs because you're now neutral, taking an objective perspective of both yourself and the others involved.

   What would this impartial person advise you to do or say? How would a third party suggest you behave? Imagine that you're looking in on the scene. Listen for intuitive signals about what can help you.

Bringing out the best in one another

Whether at home or at work, you can focus on bringing out the best in others. After all, you want other people to bring out the best in you. Like any other behaviour, though, people can get into negative habit patterns. Before you're even aware of it, within five minutes of getting together you start to bicker or put the other person down. At this point, call a halt and decide to re-engage with the good qualities you both enjoy in one another.

Consider the relationships you're in and the individual needs of those people. Work out what's necessary to focus on when helping them to be happy and to blossom. A mutual benefit exists in this process, because you feel better about yourself when you focus on the positive and help another person to do the same.

If you've been dancing the 'misery dance' together, you're going to have to switch your style. The decision is yours. So why not change the music, choose a different dance step and start to dance the 'joy waltz' or the 'collaboration polka'. Make some changes and see what happens.

Chapter 10

Getting Through Tough Times

· ·

In This Chapter

▶ Moving from grief to acceptance

▶ Recovering courage and self-belief

▶ Overcoming rejection at work

▶ Becoming whole again after separation or divorce

· ·

*T*he only certainty in life is that at some time you're going to find yourself experiencing tough times – responding to loss, dealing with fears, being rejected and ending relationships. How you respond to such events not only affects your ability to find a way through to positive feelings again, but also whether you're able to maintain optimum health.

Your ability to find ways to hold on to your *self belief,* which represents the confidence in your own abilities and judgement, becomes crucial in tough times, and this chapter offers ways to recover and maintain courage and self-esteem. Our aim is to build on the ability to self-observe – to surf the stress wave and enjoy the ride – rather than be thrown dangerously into the water.

Working Through Grief

Humans become emotionally attached to one another, and because life is finite, all relationships end at some point. Therefore, loss is an essential part of being human, and yet the brain makes the experience more painful because it interprets any experience that threatens security as bad and tries to make sense of what's happened.

The loss of a loved one brings you face to face with your own mortality. The experience also opens up your own memories of attachment to your first care-giver, usually your mother. Poor mothering with problematic attachment can interfere with your ability to adjust in a healthy way to loss. You may become reconnected to old patterns found in your earliest relationships. If, in addition, you felt you weren't 'good enough' growing up, you may end up feeling even more vulnerable. In this case you may benefit by returning to a reliable relationship with a counsellor where you can re-experience what was missing emotionally for you and move on.

You're a conscious being who seeks to be loved unconditionally. The ability for you to both give and receive attention is the foundation for secure relationships. Loss threatens these essential needs. You're likely to compare your experience with those of others and think things such as 'Why me?' and 'Is something wrong with me that I suffer so much?'.

Grief is the normal emotional response to losing someone – or something – that you're connected with through attachment and love. Grief may come about after the death of someone you love, after a relationship ends or following disability or loss of capacity in yourself. Healing occurs when you accept your loss and begin to move on. Grieving is a fluid process involving a variety of interchangeable phases, which we explore more fully in the following sections.

Understanding the phases of grieving

How you respond to loss is very personal. The phases we present in the following list are the most commonly reported and don't follow this (or any) specific order. We provide this list not to tell you how you should grieve but instead to help you understand what you may experience – and show you that a wide range of reactions is normal. Common phases of the grieving process include:

- ✔ Anger
- ✔ Anxiety and panic
- ✔ Bargaining (making deals with God or the Universe that your loss be restored in exchange for specific benevolent deeds)
- ✔ Bursts of emotional release (for instance, sadness leading to crying)
- ✔ Disbelief or denial
- ✔ Feelings of flatness and self-pity
- ✔ Guilt
- ✔ Numbness
- ✔ Yearning (for what has been lost)
- ✔ Acceptance and moving on

You can move through these phases and through the grieving process in different ways. One phase may dominate, and others may merge together. You may find yourself going back and forth between different phases: no prescription or set time is right or wrong. Whatever your personal process, the most important aspect is that you experience the pain fully, however uncomfortable it is. A full experience helps you to recognise and release your attachment – for example, to the deceased loved one or to the loss of social standing resulting from redundancy.

Some counsellors see phases of grief as steps you need to work through, as the work of Elizabeth Kubler-Ross describes. Counselling professionals now more generally accept that individuals flow and even jump between phases, rather than proceed in linear fashion. Your progression may occur naturally – or if you get stuck in a phase of grief, you may find a counsellor's assistance helpful.

You arrive at acceptance when you feel that you can talk or remember the loved one without re-igniting the other preceding phases of grief. You experience a sense of completeness, although normal sadness and the need to remember and honour the person or situation is part of reaching acceptance.

Friends and family may make unhelpful remarks such as 'you ought to be moving on by now' or 'it's not good for you to bring back old memories' or 'you need to just get on with your life'. No one can tell you how to grieve. Rest assured that what you're experiencing is normal.

Adjusting gradually

John had been married for 20 years when his wife Susan developed breast cancer. At 44 years of age and with a family of three children, he became immersed in his wife's fight for survival and dropped many of his own interests. Susan's cancer was aggressive, and despite a remission induced by chemotherapy, she eventually died.

As the weeks passed, the initial support of friends and family reduced and John became immersed in feelings of sadness and self-pity. He reviewed with all who would listen what may have happened to prevent her death and eventually became certain that he was becoming ill himself. John's GP found that he had hypertension and also referred him to the practice counsellor.

The counsellor allowed John to express feelings of anger and powerlessness and encouraged him to return to scheduled activities and get back to work. The family decided to buy a puppy, and in solitary walks John was able to release feelings as he identified with the playful qualities of this young life.

Gradually after a period of two years John was able to accept, remember what he and Susan had enjoyed together, and become more fully alive – without forgetting their love for one another. A memorial fund and scholarship was set up at the local university to help students succeed despite illness or disability, which helped to keep Susan's memory alive as a positive legacy.

Tuning into your grieving process

Although people go through their own, personal grieving processes, many people are predominantly thinkers or feelers.

Table 10-1 allows you to work out whether you're more of a thinker or a feeler and helps you determine how best to understand and navigate your own journey of grief. The aim is to help you expand your dominant style of relating to the world so that you both express and process your grief, using feeling and thinking.

Table 10-1	Thinking versus Feeling during Times of Loss	
	Feeling-Dominate Reaction to Loss	*Thinking-Dominate Reaction to Loss*
As you look at the columns on the right, is one dominant?	Feelings fill your waking moments. Your dreams are often vivid.	Thinking dominates your waking thoughts and you're reluctant to allow feelings to emerge.
What is your emotional experience?	Crying and emotional release is your natural way to respond to upsetting events.	Control and self-restraint are your natural responses in the face of difficulties.
What's your preferred method of problem-solving?	You prefer to experience, allow your feelings to emerge and then choose your approach to feeling better.	You prefer to think things through, analyse the situation and then choose your approach to restoring control.
When challenged how does your mind work?	You may be unable to think clearly because your emotional brain dominates and overwhelms your thinking brain. Anxiety and persistent tiredness may occur.	Obsessive behaviour may take over. You focus on doing rather than being.
Trying some new ways to grieve	Try scheduling your day to give you structure and stability if you're a feeler. Ensure that you're getting things done as well as releasing emotions. Stop and review your situation: how are you thinking about the future?	Allow some time for unscheduled activities to help you relax and let go of constant busyness. Take time to enjoy being as well as doing, allowing yourself to find the time to express your grief.

Different counselling approaches work better for different people. Thinkers may prefer cognitive behavioural therapy, and feelers may feel more comfortable with interpersonal therapy, although a structured approach may be of benefit. If you find that a counselling approach doesn't work, ask yourself whether the mismatch relates to your thinking or feeling preference.

See the Appendix for more information about using resources associated with both of these approaches.

Boosting immune function

The stability of your inner physiology is profoundly affected when you lose a loved one or something else to which you're deeply attached. Emotional adjustments throughout the grief process (see the preceding section) set up a struggle state in your body and mind, which changes your internal chemistry and creates the chronic stress response.

The *chronic stress response* is the continuous stimulation of mind, body and emotions which reduces the effectiveness of your immune system. This level of stimulation can result in one or several symptoms, including tiredness, sleep disturbance, abdominal distress, muscle fatigue and skin complaints. If stress intensifies without release, it eventually drives you to express your doubts, fears and difficult emotions. As pressure is released, your body – particularly your immune system – returns to normal function and you rebuild resilience (see Chapter 8).

However, we find that some individuals – more frequently men – work to ignore their bodies' chronic stress responses by staying busy, trying to right wrongs, mourning alone or remaining silent. Unfortunately, trying to carry on as usual only increases the pressure on your limbic system (see Chapters 2 and 5). You must monitor and move through your grieving process consciously, releasing pent-up feelings and restoring your immune function.

Because holding in grief can result in ill health, here are some tips to help you express and release your emotions and also help your immune system to stay strong following significant loss:

- ✔ **Emotional release:** Don't bottle up those feelings! Allow their free expression. See Chapters 6, 8 and 15 for some emotional release ideas.

- ✔ **Reduce arousal:** Find out more about reliable relaxation/breathing techniques (see Chapters 2 and 13).

- ✔ **Social support:** Maintain contact with supportive friends, family and people who listen without judging. You can find support in unexpected places with people you may not know well but who have lived through a similar experience and come through the other side.

✔ **Talk:** Explore options for one-on-one counselling or group therapy.

✔ **Touch:** Engage in massage or body therapy on a regular basis. See Chapters 6 and 15.

✔ **Volunteer:** Give your time and effort to helping others; doing so encourages a return of self-esteem.

✔ **Write:** Keep a journal and tell your story as it unfolds, including your thoughts, feelings and actions.

Overcoming Fears

Fear is the main driver and the basis of survival-oriented fight, flight or freeze strategies (see Chapter 2). Fear, when it overwhelms you, suddenly cuts off your ability to think.

A fear may be understandable and relate to a real threat, such as fear of a terrorist attack. A fear may also be deeply held and based on past or even evolutionary experience, such as a fear of spiders, which were more commonly poisonous many millennia earlier.

A fear becomes a *phobia* when the fear feels real even though the risk may not logically bear any relationship to the actual danger. Phobias can seriously disrupt lives. Individuals with agoraphobia perceive threat everywhere outside their immediate surroundings and cannot venture out. Fear of flying may prevent you from visiting family abroad.

The following sections cover fear of failure and fear of sadness, two common fears with strongly emotional components. As with any fear, your response may be rational and realistic based on past experience or carried over from your family conditioning. Whatever the origin of your fears, we provide ways to become aware and then release your old fear patterns.

When dealing with any fear, you need to create a strategy so that the fear doesn't incapacitate you. Recognising the inner signals of your fear response is essential (see Chapter 2). When you're fully aware of how fear feels in your body, you can stop reacting with yet more fear, accept the situation and reduce your fear response. Your ability to think then re-emerges.

Fearing failure

Fear of failure is a common problem leading to unfulfilled lives and limiting ambitions. People feel powerless and unable to take action to change their situations, which can lead to internalised rage or depression, negatively impacting relationships and careers.

The first step to overcoming a fear of failure is to notice when the fear becomes active for you. Your emotional brain patterns match to previous events that you associate with similar feelings. Therefore, you need to recognise your old patterns by listing situations in the past when you feared failure so that you can then counterbalance this experience with a future vision of success.

The following activity explores your fear of failure and helps cast these fears in a different light:

1. **In your journal or on a sheet of paper, list at the bottom of a page past situations where you failed or feared you may fail.**

   As you write down these situations, think of them as old, redundant and in the past.

2. **At the top of the page or paper, list situations where you successfully overcame difficulties and felt pleased to have achieved success.**

   Anything counts here – from a successful driving test to a planned holiday that was enjoyable. Write out what went into the ingredients for your success – for example hard work, persistence and determination.

3. **In the middle of the page or paper, list techniques that help you to change your emotions – in this case, from fear and alarm to calm.**

   An example of an effective technique can be a positive statement 'I can manage this situation calmly' and remembering how your body feels when you're calm and successful.

   Think of this list as your emotional toolkit (see the Cheat Sheet). Turn to these techniques whenever and wherever you need them.

See Chapter 13 for ideas of relaxation, mindfulness and breathing techniques that you may find helpful. Practise these techniques *before* potentially fearful events so you feel confident that you can calm yourself quickly.

4. **Identify a future event where you want to overcome your fear of failure.**

   List your goal, describe your specific fear and give this event a 'fear rating' on a scale of 0 to 10, with 10 being your highest, most terrible fear. For example:

   > **Goal:** Confess a mistake to my boss
   > **Fear:** Drying up and leaving the room
   > **Fear Rating:** 9

5. **Be with your fear and calm your fear response using as many tools in your emotional toolkit as necessary.**

   For example, to respond to your fear of confessing a mistake to your boss, you may choose to:

1. Think through all the possible physical/physiological responses (pulse racing, hands clammy, over-breathing and so on).

2. Apply relaxation/breathing techniques to create calm inside.

3. Counter automatic negative thoughts with positive affirmations, such as 'I will do this well enough'.

4. Prepare thoroughly what you want to say in advance.

5. Rehearse the situation in your imagination. Practise until the fear response is minimal.

6. Practise with a coach or a friend until calm, confidence and control return.

6. **As you try each tool in your toolkit, reassess your fear rating.**

   If one of these tools helps to lessen your fear by even one number, consider it worthwhile to employ during an actual fearful situation.

Your fear may never go completely away, but you definitely can lessen its intensity and power. A degree of arousal is necessary, but the problem occurs when your arousal becomes overwhelming. With practice most people can deliberately reduce their fear levels using the preceding tools.

You can apply this approach to anything that you fear – from making a presentation to a fear of flying. Going through this process may be difficult at first but with practice, you can desensitise yourself and take control of your fear.

Too scared to sell

Ralph was a very successful salesman who reached his targets year after year. After his father died, he experienced a panic attack (see Chapter 8 for how to deal with panic attacks) in a meeting where he was presenting on a new product. He had to leave suddenly, giving an excuse. From then on, he was unable to go into meetings because he feared fainting and losing control.

With the help of coaching, Ralph reminded himself of previous specific examples of success. He also reviewed negative past experiences. He recognised that his father was very critical of anything less than the highest marks and on many occasions Ralph had felt very upset and angry when he had disappointed his father. Ralph acknowledged that much of his present drive to succeed was still to please his father.

Ralph also realised that before his panic attack, he experienced early signals such as his heart racing, his pulse quickening and his breathing shifting to his upper chest. He practised a relaxation technique that he was able to apply quickly and visualised himself returning successfully to his work and giving great presentations.

Knowing that he was able to create calm in the middle of his fear renewed his confidence. He was eventually able to allow the fear to exist but went on to return to work anyway.

Avoiding feeling sad

For some people, sadness is a very uncomfortable feeling. A fear of sadness leads some to not only to avoid sadness but also to actively suppress and deny it. For some, avoiding sadness is an expression of a stiff upper lip. They fear that if they tap into their sadness, they'll never stop crying. Unfortunately, physically holding in sadness can lead you to develop a false mask of happiness, despite feeling a well of sadness inside, and even encourage certain diseases.

Expressing emotions freely may, for you, be linked with loss of control. Crying may be seen as weakness, particularly for some men. Who hasn't heard someone assert that 'tough men don't cry'?

Your earliest experiences with sadness can significantly impact your ability to feel and express this emotion. For example, as a child:

✔ Were you allowed to express sadness appropriately when emotionally upset?

✔ Were you allowed to express your hurt and sadness to the person whom you perceived to be responsible?

If you answer no to both questions, you may not be allowing yourself to acknowledge old hurts with appropriate sadness. You may still be holding sad and painful emotions inside.

When you allow fear or sadness to override your genuine feelings, you simply lock yourself into a reactive cycle, and your emotional brain stays in a physiologically aroused state that impairs your thinking, decision-making and immune function (see Chapter 2). You must recognise that your mind and body are caught up and holding on to emotion. Then you need to recognise your reasons for the sadness, accept the feeling as an emotional messenger, respond appropriately, and finally release and restore calm.

Acknowledge, accept and release pent-up feelings of sadness with the following technique:

1. **Relax your body and mind with quiet breathing or mindfulness practice.**

   See Chapters 6 and 13 for useful techniques.

2. **After you've fully relaxed, let your mind go back to a past situation where you felt emotionally or physically hurt.**

   To get your mind in the right place, listen to a piece of music or look at photos that you associate with that time.

3. **Recall the feelings you associate with this hurtful or sad situation.**

Hurt and sadness may be mixed with other complex emotions, such as disgust, resentment or anger.

4. **Explore the situation more deeply.**

What else is happening? Take note of the physical sensations you're experiencing, as well as what you're thinking and how you're behaving.

5. **Accept everything that emerges without judging the experience as good or bad.**

Allow tears to flow if they come and allow them to continue until they finish naturally. Don't be afraid if this takes some time.

Use your relaxation and breathing exercises to return to an emotionally neutral place when you feel ready.

6. **To recover, let your mind travel to a place of safety and good feelings where you can be present and relieved.**

You may have to practise this technique several times to get out of your old groove. Stick with it; the lessening of old sadness – and all the associated fears – is worth the effort.

Recovering courage

The antidote to fear is courage. Courage in real life isn't about action-movie heroics and posturing; it occurs when you act with purpose, acknowledge risk and take decisive action. To recover the ability to act with courage means that you need to move through a stuck state of fear to one of action.

Eleanor Roosevelt said: 'You gain strength, courage and confidence by every experience in which you really stop to look fear in the face. You must do the thing which you think you cannot do.' Think of the Cowardly Lion in *The Wizard of Oz* who, despite taking action courageously, didn't believe that he acted with courage until he had a medal pinned on him!

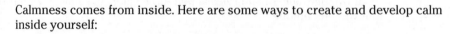

Calmness comes from inside. Here are some ways to create and develop calm inside yourself:

- ✔ **Become confident that you can quiet your breathing.** Use the techniques in Chapter 2 to bring the breath back to a diaphragmatic state in the face of strong emotion.

- ✔ **Practise calming your emotional brain as well as your breath.** Use the mindfulness practices in Chapters 13.

- ✔ **Rehearse in your imagination your ability to reduce fear and anxiety.** Prepare yourself before you return to situations in which you previously had fearful or anxious reactions. Techniques such as The Radio (Chapter 3) can be particularly helpful in this regard.

Managing Rejection

How you manage rejection – whether at work, in love or among family – depends on your ability to release negative self-talk and negative emotions while maintaining optimism that the rejection is a temporary setback. The key is not to get hooked into taking the rejection personally – but instead think through the reasons and lessons and respond with purpose and self-belief.

Locating your sense of control

How well you succeed in life depends on how you develop and use your ability to stay in control rather than feel passive in the face of external events beyond your control. People tend to divide their beliefs about control into two categories. Ask yourself which is your usual way of responding to rejection:

- **External locus of control:** You have little belief in your ability to maintain control of the events of your life. You believe that your present and future life and work is guided by fate, luck or other external circumstances. You often feel victimised.

- **Internal locus of control:** You believe that you can control and act for yourself. You believe that your present and future life is guided by the decisions you make and your own effort. You feel empowered to influence events.

Developing an internal locus of control enables you to be less dependent on external factors for your emotional wellbeing. You can increase your internal locus of control in several key ways. Some of the following strategies may be more appropriate in work-related situations, while some are useful any time you sense rejection:

- **Focus on hobbies and exercise,** in fact any enjoyable challenges that bring back a sense of control.

- **Practise your ability to reduce stress.** Use the methods we outline in this book, such as mindful breathing (Chapters 6 and 13), body scanning (Chapter 2) and relaxation techniques (Chapter 13).

- **Spend time with others working as a volunteer.** Doing so helps you to stay active and engaged in the world. You also enjoy structure in your day while looking for work.

- **Think of your situation as an opportunity rather than a loss,** and avoid immersing yourself in negative feelings.

Rebounding after rejection

Put your positive-thinking brain in the driving seat when responding to rejection with the following approach:

1. **Write down in your journal or on a blank piece of paper a description of the situation involving perceived rejection.**

   What happened? What did you expect to happen? Who was involved?

2. **List and then rate your emotions and feelings about the rejection.**

   Rate your emotion's intensity using a scale of 0 to 10, with 10 being the highest, most intense, experience you can imagine.

3. **Identify any negative self-talk and automatic thoughts.**

   Negative thoughts can include statements such as 'I'll never get another job', 'This is just my bad luck' and 'I'm totally hopeless'.

4. **Put each of your negative thoughts on trial.**

   Does any specific evidence support your negative thoughts? Write down the details.

   Does any specific evidence contradict your negative thoughts? Write down these details.

5. **Create a list of alternative thoughts and formulate a more balanced interpretation of the situation.**

   For more on crafting alternative thoughts and revising your interpretation of events, turn to Chapter 12.

6. **List your positive qualities and skills.**

   See Chapter 20 for some ideas on thinking and acting positively.

7. **Make a plan of action that draws upon your new thinking, creating steps to move forward positively.**

   Working with a coach or a peer on this step can be very helpful. Someone else's support can enable you to talk through your ideas and motivate you to act upon your plan (see Chapters 15 and 16).

You're developing your strategy to recover from any kind of rejection. By working from a single event, acknowledging and releasing emotions appropriately and creating a plan of action for the future, you can leave the past rejection behind you and move forward with renewed strength.

The Four Cs

The key qualities to develop in yourself in order to bounce back after rejection are:

✔ **Challenge:** Accept the situation as a challenge rather than resist it.

✔ **Commitment:** Set time aside to research and seek new opportunities that enable you to achieve your plan of action.

✔ **Connect:** Find and embrace sources of support. These include friends and, potentially, career coaches, education guidance advisers and other professional groups that relate to your specific goals. Use other people's experiences to tap into information, contacts and opportunities. Review your network and get in touch.

✔ **Control:** Focus on gaining internal control (as we describe in the section 'Locating your sense of control'). View the situation as a challenge, something that allows you to take responsibility for the next chapter in your life.

Putting rejection in perspective

Experiencing rejection can lead to strong emotions. You may feel unwanted and unappreciated. You must work hard to avoid taking the rejection as a personal judgement of yourself. The opinion that led to your perceived rejection is just one of many.

Whether you've been rejected at work or in a personal situation, re-discover your ability to take an objective view of your contribution. What did you positively bring to the job or situation before the rejection? To begin, change your emotional state by creating internal calm in your preferred way – perhaps through a sporting activity, a massage, body workout or a relaxation method as described in Chapters 2 and 13.

Avoid alcohol or drugs as methods of distancing yourself from your true emotional state. They distort reality and don't give you a long-term solution.

After you've been rejected, work to accept the situation rather than react to it. Behave like an athlete who feels disappointed when she fails to win a race. You can hold on to your sense of self-esteem and focus on increasing your general fitness and skills. In this way, like that athlete experiencing a setback, you're much more likely to find another job or opportunity – or win another race.

Here are some tips specifically to help you achieve success following a loss of job or redundancy:

- ✔ Ask yourself how you can add to your skills and focus on increasing your likelihood of being selected for another job next time.

- ✔ Consider any transition as an opportunity to evaluate what you enjoy and your skills, and an opportunity to change to other types of work. For example, a recent survey demonstrated that people in service occupations such as nursing, hairdressing and beauty therapy were happier than those in managerial or administrative posts.

- ✔ Evaluate your own performance. List your strong points as well as the gaps in your skills, so that you can start to add to what you can offer in the workplace.

- ✔ Maintain your self-belief and make new plans. Create fresh goals and obtain new skills and you will find new opportunities.

- ✔ Practise presenting and talking about your strengths and skills so that other people know about them. Practising the words out loud is essential for you to be comfortable presenting yourself convincingly. You can practise at home into a recording machine and listen to it back. Or better yet, practise with partners, friends or colleagues so they can give you feedback.

- ✔ Remind yourself that *you* are the best person to list your strengths and present them to others.

Separating from Significant Others

Separation brings you face to face with the loss of attachment and grief (see the earlier section 'Working through Grief'). A previous separation may have left emotional wounds that threaten to re-surface. For example, you may have avoided commitment to a fresh relationship because of the fear of re-awakening old wounds.

Coming to terms with separation and welcoming fresh opportunities means acknowledging, working through, taking on board lessons, and then moving on – and we cover all these aspects in the following sections.

Humans are biologically designed to avoid returning to situations that previously caused pain. You need to anticipate that any separation results in difficult emotional responses that you need to work to accept. Anticipate the phases of grief (which we discuss in the earlier section 'Understanding the phases of grieving') that you're likely to experience so that you'll recognise them as they arise.

Mending your broken heart

The breakdown of a relationship you care about is never undertaken lightly. Love and attachment create an emotional memory that remains, and loss requires you to work through periods of both bereavement and adjustment.

When a relationship ends, your dreams and expectations have been shattered. You probably imagined a future with the other person. You may also have experienced betrayal, rejection, infidelity or abuse. All these factors can remove your sense of trust in others and in the reliability of your judgement.

Loss involves more than physical separation. You miss touch, talk, sharing and intimacy. You may also turn the rejection inwards, losing self-esteem and confidence in your ability to attract love again.

To re-affirm your sense of belief and self-worth, take some time to allow your feelings to work themselves out. Talk with friends or write a letter to your ex expressing your feelings, including both positives and negatives (we don't recommend you send it). Talking or writing about the end of a relationship helps you to:

- Consider what you may do differently in the future.
- Re-discover your initial sense of trust in your own choices.
- Reflect on your part in the situation.
- Remember why you were attracted to the person in the first place.

After releasing some of your raw emotions, you need to start to build up your own sense of appreciation for the person you now are. You're more likely to mend a broken heart when you create a loving relationship with yourself first. Re-connect with that sense that loving support does exist and remind yourself who to go to and how to find it. Return to hobbies and activities that provide you with a sense of enjoyment and competence. Remind yourself how to meet your own needs and enjoy life again as an individual.

Working towards reconciliation

Sometimes when you separate from another person – for example, after a divorce or end of a working partnership – you still need to co-operate with the other individual, perhaps for the sake of children or a business requirement. Both you and the other person must go through a period of adjustment where your abilities to think rather than return to difficult emotions is essential. This section includes methods to help you re-establish a dramatically altered relationship on a new footing.

You're working through the phases of grieving, whatever happened. Allow yourself to fully grieve, in addition to working towards co-operation and reconciliation.

To find a state of goodwill within a dramatically altered relationship, both parties need to agree on what to focus. Shared focus enables you to discuss specific goals that are mutually beneficial and serve the ultimate purpose, which may be taking care of the children, completing a business project or selling a house while separating.

Much depends on the ability of you and your partner to use language clearly and to stay focused on your goals. Agree, if possible, to leave negative emotions, particularly blame and judgement, aside, as you work together on your agreed commitments. Should emotions arise, agree on the need to allocate time specifically to these separate conversations. We share a reconciliation process below to help you manage these discussions:

1. **Arrange a quiet place for discussions, where you won't be interrupted or reminded of old conflicts.**

   If possible, choose a place outside your own homes or offices.

2. **Agree to goals for the meeting.**

   What is the best outcome of your conversation for you both? You may want to write down a description of this outcome and keep it on a piece of paper in front of you.

3. **Outline principles of behaviour that can help you both achieve these goals, including what to do when strong emotions surface.**

   Some principles may include calling time out, listening rather than commenting, and using phrases like 'I think' or 'I feel' rather than blaming the other person.

4. **Be responsible for your own emotions.**

   Decide how you want to feel during the conversation and use some of the techniques in this book to calm yourself and access a positive emotional state (see Chapters 2, 3, 6, 8 and 12).

   If you find yourself getting physiologically aroused during the conversation, re-establish self-calm by focusing on your mind. If you start to feel angry. try to focus silently on some aspect of the other person that you value or admire in order to bring yourself back to a willingness to co-operate.

5. **Communicate clearly and assertively.**

   Assertive communication involves mutual respect; you speak your needs clearly but also allow the other person to do the same. Each of you has a right to express your personal experience of the situation. You may not agree with the other's interpretation, but each of you has a right to your own opinion.

6. **Reconcile differences in an effort to move forward.**

   Try to end the conversation by pulling together goals and actions on which you agree. Agree to disagree on areas of difference and put these topics clearly to one side.

This process can also be useful after infidelity or when your partner has let you down in some way. You must consider both feelings and thoughts, taking the bigger picture into account. Beware of all-or-nothing thinking! Just because your partner has let you down once, doesn't mean that she's going to again.

Should you be considering separation after a hurt or betrayal, stop and ask yourself whether you really think that you're going to be happier without the relationship than you would be by working things through. Cost-Benefit Analysis (see Chapter 1) can be a useful method to weigh up your options.

Daring to date

To date again after a relationship breakdown takes courage. The key is to spend some time re-connecting with yourself (see 'Mending your broken heart' earlier in the chapter).

Establishing your own ability to be independent means that you don't try to live through another person. The two people who come together in a relationship need to bring their separate identities. The new bond flourishes only when each party discovers how to accept the other and supports the other person in both work and life goals.

Use the following approaches to reconnect to certain essential qualities that enhance the success of your new relationship:

- ✔ **Allow yourself to argue.** Arguing is a sign of health in a relationship, particularly when both people are able to put their point of view and reach an agreement.

- ✔ **Be prepared for compromise and change.** You're in a new, different relationship now; you're going to do things differently from previous relationships. Besides, why would you want more of the same?

- ✔ **Devote time to being together and sharing interests and experiences.** As the relationship moves from initial interest and romantic attachment, setting aside time to be with each other becomes the most important priority.

- ✔ **Enjoy the qualities that you see in your new partner.** Get to know the other person and, in particular, live with them, if possible. You then know and approve of their habits and qualities. Focus on the positives.

✔ **Give appreciation freely.** Warm words of encouragement and support sustain relationships and build confidence and trust.

✔ **Keep touching.** Touch is a vital form of communication. Touch calms and reduces blood pressure and is the non-verbal way of saying 'You matter to me' and 'I love and appreciate you'. Also, touch releases the feel-good chemical oxytocin in the brain and encourages stronger bonding.

✔ **Love yourself.** Enter a new relationship with a healthy sense of self-esteem. Practise the loving-kindness meditation in Chapter 13 to bring back a sense of enjoying yourself.

✔ **Talk with each other and express what you're feeling.** Communication is particularly important when you disagree. Some couples set aside a regular weekly uninterrupted time together where they light a candle and share what pleases and what annoys. The sharing of needs often emerges from this type of discussion.

Chapter 11

Coping with Life's Transitions

· ·

In This Chapter

▶ Reviewing life's changes

▶ Leaving pain behind

▶ Acting like an adult

▶ Accepting the inevitable

· ·

*E*very person's life goes through many transitions between birth and death. Each transition is an opportunity for you to review your approach and let go of habits that disturb your emotional balance. You can identify and develop fresh behaviours that help you to be happy as you go forward in life, but often people don't take the time to acknowledge and honour this process.

You don't need to drag old emotional burdens and pain along with you through every transition. Your past doesn't have to determine your future. You can focus on new thoughts and experiences that override previous problems. You aren't exactly the same person now as you were when you were a child; you've discovered new ways of being and behaving since then. Similarly, you aren't going to be the same person in ten years' time as you are today, although you do have a core of identity, experience and memories that are always with you.

A transition presents you with an occasion to stop and plan consciously what your goals are and what feelings and approaches best enable you to achieve those goals. And, more importantly, transitions are about moving forwards in a way that makes you feel good.

In this chapter we offer some strategies to make transitions into powerful experiences that create positive, not negative, changes. We acknowledge that some emotional turmoil may occur as life changes but suggest that this upheaval doesn't have to paralyse you. We help you to focus on finding ways to free yourself from unhelpful emotional memories so that you choose to move into your next phase with hope and optimism.

Riding the Waves of Change

Like the sea, your life is constantly on the move. Some waves are gentle and consistent; others come in with the force of a tsunami. Some tides bring in beautiful fish and shells, others bring in rubbish. Reading this book gives you an opportunity to stop and consider what your life has been bringing you and to choose what you may like it to bring you in the future. If you feel you have had more rubbish than beauty, now is the time to consider how to focus your energy on bringing in experiences that make you feel happier on a daily basis. If your life has brought you beautiful things, you need to bottle those experiences and consider how to continue to enhance your emotional happiness in future.

No life is without challenge and comparing your experiences with those of other people does little good. You only have to look at the lives of celebrities to realise that lurking beneath a supposedly perfect ideal of a millionaire lifestyle, complete with mansion and fast cars, may be deep pain caused by personal tragedy or feelings of inadequacy and struggle. Instead, focus on making your own life better. You can develop emotional resilience so that you feel confident in riding the inevitable waves of change.

Reviewing your peaks and troughs

Sit quietly and think back over your lifetime. Recall the challenges, joyful events, surprises and experiences. Did you have periods of gentle waves of stability? Did you have some tsunami moments? What about the times when you felt life threw rubbish at you? And the times of beauty and joy? Allow your mind to flow back over your life. Notice the experience and emotions that the memories stir up in you.

Making a graphical representation of how your life has flowed to this point can help you recognise the ups and down, and the transitions between. Take a piece of paper and a pencil and draw a line that symbolises your life so far, with peaks representing good times and troughs representing bad times. Note down those experiences that brought you happiness and those that were challenging. See whether you can notice the following:

- Moments of change or insight
- Patterns of behaviour or experience that repeat
- Periods with noticeable transitions between one phase and the next
- Whether your general level of happiness has changed over this time

Figure 11-1 gives you an idea of how a life review graph may look.

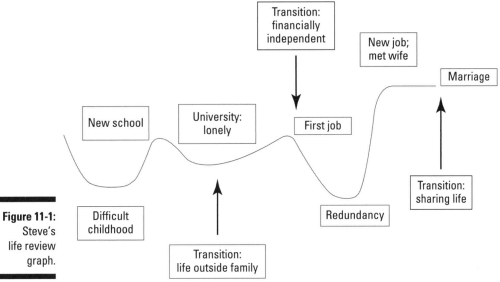

Figure 11-1:
Steve's
life review
graph.

Reflect on your graph and make some notes about what you notice. Try answering these questions:

✔ Do you need to be more proactive about making changes?

✔ How do you feel about the future? How would you like to be feeling? Who and what will support you?

✔ How do you want to manage difficult situations in future?

✔ What experiences do you want to leave behind?

✔ What helps you to feel happy? What prevents you and how can you overcome this barrier?

✔ What strengths can you build on to take into the future?

You can use this review process again to keep re-assessing your life.

Gaining emotional maturity: Considering perspectives

You can't always change the situations you find yourself in, but you do have a choice as to how you approach them. You can achieve emotional maturity and resilience by considering whether you're approaching your life experiences in the best way possible for you. You need to look back at your life and review your perspective on things.

The legacy of some people's childhood clouds their perspectives, and they can get stuck in childhood beliefs and habits. Childhood is the most influential period of your life. You're small and helpless, and so tend to take the opinions of your elders as facts. Some people go to their deathbed still believing a statement that a teacher or parent made to them when they were a small child, not recognising that this statement was one person's opinion at one stage and that it doesn't represent the truth.

Don't confuse opinion with fact. Other people sometimes make negative comments because they're jealous, or under stress. You don't have to believe them.

Here are some useful reminders to help you gain perspective on painful elements of your past:

- ✔ If you're beating yourself up for a mistake you made, tell yourself that this one thing going wrong doesn't make you a failure.

- ✔ If someone acted in a hurtful way – perhaps rejecting you or ignoring you – try to recognise that this event may not have been your fault. Try to see the other person's perspective now and realise that his actions may have little to do with you or your behaviour.

- ✔ If you're still holding emotional pain about a comment someone made many years ago, try to accept that the comment was based on just one person's opinion and that the comment doesn't make it a reality today.

- ✔ If remembering a past event brings you down, try to find a way to switch to positive thoughts and think about the situation in a way that helps you feel good about yourself today.

As you mature you're better able to put people's comments and actions into perspective. Gradually, you become less emotionally upset by other people or situations. You also take responsibility for your own emotional reaction.

Each decade of your life offers a context within which to review your perspectives. But as you do so, be careful to avoid stereotypical thinking that leads you to associate certain emotional events with a particular time of life. For example, don't set yourself up to believe the following clichés:

- ✔ After seven years in a relationship, you experience the 'seven-year itch'.

- ✔ All children in the 'terrible twos' have tantrums.

- ✔ Around the age of 40, you go through a 'mid-life crisis'.

- ✔ Everybody's teenage years are difficult.

- ✔ Students have a carefree life of fun and freedom.

- ✔ You retire at between the age of 60 and 65, and from then on you decline and lose your memory.

None of these events automatically happen to you. When you look back, you may find that you were an angelic toddler and a happy teenager. So when you look forward, don't set expectations for the future based on these stereotypes.

Emotionally mature people recognise that their way of seeing the world isn't the only way. They're willing to reflect on their approach to situations and consider whether their perspectives are realistic and helpful. They manage their emotions and are open to listening and discovering from others, but are able to stand up for the things they care about.

As you grow older and mature both physically and emotionally, you tend to gain the skills to manage life's ups and downs more easily. As a young person, you have little information to compare or reference what makes you happy and what doesn't. But in fact a young person can sometimes be more intuitively emotionally mature than someone older. (For example, children sometimes see to the heart of problems that adults are trying to ignore.)

Flowing with the endings and beginnings

Life is full of beginnings and endings. Nature is about birth, growth and death – transitions most cultures honour with rituals. People change jobs, get married and move to new shores, sometimes from choice and sometimes not. Such is the natural progression of life.

You may have experienced some unexpected events that shifted your life, such as bereavement, accidents, illness, change of home or location, redundancy, divorce, unplanned pregnancy, stillbirth or miscarriage, or war. Each event has an emotional impact and represents both an ending and a beginning in which you're driven to alter your expectations of life. Some people are able to be philosophical and accept life's challenges easily; others hold on to the hurt and bitterness of a bad event for years afterwards.

A crucial point to understand is that the external event is not, in itself, what disturbs people: instead, people's views of the change are what impact on emotional stability. A divorce may devastate one person, whereas another may feel released. Each transition contains the ingredients of both happiness and sadness. Even the 'happy' transitions of marriage and parenthood involve an ending of aspects of yourself and your life, as well as a beginning of new ones.

The Transition Review can help you through times of transition. For any transitions you're experiencing, consider how they're affecting you. What is changing? What emotions are involved? What do you have to release as one phase ends? What can you welcome in as a new phase begins? Table 11-1 outlines a reflection process to honour the change you're going through. We include an example to help you get the idea.

Table 11-1		The Transition Review		
Transition	*What is beginning?*	*What is ending?*	*What can I honour and value that I am leaving behind?*	*What can I release that no longer serves me well as I go forward?*
First baby	Life as a parent; the excitement of a new life	Life as free adults without too much responsibility	The enjoyment of our times together without children	The need to have the undivided attention of my partner

You can apply the Transition Review to past experiences as well, to help you see how transitions affected you.

Ask yourself whether your emotional life today is still being negatively influenced by past events. Can you now let go of pain or disappointment in order to transition into a new phase of your life without this burden? What thoughts and behaviours can you now focus on to help you to move forward?

Shedding redundant emotional skins to achieve happiness

Transitions allow you the potential to shed a skin. But this process doesn't mean you become a totally different person. Just as a snake sheds its skin over its lifetime but is essentially the same snake, so a core of you remains the same through your transitions. You simply choose to take on some new colours and to integrate some wisdom from previous experiences.

Your emotional state is the most defining influence on your quality of life. Your inner life shapes your experience more than your outer. Many people say that they'll be happy when they become millionaires. But if you're miserable now, research demonstrates that money itself doesn't change that. Better to find a way to be happy now.

Work out what's going to make you happy as you move into a new stage of life. Try to identify:

✔ **Your state of happiness:** Remember or imagine a time – whether recent or long ago – when you felt happy.

  • What does it feel like emotionally?

- What do you feel like physically?

- What thoughts help you to be positive and happy?

- What language would you use to express happiness?

- What clothes, environment and choices reinforce your emotional wellbeing?

✔ **The emotional skins you need to shed:** What may you need to stop doing in order to be happy in future? For example, you may focus on the negative; or hold anger at your parents; or get irritated with your children for no good reason. Identify which thoughts, habits, behaviours or relationships may hold you back so that you can choose to focus on feeling happy now.

Growing Up Emotionally

Becoming an adult is a major transition. The human being is a child for a very long time: many people don't leave home until they're in their 20s. People can get stuck, imagining that some parental figure is going to tell them what to do – what time to go to bed or get up, what to eat, when to exercise. These small disciplines support your wellbeing. If you don't find out how to do them for yourself, you can lose confidence and feel out of control. (See Chapter 8 for more information.)

The process of growing up therefore demands that you become your own parent, letting go of childhood ways, dependency on or attachment to anyone else, and being able to make your own decisions. This process in turn raises self-esteem.

Listening to your inner child, adult and parent

You need to understand that three different states are working within you: the parent, the child and the adult. A well-adjusted person makes room for each of these elements internally. You need to identify these aspects of yourself and get them talking to one another:

✔ **The Parent:** To activate your 'inner parent', identify your own idea of what a good parent is, so that you can adopt these qualities and behaviours within yourself – and for yourself.

Develop a part of yourself on whom you can call for comfort, care, self-discipline and encouragement. The benefit is that you're able to sense what you need and take action for your own wellbeing, rather than waiting for someone to prompt you.

✔ **The Adult:** This adult part of you thinks, reasons, sees clearly, solves problems and develops solutions for you.

✔ **The Child:** This part is your emotional core that, however old you may be, gets upset, frightened, lonely or angry; it also likes to play and be creative. Become familiar with how your inner child responds to situations and listen to your own needs. Allow yourself time for creativity and play, because this feeds your sense of emotional wellbeing.

The next time you feel emotionally upset follow this process:

1. **Acknowledge your 'child' and the emotions you're feeling.**

   Say 'Yes, I'm feeling fed up/tired/miserable', and allow yourself time to experience your feelings. Cry if you need to; yell or punch your pillow if you're angry.

2. **Activate your inner parent and comfort yourself.**

   Metaphorically take yourself in your arms and give yourself some love and comfort for a period of time. Remember that underneath anger is hurt. Nurture your emotional needs.

3. **Activate your adult to analyse the situation.**

   Work out what you can do practically to resolve the problem upsetting you. You may need to take action or express your needs. Ask yourself what needs to happen to help you feel better.

Taking responsibility in the adult world

The adult world is full of practical challenges. You have to decide where to live, how to manage your money, decipher your way through the tricky experience of adult relationships and find work to support you. This process can be overwhelming and is a time when many people feel vulnerable. No wonder that research indicates that up to 25 per cent of students suffer from depression.

Accepting accountability for your own decisions can be frightening. You move from the child, who's passive and looks to others for survival, through the teenage years, when articulating your needs is difficult.

Adults can get into behavioural habits that can be hard to change. At times they may be aggressive, use passive-aggressive behaviour, or remain entirely passive. In adult life you need to let go of these approaches and become an assertive adult. From this position, you can communicate well with others, treating them as equals, collaborating and problem-solving together.

Where are you operating from? Take a look at the following list and see which type of behaviour applies best to you:

✔ **Child:** Children are passive and helpless, looking to others to direct their lives and meet their needs. They can be accommodating until they grow enough to stand up for themselves.

Some people retain a child-like passivity into adulthood. They are indirect communicators and avoid conflict where possible. They can be paralysed about making decisions because the commitment is too much and they're uncertain of themselves. They use phrases like 'it's up to you', 'I don't mind' and 'whatever you like'. They need to build confidence in themselves and feel that they have the right to express their needs too.

✔ **Teenager:** Teenagers can make you feel bad just by sitting sulkily in the room. They're often unaware of the impact they have on other people. They use body language such as a raised eyebrow or a shrug of the shoulder to express their opinion.

People displaying this type of passive-aggressive behaviour can be difficult to deal with, because they aren't confident enough to express their opinions and needs. They get what they want through emotional blackmail. They blame others when accused of a mistake, using phrases like 'how could you have done that?', 'you shouldn't' and 'they made me.' They need to develop confidence to feel able to express their needs directly instead of indirectly.

✔ **Dominant parent:** People locked into this role behave aggressively, dominating others and not caring about their rights. They impose their own needs, blaming other people for things that go wrong, humiliating and putting them down. Their body language is bullying and they use phrases such as 'you must,' 'you should' and 'you ought to.' They need to develop the inner confidence to listen to and heed the needs of other people and realise that this approach enhances rather than diminishes their position.

✔ **Adult:** Assertive adults respect their own rights and the rights of others. They're secure in themselves and listen to other people's opinions and express their own. They manage life with confidence and seek compromise that enables both parties to feel good. They use collaborative phrases such as 'let's' or 'shall we see what we can both agree on?'

Triangulating: Acting in threes

The passive, child position (see the preceding section) is particularly problematic because people who continue to withhold their needs can become victims. *Victims* express themselves directly or take responsibility for their parts in problems, which in turn can create two additional roles that function in a triangular fashion:

✔ The victim pushes another person into the role of *persecutor,* blaming this other person for the situation.

✔ The victim may also share the issue with a *rescuer,* a 'safe' colleague or friend. Although gaining support can be useful, avoiding confrontation just reinforces feelings of inadequacy and helplessness.

People in triangular situations – sometimes called *drama triangles* – need to address their problems directly, in an adult way, with their perceived persecutor.

The triangular relationship between persecutor, rescuer and victim can cause great emotional pain. Persecutors may be totally unaware of the situation and can switch into feeling like victims when accused. Fear of the consequences of facing up to perceived persecutors may paralyse victims, and this suppression can lead to ill health. Rescuers are often in no-win situations because if they truly rescue their victims, the triangle switches and self-perpetuates.

In this type of triangular situation, the best solution is for each person to step back and not play the game. Even if one person pulls out of the drama, the triangle is broken.

If this situation rings a bell with you, and you need the courage to face up to someone directly, ask yourself:

✔ What is the worst that can happen if I express myself?

✔ What exactly is frightening about this person's anger or disapproval?

✔ What do you really want to happen? In how many different ways can you express that desire assertively?

✔ What is the pain of doing nothing versus the pain of having the courage to change things?

Rehearsing the conversations with a friend or coach can help build the language to re-address this pattern of miscommunication. See Chapter 12 for an exercise that helps you to predict the response of the other person involved, and plan the conversation.

Spotting and rewriting scripts

The shape of your life to date has depended on the messages you were given as a child or have told yourself since.

You may also have been following a *family script*, an overt or covert message from your parents about their expectations of you. For example, your script may dictate what career you should go into, what type of behaviour is acceptable or what sort of person you are. Your script may have put labels on you and your siblings, such as 'the clever one' or 'the sporty one'. You may look back and discover that your script has been handed down through generations, and that your own life has mirrored a pattern similar to that of your parents or grandparents.

Ask yourself about the scripts that have been running through your life:

✔ Have you experienced transitions between one chapter of your script and the next?

✔ Did these past scripts give you the feeling that you can choose from your own talents and achieve personal goals – or have they undermined your confidence and paralysed you, preventing you from taking action?

✔ Have you followed the expectations of other people?

✔ Are you able in your life now to define what your own skills and goals are, what you personally care about and to express this clearly? Are you able to live a life that reflects your personal aspirations?

You can break the pattern of following a habitual script and write your own story instead. You can make choices that are right for you rather than for others. After identifying scripts that have shaped your life, think about the new script that you want to realise for your future.

✔ What story would you like the next part of your life to be about?

✔ What theme would you like to give it?

✔ What emotions would it conjure up?

Your success in creating a good life for yourself now depends upon how powerfully you shape your story going forward. Start acting this part now. Your energy and commitment brings the new script into reality. See Chapter 16 for more on setting long-term goals.

Making Sense of Illness, Ageing and Death

Believe it or not, you can find peace and happiness amid illness, ageing and even the thought of death. You just need to have the right attitude.

Dealing with illness and disability

Many people imagine that old age is punctuated by illness, but in fact statistics show that the majority of health costs occur in the last year of life. Although many 80-year-olds do experience symptoms of ill health, most continue to function well. Some people, however, are less fortunate and experience ill health for a substantial part of their life. You may be one of them.

The illness itself doesn't signify whether you feel emotionally unhappy. Your happiness depends on how you approach your illness and how you think about it. One person can remain upbeat, and another may fall to pieces. If you focus on negative thoughts, such as 'how could this happen to me' or 'it's unfair,' you diminish your ability to cope. Although these thoughts bubbling up from time to time are understandable, stress and negativity deplete your immune system.

Focus on what you can feel positive about, because this outlook enhances both your health and your feeling of control. Consider what you can be grateful for and identify what makes you feel good, so that you can focus on these feelings.

Managing a chronic illness or disability represents a major transition. You must adjust to a new way of living life, a new state of being. This new approach may well impose on the practicalities of your life, making each day more complicated or meaning you need a carer to help you with things that you used to do yourself. You need support and rest.

You may suffer grief over the loss of your previous healthy self. One physical identity is fading and another developing. This period is a time to go gently with your emotions. Listen to them and acknowledge them. Emotions simply exist: don't think in terms of what you 'should' or 'shouldn't' feel.

Although some aspects of your previous life may end, the emotional strengths and resilience you had earlier in your life can stay with you. You need to choose how you manage your situation, which emotions to concentrate on and how you plan to develop this different stage of your life. Here are two areas to focus on:

 ✔ **Accepting the truth of your illness or disability:** Pretending that everything is fine doesn't help you address the situation honestly. What is the prognosis? What is feasible and what isn't? Acceptance doesn't rule out optimism but in fact is a first step to making some decisions about how you're going to live with your illness or disability. Acceptance frees you to focus on living life fully in your current capacity.

✔ **Identifying what's going to help you to manage:** This help may be supportive people, a change of environment, and a positive attitude that helps you to look on the bright side of life and find things that you enjoy. Talking to other people who have made their life good despite problems can be inspiring. Neither disability nor sickness have to destroy your emotional wellbeing. What you choose to focus your mind on shapes your emotional health.

Caring for a loved one who's suffering can also be very difficult. Address your own needs by asking for support and giving yourself some loving care. You can find contact details of support groups in the Appendix.

Managing the ageing process

In the modern era everyone celebrates youth. But being young doesn't signify happiness. In fact, many report being happier in older age. People are living longer, healthier lives than previously, with access to sports facilities, travel and education that didn't exist in earlier times.

Life doesn't have to slow down as you get older. 'You're as young as you feel' is an accurate saying. You don't need to imagine that old age means creaking bones or wrinkled skin. Keep active, keep fit, keep mentally alert and use moisturiser! Prevent the slippery slope of 'I can't do this anymore because I'm this age'. Challenge your beliefs about age. Being 80 is no block in itself to going to university or climbing a mountain.

Focus on the inner you. Your beauty lies within, and is about your personal qualities and how you share them with others, not what you look like. Value your rich experiences, wisdom, friends, events, things you can be proud of and the family around you.

Life is made up of moments. Look back over your photo albums and revel in the people you've known, the places you visited and in the moments of joy. These things remain a part of you forever. Then look forward and identify how you want to feel as you grow older. Retaining enthusiasm, optimism and curiosity keeps you young at heart.

If you're caring for an elderly person, see beyond the external: everyone was young once and everyone has interesting stories to tell.

Facing death in peace

Feeling at peace when you face death takes thought and attention. Everyone dies someday and no one knows what the new day may bring. Accept death as part of being a living being: this is nature's way.

Many people with terminal illness talk about 'each extra minute being a bonus' and yet other healthy people squander hours, days, weeks and even months complaining about the small irritations of life. Living each day to the full and in a way that you're proud of helps you achieve a state of grace as you face death. Whether you're religious or not, consider what helps you to feel at peace as you think about your death:

- ✔ Can you let go of old grudges and tell people that you forgive them?
- ✔ Can you tell the important people in your life that you love them?
- ✔ Do you need to make a will or arrange practicalities?
- ✔ Do you need to say something to someone in particular?
- ✔ Do you really want to experience something specific before you die?

Do whatever feeds your soul. Make the most of every moment, whether watching the clouds go by, taking a world cruise or spending more time with those you love.

Part IV
The Emotional Healing Toolkit

'Emotional healing is certainly allowing
your one unique gift to shine, Mr Treadvole.'

In this part . . .

We focus on four powerful and practical strategies to manage your life in future. We introduce you to the power of your mind and show you how focusing on constructive thoughts that support your life goals can help you feel happy. In addition, mindfulness and body scanning techniques still your mind and make you more aware of your body-mind signals and symptoms.

The lifestyle models we share enable you to express your needs and develop more creative solutions to manage your problems. We also suggest new behaviours to make the goal of becoming an emotionally healed person a reality.

Chapter 12

Managing Feelings with Thinking Strategies

In This Chapter

▶ Recognising the link between thoughts and feelings

▶ Analysing how your mind distorts situations

▶ Managing your emotions through more helpful thinking

▶ Lightening your mood with laughter

*H*ow you think affects how you feel; how you feel affects how you think. An effective way to manage your emotions is to become attuned to the conversations that you're having in your own head, which enables you to observe your thoughts and notice how they're influencing your feelings, behaviours and actions.

Thoughts in themselves can raise or lower your mood. You can check whether your thoughts are leading you down negative spirals that block your ability to live life fully. If you discover that they are, you can then redirect your focus.

At certain times you may upset yourself by obsessing about past pain or imagining things that may go wrong in the future – things that may never happen. What you choose to focus on influences your emotional response to a situation. You can develop the ability to analyse your thoughts with an objective eye and decide whether they're helping you to reach your goals and enjoy life. Controlling your thoughts helps you to manage your feelings.

In this chapter we help you understand the role that thoughts play in emotional healing. And we provide you with activities to transform your emotional response through thought, so that you can enhance your sense of happiness and ease.

Seeing How Thinking Impacts Feeling

Each thought influences your emotional equilibrium. As we explain in Chapters 1 and 2, your thinking brain can stimulate stress or calm in your emotional brain.

People need to manage challenges and difficult situations in their lives. Each person responds to situations in a different way depending on personal experiences, expectations and perspectives. How you think about difficult situations can either help or hinder your ability to manage them.

Imagine that three people find out that they have to make a presentation at work:

- ✔ **John thinks:** 'Great, here's an opportunity to demonstrate that I'm good at my job.' This response helps him to feel confident, which enhances his ability to be at ease with his audience.

- ✔ **Jane thinks:** 'Help, I hate presentations and I always forget what I was supposed to say.' This thought makes her anxious. Her anxiety triggers stress, which impairs her thinking, voice tone and memory. She doesn't give a good presentation.

- ✔ **Judy thinks:** 'I find presentations challenging, but I shall focus on feeling calm and doing the best I can.' This approach acknowledges the difficulty of the situation but creates a thought that helps her to focus on the positive.

The situation is the same for each person but how the person thinks about it determines the emotional response. Thinking, therefore, has a big effect on feelings.

Examining self-generated emotions

Disturbing yourself with your own thoughts is surprisingly easy. You may be safely at home alone, but your brain can be ticking over, upsetting your peace. Sometimes you can feel as if someone else is inside your head, sitting in judgement over you, criticising you and undermining your confidence.

Your thoughts don't define who you are and may well not even be facts – they are just thoughts. You may need to put them kindly in their place!

See whether any of these negative phrases sound familiar:

✔ How could I have said something so idiotic?

✔ I hate myself for being so irritable with my children.

✔ I'm hopeless; everything I do goes wrong.

✔ I'm so stupid.

✔ Why didn't I manage to finish my work in time?

Start to notice how your thoughts impact your feelings. Are they helping you feel good? If not, can you change the way you think?

The ABCDE exercise helps you notice how your thoughts affect your emotions by logging your reaction in certain situations. Within any Activating situation you have a Belief, thought or expectation that has a Consequential feeling. If the Belief is negative you can Dispute it so as to Exchange any negative thought for a supportive one. Table 12-1 gives you an example of the ABCDE exercise in action.

Table 12-1	Bob's ABCDE Exercise
ABCDE Process	*Bob's Response*
A: Activating situation	I was unable to get to my son's football match because I had a meeting at work.
B: Belief, thought or expectation	I know how important my being there was to him. I feel awful that I couldn't make it. I'm a terrible parent.
C: Consequential feeling	Regret, self-criticism and anxiety that may put pressure on the family.
D: Disputing beliefs	Is it rational to feel that I'm a bad parent just because of this one event?
E: Exchanging negative for supportive thought	I can think something like 'I take good care of my son most of the time and am a good parent.' This makes me feel better.

Being a perfectionist can disturb your emotions and lead to self-criticism and disappointment when you or other people don't come up to your standards. Living up to perfectionist ideals can be exhausting. Words such as *should*, *must* and *ought to* denote that you have set rules of behaviour, such as:

✔ I must get everything right.

✔ Other people must always approve of me.

✔ I ought to be in a relationship.

✔ I should have won that argument: it's awful when things don't go my way.

These thoughts are rigid and make you miserable. They also lead to self-doubt and reduce your self-esteem. Perfectionism is subjective and can be irrational: a mathematical equation may have a perfect answer but there's no perfect report and no perfect parent, husband or wife! The pursuit of excellence rather than perfection is rational and achievable and allows you to accept that life is uncertain and everyone makes mistakes sometimes. You can only do your best.

Be compassionate with yourself and others when life doesn't live up to your ideals. Ideals are seldom set in stone and are often based on cultural or parental expectations.

Transform self-defeating and judgemental thoughts to ones that reinforce acceptance of the fact that even when you try your best, you occasionally get things wrong. And that's okay because you're human. For example instead of judging yourself as no good for having lost your temper, you can dispute this all-or-nothing thinking (see the following section) and exchange the thought for: 'I accept myself despite losing my temper occasionally.'

When you exchange and develop new thoughts, soften the tone of your inner voice so that it's gentle and supportive. Identify a phrase to replace the old thoughts, such as:

✔ 'I'm okay: I don't get everything right but no one does.'

✔ 'I'll do the best I can.'

✔ 'I can love and accept myself as I am. I can change my responses in future.'

You have enough challenges in the outer world – don't upset yourself further by allowing your own thoughts to give you a hard time in your inner world.

Switching out of distorted thinking

Specific patterns of thinking exist that can upset your emotional wellbeing by distorting your reason and perception of events. Even the most logical brain can come to the wrong conclusions.

We can divide distorted thinking habits into categories:

- ✔ **All-or-nothing thinking:** You think in black and white, missing shades of grey: 'It's completely useless.'

- ✔ **Being impatient:** You have a low frustration tolerance and get impatient so that you don't finish a task, even though doing so would be beneficial: 'I've had enough of this.'

- ✔ **Being too tolerant:** You have a high frustration tolerance and stay in a damaging situation too long: 'It's okay, I can manage.'

- ✔ **Blaming:** Whatever happens is always the fault of another person so that you feel victimised and don't take responsibility for your part: 'It's all her fault!'

- ✔ **'Catastrophising':** You make more of a situation than it is: 'It's simply awful and I can't stand it!'

- ✔ **Emotional Reasoning:** You come to a conclusion because of feelings rather than facts: 'I feel so miserable that I'm sure this meeting isn't going to go well.'

- ✔ **Labelling:** You brand yourself or others with a label as a result of one instance: 'He's stupid.'

- ✔ **Making assumptions:** You assume something about a situation or person without evidence to support your conclusion: 'They're planning something against me.'

- ✔ **Magnifying:** You grossly magnify the importance of an event: 'This is the worst thing that can possibly happen.'

- ✔ **Minimising**: You play down the importance of an event: 'It's not really a problem.'

- ✔ **Over-generalising**: You draw some general conclusion as a result of one or two isolated experiences or events: 'This is never going to work.'

- ✔ **Personalising:** You take personal responsibility for an event despite others being involved; 'I must have done something wrong.'

- ✔ **Selective thinking:** You concentrate on one detail from an event or experience while ignoring other factors: 'No one appreciated my efforts.'

Spend a day this week noticing your thinking, particularly when you're involved in uncomfortable situations. Write down your emotionally charged thoughts in your journal or notepad. Review the thoughts and see whether some of them fit within the preceding categories so you understand which type of thought distortions you're experiencing. Consider how your thoughts impact the way you feel, behave, interact with others, perform work tasks, and enjoy life.

Note down each type of distorted thinking, record the situation that triggered that thinking, and then consider the consequences. If you find that the thinking is having a negative effect on you, you can replace it with a new perspective.

Table 12-2 gives you a framework for recording your thoughts. We fill in an example for you on over-generalising, but you can use this table to consider all the different categories of distorted thinking.

Table 12-2	Working on Distorted Thinking		
Thinking Style	*Situation that Triggered the Thought*	*Thought and Consequence of Thought*	*New Perspective*
Over-generalising	Anxiety about a job interview	Thinking 'I'll never get this job' leads to sweaty hands and stress, which impacts my confidence and voice	Just because I've had two rejections, doesn't mean I can't get this job

To make distorted-thinking analysis a habit, specify a daily time to self-observe so that thinking about how you're thinking becomes a natural part of your life. (See Chapter 13 for mindfulness-based approaches that can complement these exercises and allow you to develop a way of tuning out negativity and bring enjoyment and happiness back into your life.)

Stuck in anxiety

Heather had a fear of doing presentations ever since she forgot her lines in front of her senior manager. She experienced fear and sleepless nights before any presentation, even a minor one. Her mind imagined the worst outcome, making the assumption that all her presentations are and will be failures. She over-drama-tised the situation so much that she convinced herself that she was in danger of losing her job. Her fear of failure, in fact, set her up to fail, making her even more nervous and tongue-tied.

When Heather analysed her thoughts, she saw that they were heightening her anxiety rather than helping her. Instead, she developed supportive thoughts for the future, such as 'I've prepared well' and 'I shall just do my best and not get worried if I have to look at my notes.' Her presentations noticeably improved and her confidence built as she broke the anxiety cycle.

Thinking rationally

Challenge whether your thoughts are rational. Don't allow distorted thinking (see the preceding section) to make a situation worse than it really is, or linger over past pain or fret over a concern that may never happen. Imagining that when one thing goes wrong in your life all other similar situations are also going to be painful isn't sensible or helpful. Instead, develop thinking that helps you manage the experience.

Sarah's ex-boyfriend was unfaithful to her, and now she thinks she can't trust any man. When she starts dating Ben, she's defensive and suspicious of him. If he doesn't call, she thinks, 'I bet he's out with someone else.' Ben is frustrated by Sarah's lack of trust because he's not cheating on her. Their relationship starts to break down.

Sarah needs to change the way she's thinking. We recommend that she answer the following questions to dispute the rationality and helpfulness of her thoughts:

- ✔ Is it rational to think that because one partner has been unfaithful all partners are going to be unfaithful? (Rationally, the answer is no. Some partners are faithful and can be trusted.)

- ✔ How does thinking that this person can't be trusted help Sarah? Although at first she may think that recognising some people are unfaithful is realistic, she then needs to appreciate that no evidence exists to support her specific suspicions of Ben. By focusing on her past pain, she's impeding the enjoyment and progress of her new relationship.

Sarah needs to switch to a new focus on what's positive about the situation, exchanging her thoughts and putting things into perspective. For example, her new thinking can be, 'Just because one partner was unfaithful doesn't mean that this one will be. I shall relax and enjoy this relationship.'

When your thoughts are making you unhappy, ask yourself the following questions:

- ✔ What am I thinking?
- ✔ Is this thought rational?
- ✔ Is this thought helpful?
- ✔ How else can I think?

Choosing thoughts that make you feel good

You can train your brain. Whatever your age, your brain can develop new ways of thinking. Even if you've been thinking negatively or pessimistically for many years, you can become a person who now focuses on the positive. This way of thinking doesn't mean that you pretend that everything in the world is perfect, but you can identify the good things within a situation to balance your perspective and help you to manage.

The **Five Is exercise** helps you to plan thoughts so that you can manage difficult situations. Here's how it works:

1. **Identify the difficult situation.**

   For example, you want to raise a difficult topic with your partner.

2. **Identify the positive outcome.**

   What would you like the outcome of your conversation to be?

3. **Identify the emotion that helps you to manage this situation.**

   For example, you may want to feel calm and confident.

4. **Identify a constructive thought that helps you to access this emotional state.**

   For example, you can think: 'I have the right to raise this issue. I can keep calm and discuss this topic with confidence.'

5. **Imagine the successful outcome.**

   Build pictures in your mind of the meeting going well. Imagine yourself raising issues and discussing your needs, but also listening and being flexible to your partner's needs. Have positive expectations of yourself and your partner being able to reach an understanding.

Getting over a bad experience

Matt's life had been relatively easy but at the age of 24 he was mugged. The experience shocked him and jolted his sense of peace and security. He began to imagine muggers on every street.

Through coaching he realised that this view wasn't realistic, and that the majority of people are neither violent nor criminal. He acknowledged that one mugging doesn't signify that all people are bad. He developed coping thoughts, such as: 'I had an unlucky experience but that doesn't mean it will happen again'; 'I've lived 24 years and this is the first time I've had such a bad experience'; and 'Most people are law-abiding.' Gradually his perspective and sense of safety returned.

Changing takes practice and repetition to build up your new habits of supportive thinking. You may have been thinking in a particular negative pattern for many years. Switching and embedding new thoughts takes time and effort but is worth every moment. As Shakespeare said 'There's nothing good nor bad but thinking makes it so.'

Controlling Your Emotional Responses

You can control your emotions, but many people don't know how. Acts of violence such as road rage occur when the emotional brain hijacks the thinking brain (see Chapter 2). Under physical threat you may react to protect yourself. You respond automatically, without thought of the consequence (see Chapter 1).

In the majority of the situations you face in everyday life, however, the threat is more frequently to your emotional security, but the instant physical reaction in your body is the same as if you're facing a physical threat.

Between feeling the emotion and the action, though, a gap exists (albeit short) in which you can stop and choose how to respond, planning thoughts, language and physiology, which helps you manage the situation without negative repercussions. See Chapters 9 and 16 for more on using this gap between emotion and action to heal emotionally.

Living in the Moment

The quality of your day depends on your ability to be present in the moment so that both your mind and your body are in the same place, fully engaged with what you're doing. However, the human brain is easily distracted and wanders into fretting about old difficulties and fearful thoughts about the future. As Mark Twain said, 'I've known a great many troubles but most of them never happened.'

Paying attention to the moment enhances your quality of life and your relationships. You can control the focus of your mind to concentrate on where you are and what you're doing now.

Focusing on the present

You can upset yourself by letting your thoughts focus on potential disaster. You imagine that the plane is going to crash, that your child won't come home safely or that you're going to lose your job. If anything goes wrong, you're probably already so anxious that you're unlikely to manage the situation calmly. Your mind may also grind over old woes, grudges and events.

By extension, you can easily be physically close to another person – even someone you love deeply like your child or partner – and yet your mind is somewhere else. When you aren't in the current moment, you diminish the quality of the experience by being absent or only partially present for the person you're with.

Discover how much time your mind spends in the present moment. Notice the proportion of time you spend ruminating on the past or being anxious about the future. Start to adjust the focus so that you live in the present. Train your mind to focus on the current experience by:

- ✔ **Noticing the sensory experience you're having:** Where are you sitting? Who are you talking to? What are you hearing? What are you seeing? Be right there, right now.

- ✔ **Identifying what you specifically need to do right now:** Is there something you need to say or do? How can you consciously choose to bring yourself back into the present moment? (See Chapter 13.)

- ✔ **Focusing on the positive realities of the moment:** What can you be grateful for right now? Do you have money in the bank? A home to live in? An income? Someone who supports you?

Curbing your assumptions

Don't waste time thinking about things that may not even exist – stay in reality, in the here and now. Imagining what another person is thinking is an imperfect art because you can never fully see into another person's mind. Although considering how someone *may* react to a situation can be worthwhile, making assumptions about another person's behaviour can lead you to the wrong conclusions.

Josie came to coaching very stressed; she was sure that her boss had turned against her. She wasn't sleeping well and an old back problem had reactivated. 'He doesn't like me,' she said, 'But I don't understand why because we used to get along so well.' We encouraged her to seek evidence about this assumption, including arranging a meeting to check out whether she had, in fact, done anything to annoy her boss. During this meeting, Josie's boss told her that he was going through a divorce. He'd been so stressed that he hadn't realised he'd been unfriendly towards her. Josie had done nothing wrong, and her assumption was erroneous.

As the saying goes: assume nothing, because to assume makes an *ass* out of *u* and *me*! So check your facts. Look for evidence to back up a supposition. If you're concerned about something, ask the person.

In order to relate accurately to the situations in your life that require emotional healing, you need to check facts and clarify information. Otherwise you may reach the wrong conclusions and act inappropriately. Here are some questions to help you ascertain whether the information you have is correct:

- ✔ Have I checked whether my assumption is based on fact?

- ✔ Have I communicated my assumption to the other person? If not, how is she supposed to know what my problem is?

- ✔ Does a universal rule exist to say that all people would respond in a particular way to this situation?

- ✔ What facts do I know about this situation? Which other facts do I need?

Embracing the Healing Power of Laughter

Your thinking influences your mood. So thinking happy thoughts makes you feel happy! When you're fearful or depressed, you can forget what makes you laugh. Regaining your sense of humour helps you to heal, lightening your mood and helping you to think positively. You need to make a conscious decision to re-engage with that part of you that previously enjoyed laughter.

Remember what feeling happy is like and retrain your mind to focus on positive things. Here are some tips to get you giggling:

- ✔ **Laughing over memories:** Think back over your life and remember situations and events that made you laugh. Remember that time your Aunt Bea had one too many sherries and did the conga around your dining table? Chuckling is easy when you reminisce.

- ✔ **Chuckling at comedians:** Read a funny book or watch an amusing film or TV programme. Check out your television guide for comedy programmes so that you focus your mind on laughter. Visit a comedy club. See how many things you can find amusing.

- ✔ **Visiting comic websites.** Look for animation, audio or video files to get you smiling.

> ✔ **Enrolling in workshops.** Seek out clinics dedicated to laughter yoga, happiness, and laughter therapy.
>
> ✔ **Cracking up in company:** Hang out with friends and family members who tickle your sense of humour. Get together and have fun.

People influence your thoughts and emotions. If you've been through a low patch or difficult experience, spending time with others who have had a similar experience can be healing. However, after a time you may find that you become stuck in the 'problem' that you share. Review your social network and consider whether it's helping you to think positively. If not, consider forging some new friendships with some more upbeat people. You don't have to drop your old friends, but as you heal, you're likely to attract to you a group of friends who share the joys, conversations, interests and sense of humour of the 'new' you rather than the old you.

Smiling: the simplest pick-me-up

Smiling releases healing endorphins into your body, and so your health benefits when you smile more frequently. Practise smiling:

✔ First thing in the morning as you wake up

✔ As you brush your teeth

✔ When you look in the mirror to shave or put on your lipstick

✔ At a child or elderly person in the street

✔ When you find yourself doing something silly

Remember the saying, 'Smile and the world smiles with you'? Well, it's true. When someone beams at you, not grinning in return is difficult. So when you smile, you're not only improving your own health, but also improving that of other people.

Chapter 13

Finding Insight through Mindfulness

In This Chapter

▶ Remaining present and aware

▶ Acknowledging and accepting emotions

▶ Setting up your day for mindfulness

▶ Practising simple visualisations and meditations

*Y*ou're likely to have many pressures in your life that seem to demand attention and productive use of time. You need to use your energy wisely. Everyone has limited resources, and so the ability to focus on what's important to you and filter out the inessential is an important skill.

When *practising mindfulness*, you're able to be present and fully engaged in what you're doing. Practising mindfulness means you pay greater attention to what's going on in your mind, body and emotions – moment to moment and free of judgement.

Mindfulness is about connecting to real experience. Mindfulness practices help you feel anchored to a deep sense of stability and calm in the midst of threat. Mindful practice enables acceptance, calm and appropriate action. This practice isn't about mastering a particular technique. Rather, it's about allowing yourself to develop greater awareness of your immediate experience as you go through life.

This chapter introduces you to ways to be present and at the same time detached. The goal is to become a skilled observer of both inner and outer pressures that disturb your emotional balance. Mindfulness practices allow your observing, compassionate self to become present and restore perspective. You can begin to accept that 'this too will pass' and see the future as fresh and full of opportunity for growth and enjoyment.

Stilling Your Mind

Mindfulness practice, like any skill, requires that you set time aside to practise. The core skill of mindfulness practice is finding *your* own way to still your mind and deliberately introducing periods of simply being an observer of the ebb and flow of your breath, body sensations, emotions and thoughts.

Within the space created by stilling your mind you become a dispassionate observer of your own experience. You find that you can more fully consider the interplay of your emotions, thoughts and habitual responses. You can take more control of your actions, move away from automatic responses and choose the way you want to behave (see Chapters 2 and 3 for more on automatic and chosen responses).

The following sections walk you through the process of stilling your mind, relaxing your body and developing a non-judgemental point of view.

Becoming aware

You may think that you're very aware – but are you really? For example, what's your breathing rate at this very moment? Are sounds or smells occurring in your environment right now that you hadn't really noticed?

In the still of his mind

Dan had three children under five years of age, with his partner Emma. As a builder's labourer, he worked long hours, particularly at weekends. His real desire was to train as a landscape gardener, but he felt powerless to change his work because his family depended on his income. His temper occasionally got the best of him and he sometimes lost control – shouting, breaking furniture and once grabbing and bruising Emma's arm.

Dan came to counselling after being thrown out of his house. The reasons for his frustration quickly became clear: He was doing a job he disliked. When Emma complained about a problem at home, he took her comments personally, felt angry and lost control, particularly when tired or stressed.

In counselling, Dan discovered how to pay attention to the first signals of irritation and then shift his focus to stilling his mind and body through breathing techniques (see the following section 'Becoming aware' for more details). He eventually met an educational adviser at his local college and found a way to train part time as a landscape gardener and gain government support for his lost income. Emma and Dan discussed their argument triggers, which helped them consciously to avoid difficulty. They stayed together.

The intention of becoming aware is to acknowledge and accept all facets of your experience without feeling that you're doing anything right or wrong. (*Intention* in this context means paying attention on purpose.) You're simply watching moments unfold without trying to change, improve or judge anything that arises.

You can practise awareness with the following simple sequence:

1. **Find a quiet place to sit comfortably for approximately ten minutes uninterrupted.**

   See the later sidebar 'Relax to the max' for ideas on how to create a relaxing space and mental state.

2. **Notice your breath and follow each in-breath and out-breath.**

   Silently count ten complete in- and out-breaths. When you reach ten breaths, go back to one again. Continue breathing this way for several minutes until your mind becomes quiet.

   This isn't a competition. If you go beyond ten breaths before realising where you are, simply choose to pay attention the next time.

   See Chapter 2 for more on breathing techniques.

3. **As your mind quietens down, silently label any thought, emotion or bodily sensation that pops up.**

   Labelling of these experiences is important; doing so helps you notice when something new arises in your stream of consciousness.

   See Chapter 12 for more on labelling thoughts, emotions and sensations.

4. **After you label an experience, let it go.**

   Recognise the fleeting nature of all experience. As you let your labelled experience go, realise that nothing in life, good or bad, lasts.

Recognising that all your present experience is transient allows you – even in the midst of very unpleasant events – to know and believe that nothing remains the same. The expression 'this too will pass' is both comforting and true.

Body-mind scanning is a great technique to help you get in touch with your body and mind. As the phrase *body-mind* suggests, information flows continuously between your body and your mind, in both directions. Body-mind scanning helps you to feel centred and deepens your understanding of how your present situation affects your body and emotions. See Chapter 2 for more on body scanning and Chapter 6 for information on mindful walking.

Relax to the max

Relaxing your body and mind is essential for cultivating awareness. When practising any mindfulness activity, take a few moments to see that you're encouraging relaxation in the following ways:

✔ **Place:** Find somewhere to sit that feels welcoming to you. Calming colours, religious or spiritual icons, and objects that evoke warm memories can all help.

✔ **Connection:** Choose a chair that allows you to connect firmly with the seat and the floor. A chair without arms is usually best because you can place your own arms as you wish. Plant your feet firmly on the ground and adjust your back to an comfortably upright posture. Notice how the chair and the ground support your body.

✔ **Body:** Keep your posture 'alert', just noticing whether you move or fidget. Try resting your right hand in your left or touching your thumbs and middle fingers together.

✔ **Time:** If possible, choose the same time of day for mindfulness practice – early morning or evening are ideal. And set a time limit. We suggest no more than ten minutes initially. A timer can be helpful.

✔ **Clothing:** Wear something loose and comfortable. Avoid anything that makes you feel too hot or cold.

Finding your observing self

Engaging your ability to self-observe allows you to stand back from stressful situations and notice what's right for that particular moment.

Self-observing is looking in on yourself as a dispassionate and kindly observer of your total experience in that moment. By stepping back, you're able to experience more of what's going on. In this state, you can access your thinking brain, rather than your stressed-out flight, fight or freeze brain, which may still be giving you physical signals (see Chapter 2 for more on how your brain works).

In the observer state of conscious awareness, you can explore your own needs. You can find calm in the face of sustained stress, which enables you to experience a greater sense of personal control within the situation. You're more capable of seeing a broader range of options – and then knowing what action is right for you.

The educational system tends to emphasise right versus wrong. Although only one correct answer exists for a mathematical problem, much of life consists of situations where no true right or wrong exists. Instead, you have many paths and many answers. Rather than judging your actions, feelings and thoughts as good or bad, right or wrong, shift to simply observing your actions, feelings and thoughts.

The poem 'The Guest House' by the 13th century Sufi poet Rumi (translated by Coleman Barks) may help highlight your ability to stay with experience in life without judgement – to observe simply what happens to you:

> *This being human is a guest house; every morning a new arrival.*
> *A joy, a depression, a meanness;*
> *Some momentary awareness comes as an unexpected visitor.*
> *Welcome and entertain them all even if they're a crowd of sorrows*
> *Who violently sweep your house empty of its furniture.*
> *Still treat each guest honourably.*
> *He may be clearing you out for some new delight.*
> *The dark thought, the shame, the malice;*
> *Meet them at the door laughing and invite them in.*
> *Be grateful for whoever comes.*
> *Because each has been sent as a guide from beyond.*

As this poem suggests, the way you relate to your experience determines your happiness. So embrace all your experiences without judging them to be good or bad. Attitudes about what's good or bad depend on the judgement of others and what's acceptable within your culture.

If you feel caught up in doing too much or in being stuck in an uncomfortable situation where you have difficulty deciding what you need to do, take conscious time to access your observing self. Doing so can enable you to understand what's locking you into your current situation. After going through the awareness practice that we detail in 'Becoming aware', do the following:

1. **Become still and tune into your breath as it goes in and out.**

2. **Allow your mind to still and focus on the difficult situation.**

   For example, you may be facing a difficult job interview, feeling sad at the death of your loved one, or experiencing financial pressure.

3. **Pose questions about the situation and ask your mind to speak to you in the voice of your intuitive wisdom.**

   Some questions you may pose include: 'As I find calm, what do I need to do to face the situation in a helpful way?' or 'What would my inner wisdom offer as advice?'

4. **Listen to what your deepest wisdom has to say about how you're responding to the challenge.**

Watch out for those conditional voices of the past. which will be saying things like 'You should do this' or 'You ought to do that'. Check that your responses and options are coming from your own authentic voice and deepest wisdom – a voice that inspires you to act in the most helpful way for you and those you love.

Your authentic voice can take several forms. It may appear as a quiet knowing of what's right for you, a sense of what to do, or a hunch leading you in a particular direction. The more you listen or pay attention to your authentic voice, the stronger it becomes and the more you can trust it.

5. **Observe the pattern of your responses without judgement.**

You have the potential to choose how you act based on your own need – rather than on the needs of others, although these will be part of your decision.

Going further

After you've taken a few minutes to encourage awareness (see the earlier section 'Becoming aware'), you can begin exploring other aspects of mindfulness. The following sections offer three practices you can incorporate into your daily life.

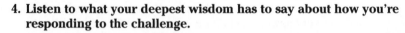

Diagnosis: Stop judging

At the age of 65, Joy came for help to understand and relieve long-standing back pain, poor sleep and irritable bowel syndrome. She had many other bodily complaints, but medical investigations had all been negative.

Her answers to various physiological questionnaires indicated that she was in a persistent 'overdrive' state – constantly pushing herself to achieve. Talking about her early upbringing revealed that she had perfectionist parents. Despite excellent exam results, she always received a comment of 'Why can't you do better?'

Her parents' judgemental attitudes resulted in an inability to slow down. As she grew older, she replaced her parents' expectations by judging herself – every thought, feeling or achievement she experienced. Nearing retirement, she experienced depression and unhappiness, as if she was unable to let herself enjoy an honourable retirement.

Over the course of several mindfulness sessions, Joy developed the ability to relax and observe herself through meditation. She noticed the strong internal judgements that drove her to continue to do more than was required. This realisation allowed her to develop a kind and accepting attitude to herself. She lost many of her persistent physical symptoms and was able to plan and move into a more satisfying retirement.

Moving into deeper calming and relaxation

The following practice is most suitable if you have a strongly visual memory. Initially you may want to try this practice in a quiet place, but when you become familiar with the process you can transfer it to different situations, such as the office or train.

1. **Close your eyes, relax your body and smooth out any tension.**

   Imagine yourself in a beautiful place – perhaps lying on a beach. The sky is blue. You can hear the waves lapping the shore. The sun is shining, and you feel its warmth on your body. You feel increasingly calm, relaxed and content as time goes by.

2. **Shift your awareness to your abdomen.**

   Place your hands on your abdomen and notice the movement as it rises and falls in response to each breath. Keep the sense of calm of the scene you created in Step 1 and count each complete breath from one to ten. When you reach ten complete breaths, go back to one again. Continue breathing this way for several minutes until your mind becomes quiet.

   Watch your breath without trying to control it. If your mind is distracted, bring it back gently to observing the breath. Stay in this state of present moment awareness for 10–15 minutes.

After you've settled into this level of deeper calm and relaxation, you may want to try other practices in this section.

Contemplating your own good fortune

This is a gratitude meditation, which helps you reconnect to a sense of love and appreciation for yourself and others. This practice reminds you of what you can be grateful for.

1. **Identify for a few minutes, aspects of your own good fortune – or those areas of your life for which you can feel gratitude.**

   Perhaps you're fortunate to have a home, job, family, money, food to eat, and live in a relatively peaceful society and so on.

2. **Contemplate each aspect of your own good fortune that you identify.**

   Think about some of the following questions:

   - What does having a good job, money, home, love or health mean to you?

   - What exactly do you enjoy about these aspects of your life?

   - How do these aspects of your life make you feel?

Spend some time exploring anything that comes to mind. As your practice develops, you may want to include any benefits that arise as a result of meditation as part of your good fortune.

Using loving-kindness meditation

Loving kindness comes up often in discussions of mindfulness and meditation. Think of loving kindness as friendliness towards yourself and others. Some people describe the feeling as similar to that felt by a mother for her child.

To develop and let in feelings of loving kindness, do the following:

1. **Think about a person you respect or admire.**

   You may want to remember someone whom you admire. This can be someone you know or someone in public or spiritual life whom you revere.

   Notice how you how you feel as you think about this person and identify the qualities that you admire. You're reconnecting with qualities you personally care about and can bring these into your own awareness.

2. **Move your thoughts to a loved one.**

   Try to think about someone other than your spouse or partner – perhaps someone who gave you wholehearted support and love in the past. Remember how you felt in the loving presence of this person and notice how you feel now that you think about him again. Bring this sense of love into your heart, with quiet breathing, so that you develop a feeling of loving kindness within you.

3. **Shift your thoughts to a neutral person – someone for whom you have no particular feelings.**

   You can think about a local shopkeeper or garage attendant. Notice any change of feelings and then reconnect with the feeling of love you remembered in Steps 1 and 2. Direct this feeling at this neutral person. This may feel like a wave of compassion and kindness that flows from you.

4. **Direct your thoughts to someone you find difficult or with whom you're experiencing conflict.**

   Hold onto the feeling of loving kindness as you continue to think about this person. Direct this energy to this person through your heart, with quite breathing and presence of mind.

This practice enables you to consciously create a state of loving kindness, which you can bring back in the midst of challenge and conflict. When you next meet that person, you can acknowledge him with compassion, without focusing unduly on the negative. It also allows you to recharge your own self-esteem by replenishing a sense of love and appreciation for yourself.

Visualising Emotional Healing

Visualisation is a method of building imaginary pictures in your mind in order to help you focus on positive events and feelings. This powerful technique tricks your mind and body into creating 'feel-good' chemicals (see Chapter 2) that enhance your general emotional and physical wellbeing. Visualisation can be part of a mindfulness practice and works well if you have a strongly visual memory.

To create a picture of yourself in which you feel fully alive, well and happy, use visualisation to build on good memories:

1. **Think back on positive memories, perhaps of a holiday or a time without pressures.**

   Looking at photographs or reading through your diary may help you recall particularly positive memories.

2. **When you identify a strong, positive memory, use your imagination to boost the colours, sights, sounds, smells and bodily feelings.**

   How you are looking? What are you doing? How are you feeling?

   If you find creating imagination-enhanced internal pictures difficult, stay with a felt sense of just being in a pleasant memory.

3. **Zoom in on your enhanced image and see yourself relaxed and calm.**

   Stay with this image long enough to fully tune into the scene (perhaps five minutes at first). Pay attention to sights, sounds, bodily sensations, feelings and smells.

4. **See yourself in the future having left behind old emotional difficulties you had in the past.**

   Try zooming forward six months and see yourself well, happy, fulfilled and enjoying life. Create some mental pictures to support this future state. How does this feel when you visualise this future?

5. **Stay in the difficult situation, but transform yourself into the healthy and healed vision you imagined.**

   Bring the feelings you visualised into your present. See a smile on your face. Know that you've let go of past emotional difficulties.

   Smile now and gently come back into the present moment.

You can use this technique when in the midst of difficult emotional feelings that prevent you from enjoying life. You can also apply it when you're making your plans for the future (see Chapter 15).

Practising Mindfulness Every Day

You gain the most benefit emotionally and physically when you're able to integrate mindfulness practices into your daily routine. Doing so may take some discipline to begin with. For example, you may need to schedule some time in your diary to sit down and cultivate awareness.

As with any new skill or behaviour, mindfulness practice may not feel comfortable at first, but the more you practise, the more you reap the benefits.

The following sections provide several strategies to help make mindfulness a part of each and every day.

Being, not doing

Humans are capable of two dominant states: doing and being. *Doing* is active and task-oriented. *Being* is a state of calm presence, where you switch off the active state and just immerse yourself in the present moment, without expectations.

Constant doing leads to exhaustion. You need to find a balance between these two states, becoming able to switch from one to the other at will. For example, you're late for an appointment. Your task is to reach your destination on time, but the train is delayed. Instead of getting anxious in your 'doing' state, you can switch into your 'being' state by applying the mindfulness exercises in the earlier sections. Being, rather than doing, enables you to conserve energy and remain calm.

Understanding how to access these two states allows you to switch out of constantly trying to find solutions to your problems through doing and allows you to access a state of inner calm, which creates space for fresh thinking. People try actively to problem-solve their ways out of situations, but these approaches aren't always effective ways to heal emotional wounds or states such as depression.

Relating to a problem through doing tries to seek answers and identify actions to remedy the problem, which can result in self-judgement and critical thinking – particularly if things don't seem to be working. See the earlier section 'Finding your observing self'.

Although problem-solving and thinking strategies can work for certain situations and can help you to gain perspective (as we describe in Chapter 12), a problem-solving focus can lead you to seek a villain, someone or something to blame for the problem. The person on the receiving end often becomes a victim. And victims often need someone else to fix their problems. Also, not all problems have a ready solution. Trying to find the solution puts you into a doing frame of mind.

Nick's experience highlights two ways of relating to difficult situations and emotions:

- ✔ **Doing:** The first time Nick was made redundant, he felt angry and frustrated. He obsessed about 'Why me' and how unfair the whole situation was. He worried and became stressed, tired and ill. He was unable to step back, accept the situation and plan a strategy to re-enter the job market. He didn't think clearly and went for jobs which were unsuitable, wasting energy and time. After six months, in desperation he accepted another job at a much lower salary.

- ✔ **Being:** A short time afterwards, finding he was unsuitable for the job, Nick was made redundant again. During his second redundancy, Nick came for coaching and developed the ability to switch states. He told himself to just accept what had happened. He became detached and reminded himself that fighting the inevitable wasn't helpful. In his being state he was able to access insights into what to do next and target suitable jobs. He used his spare time to enjoy his home, catch up with reading, and spend more time with his wife and family. He found another job within the month.

Morning rituals

Starting the day with a morning ritual sets the scene for a productive day. Vivid dreams linked to some unresolved difficulties may have disturbed your sleep, and so resetting the balance of body and mind is a helpful beginning. Try the following:

1. **As you wake in the morning, notice your breathing before getting out of bed.**

   Observe five breaths with full attention. Allow the effortless release of the out-breath.

2. **Move your attention to your upper body.**

   Let your shoulders drop and create room for the breath to come into your abdomen.

3. **Focus on your head and neck.**

   Notice that you're able to create space in your head by relaxing your jaw and allowing your tongue to settle in the floor of your mouth.

   Imagine that you're unbuttoning a shirt or releasing a scarf, thus allowing your neck to feel free and your throat to open.

Follow your breath as it moves through your nose and throat. Let the air cool your nasal passages.

4. **As you get out of bed, notice your body and particularly your posture.**

   Feel the ground under your feet as you start to walk. Be mindful of all activity, movement, sounds, sensations and scents.

5. **Take a moment to think about the day ahead.**

   Consider how you want to 'be' – physically and emotionally – so that your mind focuses on the emotional state you want to take with you into the day.

As you move into your day, pay full attention to what you're doing. Notice your body. If you find a tightness anywhere, take five breaths and breathe into the tension. On the out-breath, let go of the tension.

Responding to your activity cycles

Each day has a period when you're active and switched on to the tasks and activities that engage you. At other times, you lose concentration.

Keep a notebook and see whether you can identify your own particular rhythms. Your body may signal that the relaxation part of your nervous system needs to be turned on with a yawn or a sigh. At other times you may find yourself daydreaming or realise that you've missed a significant portion of a conversation because you aren't tuned in.

When you lose concentration, your brain is signalling that you need to shift from a dominant left brain, or *doing mode*, to a dominant right brain, or *being mode*. Relaxation encourages you to step back, review, recharge your internal batteries and restore energy for the next activity cycle.

Taking notice and taking a break allow you to continue with renewed energy. Most people need to rest after about an hour and a half of sustained activity. Typically, the body needs about 20 minutes of rest to rebalance the brain. The rest period needs to include a change of focus, from doing to being, and can include going for a walk, listening to music, or stretching. (See Chapter 5 for more information on body rhythms.)

Ignoring your activity/rest cycles is likely to leave you frustrated, irritable and, in time, exhausted and fatigued. Finding the time to take the break allows you to restore energy and often intuitive problem-solving follows.

The traditions of mid-morning breaks, a one-hour lunch and mid-afternoon tea breaks are natural and sanctioned ways for these periods of rest and rebalance to occur. In today's pressurised, overdriven culture – where persistent mental health problems occur in an increasing number of the working population – re-introducing these recovery periods may reduce the likelihood of anxiety, depression and stress-related ill health.

Moving into Meditation

The mindfulness, awareness, and visualisation practices are all forms of meditation. The word meditation may conjure up a mysterious practice, one that requires a special place, accessories, clothing or spiritual beliefs.

Meditation methods, however, can be very simple. *Meditation* is the ability to find a state of inner calm where you narrow your attention to a single focus, like your breath or a phrase. Focusing allows you to relax your body and calm your mind

You can adopt a meditation method that takes just a few seconds and enables you to practise on the bus or as you do the cooking. You can find more information in *Meditation For Dummies* by Stephan Bodian and Dean Ornish.

You can also direct your meditation practice towards a specific aim, perhaps to allow you to acknowledge that you're in the midst of strong emotions, notice what these emotions are and then choose whether to respond or not. The following sections explore some specific aims you may choose for yourself.

Changing state: Breathing space meditation

If you find yourself in the midst of anger, sadness or frustration, try the following meditation practice to change your emotional state and restore calm. You can do this practice anywhere:

1. **Bring your attention into your body.**

   Notice how you're holding yourself. Soften any bracing or holding of tension. For instance, you may let your shoulders drop and allow your back to become upright. (You may find the body-scanning technique in Chapter 2 helpful.)

2. **Ask yourself what's going on right now inside you?**

   What's going on can include thoughts, feelings, bodily sensations, a situation, and so on.

3. **Bring your attention to the breath and ask yourself, 'How am I breathing?'**

   In the face of a difficult thought or emotion, you may find that your breathing becomes shallow or moves to your upper chest, or even that you're holding your breath.

4. **Pay attention to the out-breath; with each out-breath become absorbed in movement of the breath itself.**

   Allow the in-breath to expand your abdomen with the lower ribs moving outwards.

5. **Take five gentle breaths, in which the out-breath is longer and the in-breath is quiet and gentle.**

   Just five breaths is enough to change your state.

   As you continue to breathe in this way, your turbulent emotions become a surface storm that you acknowledge and allow to pass. Your breathing practice helps you to find the calm inside that allows the negative thoughts or feelings to pass.

Choosing wise action

Making good choices when you're in a highly emotional state is very difficult. Use the meditation, mindfulness and breathing practices in this chapter to help you find calm and expand your awareness, allowing you to acknowledge with acceptance (and without judgement) whatever is happening in your life situations.

To help you develop good choices and wise decisions, you can pick any of the practices we share with you in this chapter. As you do so, you may find that the following questions help you broaden your options around life decisions:

✔ What specifically can lead me out of my present emotional difficulties into fresh thinking and better choices?

✔ If I rise above the immediate emotional storms, what insights do I gain that can help me make better decisions?

✔ Who are the people who can support my decision-making?

Listen to any inner messages and insights you may receive about how to move out of your present difficulties. These insights may come in words, images or feelings. Get a sense of a journey ahead in which you feel confident that you've made good choices and decisions and arrived at a better future.

Chapter 14

Using Day-to-Day Strategies for Emotional Healing

In This Chapter

▶ Checking your emotions and comforting yourself

▶ Sharing difficult emotions with others

▶ Sticking with a plan for ongoing change

▶ Engaging your creative mind

*H*ealing your emotions becomes an integral part of how you live each day. Alongside the joys of life, you contend with emotional upheavals – disappointments, funerals, irritations with work and so on – until the day you die. Not everything goes your way, but that doesn't mean life has to be darkness and gloom.

The aim of this chapter is to help you make a habit of noticing, feeling, acknowledging, expressing and sharing the emotions that come up so that you're better able to enjoy life.

You may also encounter times when you need to change your thoughts and behaviours to truly heal. This type of change is tough work that requires reinforcement on a daily basis. You need to become aware of your past tendencies, which may include focusing on resentment, playing the victim, or feeling the world is against you, and decide if you're going to continue falling back on these familiar responses.

In the following sections, we help you build new day-to-day habits that support your emotional wellbeing. We give you tips to make healing a daily priority and some strategies to apply as soon as you meet challenges. We also introduce techniques to incorporate creative play easily into your daily life as a tool for emotional expression and release.

Expressing Your Emotional Needs

Other people frequently play a role in your emotional upheaval. Pretending that you don't have a problem with another person or hoping that the whole mess just goes away of its own accord may seem like a good solution but it rarely works. Negative feelings, grudges, frustrations and resentments continue to lurk below the surface, which creates distance between you and the other person. You develop a false self who pretends that all is well when it isn't. Inevitably, difficulties rise to the surface, and your unexpressed feelings suddenly intensify

Honest and collaborative interaction and conversation with others is an essential everyday activity for a healthy emotional life. You may feel like you're jeopardising the status quo, but this supposed harmony may not be worthwhile. In the following sections we show you how to identify and share emotions through effective communication techniques.

Giving yourself an emotional check-up

You need to know what you're feeling in order to share and discuss your emotional needs with someone else. Take approximately ten minutes each day to go through a daily emotional checklist. Morning is preferable or at a time when you feel fresh.

Quieten your mind, calm your breath (see Chapters 2 and 13) and then ask yourself the following questions:

1. **Tuning in:** How are you feeling, physically and emotionally? Are certain emotions or physical symptoms disturbing you? If you're experiencing physical arousal, turn to Chapters 2 and 13 to help you calm and then identify the emotional content within the signal.

2. **Understanding the cause:** Why are you feeling this emotion? What actually happened to disturb you? What were or are your expectations of yourself? The situation? Other people involved?

3. **Checking patterns:** Is your emotion related to a specific event – or does it relate to a previous event or events? See Chapter 3 for more on emotional patterns.

4. **Identifying needs and solutions:** What did you or do you need to happen? How many different solutions can you identify to manage the situations you face? For more on problem-solving, see the later section 'Finding new perspectives,' as well as Chapters 9, 11 and 16. Are the needs and solutions you identify reasonable and feasible? Did you express your needs? How was your expression of need received by others? (See Chapter 1 for more information on basic needs).

5. **Caring for yourself:** Can you comfort your mind and body? Can you manage your own emotions? What do you need to do to help you feel okay? See the following section 'Taking care of yourself' for some self-comfort ideas.

6. **Communicating solutions:** Do you need to share your emotions and solutions with anyone else involved?

If the last two steps in the preceding list sound challenging, they are. The questions associated with these items help you identify actions you can take to respond effectively to the emotions you're experiencing. The following sections cover self-care and communication in greater detail.

Taking care of yourself

People can comfort one another, but individuals can also comfort themselves. As an adult you need to devise ways to nurture and heal your own problems, taking responsibility for your responses.

Managing daily life when you're feeling low, particularly after a loss or trauma, can be difficult. Discover what activities give you comfort and then take some time doing these things in order to heal. Soldiering on simply locks in the problem and postpones healing.

Write down a list of resources you can turn to and activities you can do in response to specific emotions. Your list may include any of the following:

- Allowing yourself to feel the emotion for a period of time when you're experiencing loss or rejection.

- Cooking yourself a delicious and healthy meal to raise your self-esteem.

- Engaging in a talking therapy, such as coaching, counselling, psychotherapy or group support activity. (You can find contact details in the Appendix.)

- Phoning a friend when you feel hurt, depressed or confused.

- Practising the six-breaths-a-minute exercise (which we describe in Chapter 2) to reduce your anxiety level.

- Transforming negative thoughts to focus on the positive when you're bogged down by pessimism, depression or sadness. (See Chapter 12.)

- Taking a walk in nature to clear your head and regain a sense of connection when you feel lonely or isolated.

- Turning on some uplifting or peaceful music to switch your mood and regain energy and joy.

- Wrapping yourself up in bed for an hour's sleep and recovery to nurture yourself when you feel low or fatigued.

Focus on activities that you can engage in quickly and that yield results in five minutes or so. And if you simply can't stop in the middle of your day and take a few minutes to respond to how you're feeling, make a date with yourself later that same day to address your problem and comfort yourself. You inevitably have other commitments in your life but self-care is about the deliberate and conscious choice to do what you need to do for yourself, so build this habit into your life.

Sharing solutions

You may be a very caring person who recognises that other people have their own problems, needs and concerns. You may not want to burden others with your own problems. But being able to express yourself and stick up for yourself is an essential aspect of emotional wellbeing. Taking responsibility empowers you.

Bottling up your feelings only internalises the problem and eats away at you. Repressed emotions can become 'toxic' and lead to discomfort and even illness because the altered chemistry of repressed emotion disturbs your body's balance and affects your immune system (see Chapter 2). Repressing your feeling can also lead to seeing yourself as a victim or a martyr, which is avoidance behaviour (something we discuss in Chapter 8) and doesn't help anyone because you're not speaking up for your needs.

On the other hand, you may be someone who tends to let off emotional steam easily and aggressively. Anger is a natural part of human emotion, but you must recognise that underneath anger is pain. If you're angry (and perhaps sad) all the time, you're likely not to be receiving what you want from life. Somewhere deep inside of you, you're hurting and, like a small child, you may want to stamp your feet and throw your toys out of the pram.

Reflect on how you convey your own needs. Bottling up your feelings can lead to manipulating others to do what you want in indirect ways. In contrast, if you shout and yell easily, you may get what you want – but at a cost to your relationships. Both behaviours have a disadvantage: people resent being manipulated and rarely appreciate being shouted at.

Communicating assertively

Instead of suppressing your emotions or letting them burst forth like a volcano, you can try assertively communicating your feelings and needs:

✔ **Assertive communication is a collaborative and equal conversation or discussion.** All parties treat one another with respect. You may disagree about a problem or solution, but you acknowledge that all participants have the right to their own personal perspectives. You aren't seeking to win – you're seeking to compromise and agree a solution that's as mutually satisfactory as possible.

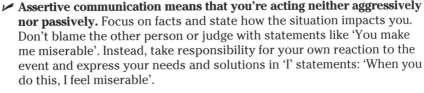

✔ **Assertive communication means that you're acting neither aggressively nor passively.** Focus on facts and state how the situation impacts you. Don't blame the other person or judge with statements like 'You make me miserable'. Instead, take responsibility for your own reaction to the event and express your needs and solutions in 'I' statements: 'When you do this, I feel miserable'.

In addition to expressing your own perspective, allow the other person to explain her perspective, without interrupting. Listen with the intention of trying to understand the other person's point of view.

✔ **Assertive communication doesn't mean that you have to know all the answers.** No one has the answers to every question. Being able to admit that you're wrong or don't know something is actually a sign of confidence. Being vulnerable and expressing your questions, fears and concerns demonstrates that you're emotionally secure. An insecure person can be defensive or take an aggressive stance.

Stepping through the Three-Step Model

Maintain positive expectations that you can resolve the situation, but don't beat yourself up if you don't reach a satisfactory conclusion immediately. Agreement and compromise require willingness from both parties, and you may find that you or the other person can't find a middle position.

To achieve the best results, structure your conversations using the following **Three-Step Model**:

1. **State *what* your problem is and *how* it makes you feel.**

   For example, rather than saying, 'I hate it when you sulk and refuse to talk to me when I ask you a question,' say 'When you seem to be upset but don't tell me what's wrong – like yesterday morning at breakfast, I feel frustrated.'

   Be specific. Focus on one occasion if possible and avoid dredging up old hurts. Try to ask one question and make one statement at a time, otherwise you weaken your point and dilute the message. For example instead of 'I'm fed up and feel dismissed, blamed and diminished when you don't listen to me. Why can't you listen – and you didn't take out the rubbish yesterday,' say 'I feel invisible when you don't listen to me. Can you please pay me attention when I'm talking?'

2. **Listen to the other person's response.**

   Listening requires empathy and an intention to understand the other person's point of view. Allow the other person space to talk without interrupting or jumping to conclusions.

   Consider summarising what you think you've heard so that you ensure that you completely understand. For example, say 'What I understood you to say was. . . .' (See Chapters 8, 12 and 17.)

3. **Suggest mutually beneficial solutions.**

For example, rather than telling your partner 'You need to start telling me how you feel', offer a suggestion that involves give and take from both parties, such as: 'Perhaps in future, we can put aside some time where you can feel safe and okay to express your problems. Or alternatively you can write me a letter if you find speaking up difficult.'

Give your partner time and space to share solutions and endeavour to come to an agreement. If you can't, you may choose to take time out and reflect or calm any emotions that you've generated (see Chapters 2 and 13). Where possible, agree a time to meet to start again. (Chapters 8 and 9 offer more ideas on communicating emotions and needs.)

Finding new perspectives

Pain can give you tunnel vision. Obsessive negative thinking is a common feature of depression, sadness, loss or disappointment.

Breaking free of emotional patterns requires that you develop new perspectives. You can't solve a problem from the same emotional state and perspective in which you created it. Instead, approach the problem as if you're feeling confident, creative and happy, and you're going to find new solutions.

As you constantly seek out new perspectives, you gradually get better at seeing around a problem or re-framing a situation in a positive light. Finding a fresh perspective can eventually become much easier and even a natural part of how you approach emotional difficulties.

Try the following thought exercises and ask the following questions to encourage the discovery of new perspectives:

✔ Create a story in which you're a superhero. How can Super You manage or view this situation? What positive outcome did Super You create?

✔ Imagine that you solved the problem and are looking back at the situation. How did you get to this point? Notice and label the steps.

✔ Imagine that you're a wise old sage. What advice may you give yourself? Conversely, how might a plucky eight-year-old schoolchild tackle the situation?

✔ How can you face this problem and feel okay within it? Does a way exist so that you can even smile through it? What positives exist?

✔ In how many different ways can you approach this situation?

✔ What strengths and benefits are you gaining through having to manage this situation?

Finding something to be passionate about can take you out of negative or incapacitating thoughts and give you a new perspective on life.

Preparing for difficult conversations

Sometimes you need to share and discuss a particularly difficult topic, problem or situation with another person. For example, you may need to tell someone that you want to divorce or finish a relationship. You may have to give someone bad news, confront her about a problem, negotiate a change of behaviour that's been upsetting you, or share a significant concern.

Knowing yourself

As you prepare for a difficult conversation, consider your own behaviour before you consider the actions of other parties. For example, consider whether your own actions have

- ✔ **Helped to resolve the situation.** Can you honestly say that you've taken specific action to find a solution?

- ✔ **Made you happy.** Sometimes you get caught in sticking to a particular point-of-view that doesn't move a situation forward. This often occurs when you focus more on blaming another person than on finding a solution. You need new perspectives to move on. See the earlier section 'Finding new perspectives'.

- ✔ **Been influenced by other people.** Are others' opinions overriding your own personal perspectives?

- ✔ **Been deemed reasonable in the eyes of those whom you respect.**

Before you go into a difficult conversation, take some time to consider how the other person may respond. Ask yourself:

- ✔ What sort of person am I talking to?

- ✔ What is the best way to communicate with that person?

- ✔ What pressure or stress may the other person be under?

- ✔ How can I prepare the other person for this potentially difficult conversation?

See Chapters 8, 9 and 17 for tips on difficult conversations.

Thinking like someone else

After considering your own actions and feelings, spend some time thinking about what the other person cares about and values in life. Determine whether the other person is motivated by

- ✔ Change, excitement, fresh ideas and new activities.

- ✔ Money, details and facts.

- ✔ Relationships and harmony.

- ✔ Routine, tradition and things staying safely the same.

Knowing what's meaningful to the other person gives you a starting place for a difficult conversation. You can then organise your discussion in a way that meets the other person's primary need.

Imagine that you've been offered a job in a new location. You're excited about the opportunity but anxious that your partner may not agree to relocating. You dread having to talk with your partner about the offer and fear you may end up in a terrible fight. Still, the opportunity isn't going to be yours much longer – you need to come to a decision very soon. Following are four ways of approaching the same topic:

- ✔ **If your partner enjoys change and excitement,** you're likely to have less of a challenge relating all about a new job opportunity because the suggestion probably excites your partner. Support your message of change by researching some of the opportunities and interests available in the new location – for you and your partner as a couple and as individuals.

- ✔ **If your partner is concerned with money,** focus your conversation on the financial benefits of the move. Talk about promotion prospects. Gather facts on house prices and cost of living. Be prepared to share the costs and benefits of the move.

- ✔ **If your partner is moved by relationships,** reassure him or her that you can maintain connections with current friends, colleagues and family. Provide ideas about how you may make new contacts in the new location.

- ✔ **If your partner likes routine,** take him or her step by step through the change process as you envision it. That way, your partner can feel safe that you aren't going to rock the boat too much. Change is difficult for people who value routine, so lead them along the journey.

Standing in other people's shoes enables you to consider what they need to hear and how best to address their needs. This process is about bridging different communication styles and preferred comfort zones in order to achieve greater understanding of a situation – not about manipulation. You're seeking to have an adult conversation where reason and thinking are uppermost. Anticipating likely reactions based on what the other person cares about is an effort to recognise, accept and reduce fears.

Bringing in positive emotions

Having positive expectations of a difficult discussion is crucial to setting up the right energy for understanding and agreement. Before you begin the actual conversation, focus on feelings that help you best manage your own emotions and the other person's emotions. Take time to:

- ✔ Consider the other person's emotions and needs. See the preceding section 'Thinking like someone else'.

- ✔ Generate positive feelings about the other person. See the later sidebar 'Making up a batch of loving kindness'.

- ✔ Engage your own positive emotions with a sense of love and acceptance of your own needs (see Chapter 1).

Before the difficult conversation, evaluate how you truly need to express your emotions. Is doing so going to help the situation – or do you just need to get something off your chest for your own reasons, or dump on the other person?

Visualise what you really want to happen by the end of your conversation and figure out what your role is in reaching this conclusion. Rehearse the meeting in your mind. See yourself and the other person:

- ✔ Hearing, acknowledging and understanding each other's points of view.

- ✔ Coming to an agreement.

- ✔ Leaving the conversation feeling good.

Try to want – rather than need – a perfect outcome. Needing a perfect outcome puts pressure on the other person and can act as a reverse magnet, pushing the other person away from a solution rather than towards it. A useful thought is: 'I'd prefer that the meeting goes this way, but I can manage if it doesn't.'

Making up a batch of loving kindness

To develop feelings of compassion for another person, even if your relationship has been less than wonderful in the past, try the following loving kindness exercise before a difficult conversation:

1. Bring to mind someone you feel kindly about. As you think about that person, focus on how gentleness, loving kindness and compassion feel in every inch of your body.

2. Turn the feelings of loving kindness towards yourself. Draw gentleness and compassion into your thoughts about yourself.

3. Think about the person or people who are causing you difficulty. Direct the feelings of loving kindness and compassion to them. Accept that you and the other people you've thought about are all human beings who are muddling along in life and just trying to do the best possible. No one has the 'right' answer necessarily, but everyone deserves kindness.

Changing Behaviours Day by Day

You are *not* your emotions. Yes, you experience an emotion, sometimes very deeply, but still the emotion isn't you. Specifically, avoid:

- ✔ Identifying too deeply with your emotions.
- ✔ Getting caught in the drama of your emotions.
- ✔ Convincing yourself that experiencing a particular emotion is your story or destiny.

All these behaviours can prolong your difficult feelings.

Instead of thinking of yourself as a 'depressive' person, think of yourself as a happy person who's temporarily experiencing some depression. Mental labels, such as 'I'm a sad git' or 'I'm an emotional cripple' can result in you adopting verbal and body language that relates to that emotion, and as a result you begin to think and act like someone who's sad, anxious or angry.

Identify language and behaviours that support positive emotions and develop habits to build up your happier self, as we discuss in the following section.

Taking tiny steps

Old habits are hard to change. And yet, change is possible, little by little. The journey of 1000 miles starts with a single step.

Change is uncomfortable – so embrace the discomfort for a while. If you're too comfortable, you're not changing! Remind yourself that new behaviour becomes more comfortable the more you practise it. Make a plan of action to become stronger. See Chapter 16 for detailed information and an example.

Motivating yourself

Developing new behaviours to boost your emotional happiness takes effort, and so you need to identify the potential benefits of change.

Spend some time considering the end result of every change that you'd like to make or are in the process of making. Having a very specific vision of your goal motivates you to action. To develop your vision, ask yourself:

✔ **What precisely needs to change in order to heal my painful emotions?**
Identify the specific new thoughts, emotions, behaviours and actions that must become part of your daily life.

✔ **What specifically do you need to do to make your vision a reality?**
Perhaps you need to make a radical shift in your environment and actions, such as changing your job or developing new friends. Or maybe the changes are more subtle and internal, such as choosing to focus on the positive rather than the negative.

Write down your responses to these questions and then use this information to create a specific daily plan for the next three to six months. Table 14-1 is an example plan. Ensure that your plan includes lists with smaller, doable actions and behaviours, and that you can check off each success as you go along. And don't forget to identify ways to reward yourself when you complete an item on your list. (The section 'Taking care of yourself' includes some easy, rewarding ideas.)

Make the most of the beginning and end of a day

You're most likely awake more than 16 hours – or 960 minutes – every day. Some of the most important minutes occur at the start and the finish of the day, so get more from these precious times.

How you start the day sets the tone. Many people find their daily commute exhausting. They lose their tempers with their fellow passengers, which clouds their daily happiness and experience of life. If you experience this problem, decide to enjoy the commute:

✔ Read a book if you're on public transport or listen to a talking-book or music in the car.

✔ Be curious about your fellow passengers or drivers. What may their stories be? Where have they come from?

✔ Notice the trees, plants, birds and buildings around you. What you see often becomes no more than visual wallpaper, but when you choose to open your eyes to any of the surrounding beauty, you can see it again for the first time.

✔ If you work at home, get some fresh air by walking in your garden, on your terrace, in the park or around the block.

✔ Do some stretches, breathing exercises or meditation to quieten your mind.

Similarly, little changes before bed can help bring your day to a happy ending. Practise the Gratitude Exercise. Before you go to sleep, bring to mind anything you can for which you can be grateful – your health, friends, family, a train that ran on time, pets, achievements and so forth. You may wish to summarise these in your journal so you can refer back to them whenever you want to lift your spirits.

Table 14-1		Sally's Healing Plan	
	Activity	*Helpful Thoughts and People*	*Reward*
Week One	Take time to identify my basic needs and tune in to my physical and emotional signals. Start a daily journal.	'I am taking control of my life.'	Go swimming once a week after work to unwind
Week Two	Make time for some creativity; join a dance class. Talk to my brother to try to heal our old rivalry. Practise mindfulness in the morning.	'I can be optimistic that we can resolve our old difficulties.'	Stay in a nice hotel when I visit my brother
Week Three	Focus on my relationship with Jim, going out once a week to make time to talk. Take breaks during the day and respond to body rhythms.	'We can rekindle some of the romance we had in our marriage.'	A beauty treatment

Be compassionate with yourself when you find change difficult. You may experience some U-turns and fall-back moments, but don't allow these to be excuses to give up. Keep the vision of success and happiness in your mind.

Injecting Creativity into Your Day

Creativity is an essential part of developing solutions to your problems. As a child you were probably immensely creative and expressed yourself through games, painting and imaginative play. But when you go to school, much of this creativity can be drummed out by having to focus on curriculum subjects that supposedly have 'right and correct' answers.

You're creative, but you may have forgotten how to feed and nurture this aspect of yourself. Creative play is good for you at any stage of your life. We recently saw an elderly couple in their 80s at a funfair. They went on some of the rides, chatting, singing and eating ice cream cornets as if they were six years old. Watching their laughter and enjoyment of that moment was delightful. Creativity keeps you younger more effectively than using Botox!

Retaining or rediscovering the childlike part of you is fun and does your brain good. One of the reasons that people find concentrating on business literature or technical documents so difficult is because the human brain prefers to be interested, to enjoy itself, to play and be curious. If you don't feed your brain with activities or information that meet these needs, your brain gets bored and starts to nudge you to take a break so it can have some fun. Making time for creative and playful activities ensures that you restore the balance between being and doing. You're re-connecting with joy, which releases feel-good chemicals and helps you heal.

Taking little creative breaks

The long-hours working culture of organisations limits people from taking time to play and feed their minds, bodies and souls. Make time. Without some fun, what is life about? Even short time-outs such as the following nurture your emotional wellbeing:

- Do something that you know makes you laugh, such as watching an amusing television or radio programme or going to a live comedy performance.
- Doodle in a notebook with a coloured marker or pencil.
- Figure out a crossword or Sudoku puzzle.
- Go to the theatre or cinema.
- Knit or crochet for a few minutes.
- Play a game – by yourself or with others.
- Play around with a small ball of clay or a handful of building blocks.
- Read a book.
- Take some exercise (see Chapter 6 for ideas).
- Visit an art gallery.

Letting go of your inner critic

Probably the greatest limiting factor on your creativity, and therefore your ability to move forward in life, is your *inner critical voice*. Everyone has one. You probably developed your inner critical voice while growing up, picking up the way that your parents, teachers, authority figures and bosses criticised you for various things. You have to acknowledge and take control of your inner critic if you want to rediscover the joy of creating and play.

Analysis and critical thinking can be useful, helping you to solve a maths sum correctly or get the right angle when building a wall. Certain aspects of life do have an objective, 'right' solution, but much of life can be said to be subjective and have many possible solutions.

Pursuing excellence is rational, whereas pursuing perfection is irrational and limiting. See Chapter 12. A search for perfection or a perfect answer can limit your creative spirit. For example:

- ✔ No perfect human being exists.
- ✔ No perfect work of art, book, painting or piece of music exists.

Yes, the world abounds with wonderful people, rewarding relationships, fabulous artistic creations and inspiring presentations. But the label of 'wonderful' is subjective. Just because 'wonderful' examples of any of these things inspire you greatly doesn't necessarily mean that they inspire someone else. People consider Mozart and Beethoven to have been geniuses, but not 100 per cent of human beings like their music.

In order to allow your own unique expression of emotional creativity to flourish, you must turn down and switch off the voice of your inner critic for a period of time. (See Chapters 3 and 12 for more on stopping certain thoughts.) Replace critical thoughts such as 'I'm not creative' with supportive thoughts like 'I shall enjoy this activity – whatever the outcome. I'm just doing it for fun.'

You can always put your analytical thinking cap back on again when you finish creating. Your analytical brain can even come in handy by asking yourself how much fun you had and whether you gained any new insights from your creative endeavours.

Developing the artist within

Emotional healing can manifest through creative expression, such as painting, drawing, music, writing poetry and keeping a journal. The outputs of these creative activities can give you insights into your emotional state. *Art and music therapy* use creative work to interpret and resolve emotional difficulties (see the Appendix). Within the process of painting or writing a poem, you may discover metaphors which help you understand, resolve and release emotional disturbance.

Begin getting in touch with your inner artist by asking yourself:

- ✔ **What have I always wanted to do?** Perhaps you always wanted to write a book or play the guitar or drums.
- ✔ **What creative activities did I enjoy while growing up?** Maybe you enjoyed doing pottery, sculpture, woodworking, ceramics or glasswork.

Any of your responses to these questions can lead you towards creative activities that you'll enjoy and that can offer emotional healing.

Get in touch with your inner artist as follows:

1. **Buy or borrow some paper and paints and pencils and set aside one to two hours, once or twice a month, when you won't be disturbed.**

2. **Decide on some general image you want to paint.**

   Of course, you can draw or paint whatever you want, but having a general idea in mind can be helpful. Here are some suggestions to get you inspired:

   • **A self-portrait.** Set a mirror about two feet in front of you to serve as a reference or look at a favourite photograph. But don't get hung up on being literal. Maybe you've always envisioned yourself as having flowing blue hair?!

   • **A house that represents your life today.** Your house doesn't need to be real or traditional. Maybe it has a waterslide off the front porch and a field for raising miniature ponies.

   • **A picture of your ideal life in two years' time.** Remove your fear and tell yourself, 'If I couldn't fail, this is what my ideal life would look like'.

   • **A childhood scene or fantasy.** Recall an inspiring story you read or experienced and put it on paper.

3. **Before you begin painting or drawing, thoroughly relax your body and mind.**

   Calm your thoughts. Quieten your concerns or worries. Switch off any fears that you may have about the exercise itself (see the preceding 'Letting go of your inner critic' section). Remind yourself of how an enthusiastic child feels.

   Relax your shoulders and neck, feel flexible in your body, including your legs, knees, hips, arms, wrists and hands. Breathe in three times counting four as you breathe in and six as you breathe out. Allow yourself to sigh on the final exhalation.

4. **Begin to paint or draw.**

   Express yourself in whatever way comes through. You're not here to produce a perfect work of art. You're here to express yourself in your own unique style that reflects your personality.

5. **Continue to paint or draw, uninterrupted, for at least 30 minutes.**

   Trust yourself to know that you'll finish when you're ready to finish. Take a short break to stretch or get a drink. Then return to another session of painting, if you want to.

6. **When complete, metaphorically pat yourself on the back and notice how you're feeling.**

   Look at your painting or drawing and ask yourself:

   - What does this painting tell me about my emotions?

   - What colours did I use? What do they say about my mood and expression?

   - Do certain themes come through to give me a message?

   - What does the style of the artwork tell me about my personality?

   - In what way does this drawing show that I'm feeling free? In what way does it show that I'm feeling limited?

Don't worry whether your painting is a work of art or resembles a three-year-old's playschool picture. What matters is that your painting or drawing is a form of expression – your expression. Through this activity, you're tapping into your creative childlike soul and giving yourself permission to play.

Playing with words: Poetry

Poetry is another medium by which you can tap into your emotions and gain some insights into how you're feeling. Poetry can help you develop solutions and even resolve issues.

Following specific poetry structures help you to make a start. Here are some simple, short forms you can try:

- A **haiku** is a Japanese structure of three phrases that can be said in one breath. The first line contains five syllables, the second line seven and the third line five. Haikus usually contain a reference to nature. Here's an example:

  Sadness pervades me
  Birdsong echoes with my grief
  On wings, it will pass

- A **limerick** is a form of humorous verse consisting of five lines. The first, fourth and fifth lines use the same rhyme, while the third and fourth lines are usually shorter and also share a rhyme:

  There was a bad moment in Blackpool
  When my partner said something so hurtful;
  I sulked for six hours
  Then he gave me some flowers
  And since I forgave him life's wonderful!

ANECDOTE

Surprises in Mariam's dream house

Mariam decided to explore her inner creative spirit (see the earlier section 'Developing the artist within') by drawing a house that represented her life today. She enjoyed the activity of drawing – something she hadn't let herself do in years – and was surprised by the picture she eventually created.

The house she drew had walls, a chimney and a roof. Trees and people were outside in the gardens. But as she looked at the picture later, she realised that she hadn't included any windows. This artistic choice indicated to her that she felt imprisoned. She recognised a need to change her life and her relationship in order to get out of the house more.

✔ An **acrostic** is a short composition constructed so that the initial letters of the lines form a word or words that relate to the subject. For example here is an acrostic on anger:

Anger before healing	*Anger after healing*
Aggressive behaviour	Allowing and acknowledging
Numbing response	Noticing and breathing
Growling voices	Giving space to what's happening
Exaggerating a problem	Exploring our options
Resolution is difficult	Releasing and resolving differences

✔ A **free-style poem** can follow any pattern of rhythm and rhyme – or contain no rhymes whatsoever. 'Fooling' is a free-style poem a client wrote as she began to heal old emotions:

Always tears, tears so close to laughter
The jumping child, jumping in my arms
One two three, one two three
Her birthday celebration.
The spring sun shines on the patio.
Dear dear Jen is there.
I weep in the little green house
The spring sun shines in the valley.
Tears so close to laughter.

Set aside 30 minutes now or some time later today and write a poem about an emotional experience to see what message or theme comes out. Choose one of the four simple forms we describe in the preceding list. Silence your inner critic for a few minutes (see the earlier section 'Letting go of your inner critic') and just keep writing.

Let the words flow

Simply writing down words on a piece of paper encourages your creative mind to express itself and can yield impressive emotional healing.

Everyday for the next two weeks, spend a few minutes free-style writing. Express whatever comes into your mind. Early morning is a good time for this activity because your mind tends to be more open. Allow your pen to flow across the page for three pages without stopping. What you write doesn't matter, just let your thoughts out onto the page, without criticism or judgement (see the earlier section 'Letting go of your inner critic'). You don't need to keep the pages.

Chapter 15

Living as an Emotionally Healed Person

In This Chapter

▶ Integrating new behaviours into your life

▶ Fine-tuning your behaviour and thinking

▶ Meeting your emotional and spiritual needs

▶ Setting your vision for the future

*E*motional healing is a lifetime's journey. Although you can heal past grievances, the nature of life is such that you're always going to experience ups and downs, challenges and disappointments all the way through your lifetime. The key is for you to be able to recognise this truth and develop the conscious awareness necessary to accept and work through difficulties without becoming overwhelmed by them.

Working through your childhood (as we discuss in Chapter 7) and past emotional pain (see Chapters 8 and 9) can lighten your load as you move forward. Finding the healing strategies that work best for you enables you to apply them in the future. All these activities don't remove the fact that you may still experience anger, pain or fear, but the techniques may give you confidence to trust that you can navigate your way through life's storms more effectively.

You can develop the ability to change your behaviour to reflect the person you want to become, rather than the person you were. This process requires you to identify thoughts, body language and words that express the 'you' that you want to be for the next stage of your life. You can then liberate fresh aspects of yourself that may previously have been hidden. As a result, you're likely to experience life in a lighter, happier and yet deeper way.

This chapter helps you to find renewed purpose and meaning in your life. We touch on aspects of mind, body, emotions, relationships and spirit – all key elements for your continued health and wellbeing.

Tuning Up Your Body and Mind

Your body and mind are intricately connected; what happens in one can have dramatic, far-reaching consequences in the other. When you make an effort to improve the health of one part, you benefit both parts. The following sections explore physical and mental activities you can engage in for long-term emotional health and wellbeing.

Getting physical

Even if you've experienced illness or disability, you can nonetheless work to achieve a level of wellbeing and fitness that helps you feel good about yourself. For millennia, general wisdom has agreed that a healthy body gives you a healthy mind. A strong body tunes up your whole system – body, mind, spirit, emotions and more. A fit body releases *endorphins*, the feel-good chemicals, which boost your immune system. You feel better, more self-confident and have more energy. Consequently, you tend to see the bright side of life.

Look to television, film and books for amazing, real-life stories of individuals who overcome physical limitations. People who return from wars or have accidents go on to run marathons despite disability, or enter the Paralympics. The human spirit is powerful in its desire to live life to the full. Embrace the possibilities and opportunities that can exist for you.

Chapter 6 gives you tons of ideas to get your body actively involved in the process of emotional healing, but here are some of our favourite ways to tune up your body (and by extension, your mind):

- ✔ **Start your day well.** Gain control of your mental state by focusing on the positives in your life and the day ahead. Specifically:

  - **Spend a moment upon waking to tune into your breath.** See Chapter 13 for more advice on starting the day right.

  - **Stretch your body.** Yoga exercises are an ideal way to focus body, mind and breath. Ask your doctor or a yoga teacher first if you're worried about physical problems. You also benefit from aerobic exercise such as running on the spot, dancing to music, skipping or running up the stairs.

  - **Spend time with a mood-affecting light source.** The morning may be the best time to spend appropriate time in front of a light source. Exactly how much time needs to be tailored both to your needs and to the intensity of the light source.

✔ **Imagine what being fit feels like – and then get moving.** As you go about your daily activities, move as if you're energised, emotionally healed and have a sense of general mental and emotional wellbeing – even if you don't feel that way at the moment. When you act as if you're energised and fully engaged, your body responds accordingly, returning to a state of aliveness. Switching into a new groove can become a habit. Eventually feeling alive and energised becomes your natural state.

Thinking your way to better health

The Buddha said, 'It is your mind that creates your life.' Every decision you make comes from a thought – whether you think about climbing Mount Everest, designing a table, starting a business or getting married.

Your brain is malleable and capable of changing its circuitry at any stage of your life, provided you train it to do so. This fact means that you can choose to be happy by deliberately developing positive thoughts of kindness to yourself and others.

Experts generally agree that negative or pessimistic thinking can lead to ill health and a shorter life (see Chapter 2). Allowing negativity into your daily life definitely reduces your inner happiness and limits your options in the outer world.

Some people claim that negative thinking is more 'realistic' than positive thinking. However, if positivity, trust, honesty and love were in the minority, humans would live in a state of anarchy. Wars, hunger and imperfection certainly exist, but so does an indomitable force that leads humans to create order and social communities where you can live in safety. Analytical and critical thinking are rational and useful. We aren't suggesting that you go through life in a delusional state of Pollyanna positive thinking, but we are suggesting that you switch out of negative thoughts that drain your sense of happiness and wellbeing.

You probably don't think twice about cleaning your teeth each day, but how often do you stop to filter out negative or doubtful thoughts? Become vigilant regarding your thoughts and how they impact your life:

✔ **Be discerning of what you read, watch and listen to throughout the day.** The music you listen to changes your emotional state, and so match the music to the mood you want to create. Also, pay attention to the television programmes you watch, the websites you visit and the news sources you examine. The tone and presentation style of the media you consume each day can affect the way you feel.

✔ **Replace negative generalisations with accurate and specific thoughts.** For example, rather than telling yourself something like 'Nobody supports me' and consequently feeling worse about your situation, actively remind yourself of the truth: 'I'm supported by my friend John.' (See Chapter 12.)

✔ **Maintain perspective within situations by ensuring that your emotional brain doesn't overwhelm your thinking brain:** For example, rather than thinking 'I can't cope', remind yourself what skills you have to manage the situation and remember when you've used those skills successfully in the past. Ask yourself how important this moment is going to be three months in the future.

✔ **Take care with what you say.** Your words are a reflection of your thoughts, so discover how to express yourself assertively but not be overbearing. See Chapters 8 and 14 for approaches that enable you to create mutually affirming conversations.

✔ **Take action based on your thoughts and needs.** If you complain about a problem, do something about it. Taking appropriate action raises your sense of control and self-esteem.

✔ **Live by your personal beliefs and values.** Be conscious of how you spend your time so that you focus on what matters most to you.

✔ **Engage in regular meditation or mindfulness practice.** These activities help you rise above problems or anxieties and gain a sense of peace and control (see Chapter 13).

Maintaining physical energy

Your mind, body and emotions are one integrated system. If one part is feeling low in energy, the other parts are impacted.

The following activity can help you examine and take control of your energy level:

1. **Think about how you feel when you're at low energy.**

   Think of your energy on a scale from 0 to 10, with 0 being very low energy and 10 being very high. How do you feel when you're at a 3 or 4? Maybe you feel like it's a grey winter's Monday morning and you have to head off on your commute to work.

   Spend some time recalling how you felt physically, mentally and emotionally:

   • **Physically:** Droopy, heavy, edgy, achy or lethargic.

   • **Mentally:** Sluggish, foggy, depressed or anxious.

   • **Emotionally:** Bleak, down, sad or angry.

2. **Consider how you feel when you have high energy.**

   Recall a time when you felt as if you were on a roll, at a 9–10 energy level. Perhaps you performed well at work or in study. Or maybe you were in a social or family environment and felt good about life.

   Recreate the feeling of being at a high energy level:

   - **Physically:** Lighter, more flexible, taller, straighter and stronger.
   - **Mentally:** More integrated, more alert with clear and creative thinking.
   - **Emotionally:** Brighter, happier or optimistic.

3. **Tune into this energy scale as you go about your day.**

   You can bring in the feelings of high energy at will by remembering the sensations you describe in Step 2. Remind yourself of this exercise two or three times a day until it becomes a habit.

Your energy impacts the world around you, influencing not only how you feel but also other people. Good energy is infectious.

Attending to Your Emotional Needs

In addition to taking care of yourself physically and mentally, you need to address your emotional needs on a regular basis. Because you're reading this book, you obviously already know that emotions can be powerful forces in your life. In the following sections, we cover some emotional aspects of day-to-day living that with a little extra effort can produce big effects.

Finding security through trust

Develop trust in yourself that you have the capacity to manage life. Without this trust, you live in fear. Humans never know what's going to happen tomorrow or whether events are going to go their way. But you've got to this point and survived so far, which shows that you must have developed some useful life skills along the way!

Create a plan of what you want to happen in your life (see the later section 'Sketching Your Vision and Goals'), but at the same time, remember that whatever life throws at you, you have the resources to work through things. Trying to control events that are outside your remit, or control the behaviour of others, doesn't work. Instead, focus on building self-reliance and positive thinking so that you trust in yourself and in the benevolence of life. See Chapter 20 for some great ideas for staying positive.

Every day, you give your trust to people because if you don't, you can't live an ordinary life. And most of the time, things go well. Yet you also need to accept that occasionally people let you down or accidents happen. Be realistic about the nature of life.

You're likely to be happier if you can let go of defensiveness and fear. Focus on being optimistic, but also maintain rational thoughts that affirm the fact that you can trust yourself to manage whatever situations come your way. Think about how many strangers you already trust on a daily basis:

- ✔ The person who changes the tyres on your car
- ✔ The builder who fixes your roof
- ✔ The driver of your plane, train or bus

Trust starts with yourself: trusting you, trusting that you matter, trusting that you can follow your own path and be loyal and dependable to yourself. If you can't trust yourself, others don't trust you and you don't trust them.

Getting intimate

Love nurtures you: bonding with other people is an essential part of human evolution. Any relationship has the potential to develop qualities – such as kindness, compassion, co-operation and altruism – which enhance wellbeing.

In today's fast-paced world, people often put work before love. The long-hours culture can lead you to be driven by your career. As a result, many more people today live alone and get married or start having children later in life.

Loneliness and lack of connection with others can cause unhappiness and be bad for your health. Rejection and isolation can increase your blood pressure and stress levels, leading to lower immune function. Creating supportive social networks has been shown to improve health. The difference in health between someone who feels isolated and someone with a good social network is as much as between a smoker and a non-smoker.

Of course relationships – especially intimate relationships – can be painful and damaging. If you're in an intimate relationship, take action to keep your love alive. If you're not in a relationship at the moment, make time for loving connection with friends and family so that you nurture yourself. And if a relationship is what you're looking for, take the risk and get out there and try to find one (see Chapter 10).

The following sections explore the intricacies of healthy intimacy.

Giving and receiving

Love thrives on gentleness and generosity. Love requires softness and opening up. If you've been hurt by a relationship that went wrong, you may build defensive walls to keep others at bay. However, defensiveness is ultimately self-sabotage because you remain isolated.

Defensive behaviours – such as stonewalling, mistrust or cynicism – can build up within a long-term relationship and create a void where you and your partner refuse to compromise. If this situation applies to you, try any or all the following techniques to begin dismantling those walls:

- ✔ **Encourage kindness and fun:** Consider what your partner really loves and treat him or her to it.

- ✔ **Go back to the beginning.** Remember what brought you together – perhaps a shared hobby or a passion for a specific cause. Find ways to enjoy your mutual interest again.

- ✔ **Let go:** Work to release past pain, hurtful memories of things that went wrong and resentment for unmet needs. Focus on the moment (check out Chapter 13 for more details on mindfulness).

- ✔ **Prioritise:** What's more important – being 'right' and judgemental or being together? Answering this question honestly can help put a relationship back on the right track.

- ✔ **Talk through difficulty:** Allow ten minutes for each one of you to offload your problems while the other just listens without saying anything (flip to Chapter 14 to gain some tips on positive conversations). Try not to blame or be critical; just relate your own experience.

  Start these types of conversations with a moment's silence. Bring gentleness and an intention to find love into your mind because these echo in your voice and what you say. Be forgiving.

- ✔ **Receive love:** Put down the barriers and allow love to come to you.

- ✔ **Welcome the change and growth of each individual:** People change – yourself included. Instead of fighting this fact, embrace it and celebrate the people you and the other person are becoming.

Finding time for touch and sexual release

Sex in a loving relationship is good for you. It reduces your level of cortisol (the stress chemical) and releases oxytocin (the bonding hormone) into your bloodstream. Unfortunately, work, children and loads of other commitments can intervene if you don't consciously make time for physically expressing love.

Making love is an important part of maintaining intimacy in a relationship. But the focus needs to be on those two words – *making love*. Sex can be a cold and lonely experience without warm feelings between you.

If you've lost some of the chemistry that you had earlier in your relationship, bring the physical aspect of your life higher up your agenda. Many couples report that their relationships get back on track when they focus on making time to make love. And if you're not in a relationship, you can still treat yourself to loving touch and find forms of sexual release that are emotionally healing.

To bring sexual intimacy back into your life and relationship, try the following approaches:

- ✔ **Set aside some time when you can be together undisturbed.** Build in a time without pressures that suits you both. If necessary, schedule this time specifically into your life. You're giving priority to the most important person in your life.

- ✔ **Create a sensual and loving environment:** Do anything that feels good or makes your partner feel good, including music, a scented candle, a coloured light bulb or a comfortable place to lie together.

- ✔ **Start slow.** Agree in advance that you're going to just touch and massage one another to begin with, so as to remind yourself of sensual and gentle touch. This approach takes the pressure off 'performance' anxiety.

  As you touch one another bring in a feeling of loving kindness. Love is a choice you make moment by moment, and so choose to focus on it.

- ✔ **Focus on intimacy rather than orgasm.** So much is written about orgasm that it can add to tension. Instead, you just want to relax into the intimate experience. Gradually you can help one another to rediscover the touch that brought you pleasure – and yes, climax – when you were first in your relationship.

- ✔ **Let yourself be touched.** Allow yourself to enjoy the feelings of your body and accept the sensations with a sense of love. You don't have to reciprocate every single touch from your partner.

If you have sexual problems, visit a counsellor with special training. Premature ejaculation and unsatisfying intercourse can be very distressing but you can overcome these challenges by following specialised sexual counselling.

Appreciating the dance of intimacy

Tradition says that men come to love through sex and women come to sex through love. Although one can't generalise, our professional experiences indicate that women enjoy sex and intimacy more when they feel loved and valued. A man may seek to 'make up' through sex, but if a woman is still brooding over a hurt or painful issue then this approach is unlikely to succeed.

Hearts, flowers and few good laughs

Make time for romance, possibly going out once a month or so if you can afford it for a romantic dinner together. Romance doesn't have to cost money, though. You can be romantic by:

- ✔ Saying loving things.

- ✔ Doing something special, such as cooking your partner's favourite meal.

- ✔ Giving a 'gift' token for you to give your partner a head massage or foot rub.

- ✔ Allowing your partner to watch sport or a weepy movie without criticising.

- ✔ Letting your partner take some time out just for him or herself – without resentment on your part.

Fun is also important. Sexual intimacy breaks down barriers and can help you remember how to laugh. You can be gentle and loving and yet not take life too seriously. Couples who are still happy together after many years tend to enjoy 'intensive companionship and sexual liveliness', but without the anxieties and tensions of early love. They're likely to be generous, calm and deeply attached, and to share experiences and avoid stress.

Ways to enhance fun in intimacy can include writing poetry to one another, singing along to a tune you both enjoy, dancing together, playing with sex toys and experimenting with new sexual positions or in different places.

Good sex begins with seeking to understand one another's point of view. Talk, mutual understanding, trust and honesty are the foundation stones of intimacy. If you're hiding feelings from the other person or don't trust him or her – to tell the truth or to take care of your needs, this secrecy interferes with the joy of love-making.

Beware of the turn-offs to sex and intimacy, such as nagging or criticism. Acting as the 'authority' or like a controlling parent with your partner quickly dampens any sexual desire. No one wants to have sex with an expert – or a parent!

Balancing Your Personal and Social Needs

You're both an individual and also a part of a group. As you become an adult, finding a balance between your individuality and your need to be part of a social system can be difficult. You can easily get drawn into habits that don't suit your personality but suit those of your friends or your partner. Asserting and explaining what you need – for instance, more time alone or a greater number of social activities – requires courage on your part.

Standing up to the demands of work can be difficult. A boss who gives you work last thing at night and expects you to have the result by the morning may be hard to refuse. Before the demands even arise, identify for yourself what's acceptable – for example, working late for a specific project – and what's unacceptable – being expected to work late every night even when no urgent need exists. Use a similar strategy to establish what's acceptable to you in terms of helping a needy friend or responding to a parent's requests.

The following sections help you clarify your own needs and develop assertive ways to maintain and meet those needs.

Finding alone time

With so many opportunities available for entertainment and engagement today, people can easily get out of the habit of spending time alone to sit, read or rest. A client commented recently that he'd forgotten how to relax. Sound familiar?

People get drawn into activities such as running errands or doing household chores, and they get sucked into things that are meant to be entertaining such as television, emails or digital games. You can easily lose yourself amid the constant hustle and excitement.

Your ability to be alone has benefits for your emotional and physical wellbeing. Find some time when you can just be with yourself, meet your own needs and not be at the beck and call of what others want to do, or want you to be. Discover how to negotiate time alone when you need it.

Many people feel guilty about taking time for themselves, so give yourself this opportunity as a gift. Build up slowly with a ten-minute mindfulness exercise (see Chapter 13) or a walk on your own. You may want to do some physical exercise (see Chapter 6) or take time for your journal.

Developing healthy boundaries

Do you feel bad when you don't give your time to people who demand it, even when you'd rather do something else? You must find ways to balance meeting the needs of others and satisfying your own needs.

Living the life

No person's temperament is fixed. Some people believe that they're born optimistic or pessimistic, irritable or easy-going. In reality, scientific research shows that the brain changes its circuitry according to how you use it, which means that you can change your temperament by choosing and practising other behaviours. Your thoughts, beliefs and expectations shape your emotions, and so changing your thinking can change your temperament.

Of course, you must reinforce new behaviours in order to integrate positive emotional states into your daily life. Start with everyday aspects including:

✔ **Your language:** Words are important because they have emotional resonance. Someone caught up in the London tube bombings described how she stopped thinking of herself as a 'victim' and chose to describe herself as a 'survivor'; this switch in language put her on an entirely different and potentially healing path of self-identity.

What frequently used words or phrases in your vocabulary do you want to change? What words or phrases do you want to add? What topics of conversation do you want to engage in – or avoid being drawn into? (See Chapter 8 and 14.)

✔ **Your body language:** The way you hold your head, shoulders, chest and arms says much about how you view yourself and how you want others to treat you. One of our clients noticed after a severe car accident that she was holding her body in a tense and defended way as if she was expecting another impact. She was able to consciously adjust her body at the beginning of the day to be more relaxed and open. This simple movement enabled her to feel stronger and more empowered.

How do you walk and move when you're feeling healed, empowered and more confident of your ability to manage difficulties in future? (See Chapter 6.)

In her early 30s and not in a relationship, Mia felt duty-bound to keep her mother company. However, through coaching for stress-related symptoms, Mia realised that *her* needs mattered too. Specifically, she wanted to find a loving relationship with a man, have time to go on dates and enjoy some relaxation time on her own in the evenings. She eventually gained the courage to explain to her mother that although she wasn't going to visit as often, this didn't mean that she didn't love her. Mia prepared herself prior to the conversation for the likelihood that her mother would try to make her feel guilty for her decision. But Mia stuck to her guns and negotiated that she would visit once a fortnight, rather than three times a week.

You need to develop a clear intent about the balance of your own needs and the needs of someone who has become demanding. Your ability to set boundaries (see Chapter 7) is an essential part of your self-care.

Satisfying Your Spiritual Needs

Although spirituality can relate to a religion, it doesn't have to.

Most people need a belief or sense of connection to bring them comfort. To feel a part of something greater than yourself is an essential human need. Some find this need fulfilled through religion, or through art, music, poetry, love, scientific discovery or by being in nature. Powerful experiences in each of these areas can lift you out of the smallness of your own existence and connect you to the universal.

Many people talk of their tragedy or their illness as a spiritual wake-up call. Individuals who have near-death experiences or recover from illness frequently report that 'every hour is more precious'. Although these responses are personal and you may not feel similarly, experiencing pain can bring personal priorities into brighter focus.

A client who lost his mother at an early age commented that he felt the experience made him a better father, because he understood the importance of giving love to his children. The memory of love received is sustaining even after a person dies. Indeed, the fact that everyone dies makes life more poignant. So value each day as precious.

You can experience spirituality in many ways, including watching a sunrise, listening to music, walking in nature or looking at the moon. Each of these experiences can inspire a sense of wonder, love and connection to something greater than yourself. Such moments can bring you great comfort in difficult times.

The following sections extend our exploration of living as an emotionally healed person into the realm of the soul.

Finding your special purpose in life

You're a unique human being. No one has ever been precisely like you before and never will be again. This fact is both exciting and daunting. You may question what you're supposed to do with this responsibility. Having a special purpose doesn't necessarily signify that you need to become a rocket scientist, prime minister or rebel; it may simply mean that you need to find a way to express your own particular ideas and talents.

Your unique spark radiates out from you and acts as a spiritual energy that touches others. As you tune into this spiritual force, you're likely to find yourself acting selflessly in the service of others, perhaps through volunteering, raising money for good causes or just being kind to a neighbour without being asked.

Finding your own purpose depends upon you being in the present moment and listening to the signals that your body gives you. Do what makes you feel happy and interested because this action is likely to lead you in the direction where your unique contribution makes the most difference. Specifically:

- ✔ Be with the people who set you alight.
- ✔ Go to the places that make you feel alive.
- ✔ Travel to the places that help you realise that you can live life in many different ways.

Follow your own conscience and take actions and decisions that come from your heart rather than feeling you always have to do what others demand of you. Heed your personal sense of morals and ethics so that you take what you yourself see to be the right action.

When you're going in the wrong direction, your inner wisdom may surface in the way of pain or illness or self-sabotage. For example your plans may be upset by an illness or by forgetting to make a phone call. Start to observe your own life and behaviours to analyse these tendencies. Doing so creates consciousness of your choices.

Simone had worked as a personal assistant to an advertising director for 20 years. She had enjoyed her work: her boss was an interesting man, and his clients were dynamic. However, as her 40th birthday approached, she found that she was becoming bored with the work. She woke up many days with a heavy feeling in the pit of her stomach and began to suffer from bouts of ill health.

Talking over the situation with her husband, she said that she felt that she was born to do more than assist someone else, but she wasn't sure what 'more' was. He suggested that she took a holiday on her own to think about her life. As she travelled to Africa, she met someone on the flight who worked for a Non-Governmental Organisation helping to educate African women. The trip and the encounter changed Simone's life. She became a fund-raiser and a powerful influence within the group. Both her health and happiness improved as she experienced the fulfilment of giving and helping others, without expectation of return.

Allowing your unique gifts to shine

Everyone has unique gifts, including you. Think of various people you know; you can easily identify qualities that are specific to each in terms of emotional energy, behaviours, personality and approach to life.

If you've been through some difficult emotional times, you may have lost sight of what others value in you. The first step to allowing your gifts to shine is to identify what they are.

Stop and reflect on what personal qualities you contribute . Remind yourself of appreciative comments that others have made about you. See Chapter 14 for more ideas for exploring and identifying your talents. Ask yourself some big questions:

- ✔ What is my life about?
- ✔ If there were one thing I wanted to give the world, what would it be?
- ✔ What beliefs do I honestly hold about life and death?
- ✔ As I reflect on my small part in the wider universe, how do I connect my energy to doing things in the service of others?

Asking for feedback can be a validating experience, not only from work colleagues – where a feedback system is more likely to be formally set up – but also from your family and friends. Ask them:

- ✔ What do they enjoy about you?
- ✔ What talents and personal qualities do they notice in you?
- ✔ What do they suggest you can focus on more in order to share your gifts with others?

Digest what people say. You may want to write down in your journal their most surprising comments. Find a tranquil moment when you can be alone and review their comments. Listen to the quiet voice that's in you. Don't put yourself down or be modest. Modesty can hold you back from taking action that may not only change your own life for the better but also can benefit other people.

Developing compassion for yourself and others

Compassion is a word that's seldom used in school or in the workplace. The world is filled with competitive sport and business battles. The capacity to win or excel is regarded as success. In addition, the industrial, scientific and technical revolutions have favoured a mechanistic way of life.

Yet compassion and altruism are an essential part of being human. (When you're *compassionate,* you share a sense of kindness and benevolence to your fellow human beings. When you're *altruistic,* you take unselfish action on someone else's behalf without thought for yourself.) A fundamental need exists to be collaborative, form communities and work in teams. To do all these vital things successfully requires compassion for yourself and others.

Compassion doesn't mean that you accept bad behaviour, but it may mean that you seek to understand the reason for that behaviour. When you forget how to be compassionate, you can easily become judgemental. Judging separates you from others and can lead to comparison, blame and isolation.

Compassion is a choice, and starts with self-love, care and acceptance of your humanity and fallibility. No human being is perfect; you make and will continue to make mistakes – just like everyone else does. Show compassion to yourself and grow from the experience. You can become gentler not only with yourself but also with others. (See Chapters 12 and 14.)

Sketching Your Vision and Goals

To live life as an emotionally healed person takes planning. You need to consider and plan for your future. To be successful, you need to put aside your fears and develop the self-belief that you can create a good life for yourself.

To develop a strong self-belief, begin by identifying goals for the following areas:

- ✔ **Your inner state of emotional wellbeing as you move forward.** This is your most important goal because it determines your daily experience. Whatever is happening in your life, you can draw into yourself a sense of being loved and loving yourself (see Chapter 13).

- ✔ **Your relationship:** Can your partner support the emotionally healed you? You may need to have a discussion or two to ensure that your partner can change his or her behaviour to encourage your emotionally recovered self to surface.

  Partners may collude in your old behaviours without realising it. Honesty can be frightening but leads you both to deeper levels of intimacy. If honesty doesn't work, a parting of the ways may sometimes be necessary to release you both from a limiting or dysfunctional relationship. See Chapters 10 and 14 for more on ending relationships.

- ✔ **Your work:** What do you want to be doing – as well as where, with whom and for what reward? Figure out what specific changes you need to make within your current job or find in a new job in order to be more fulfilled. You can review whether the work reflects your core values and purpose; you may need to articulate these more clearly to represent the emotionally healed you.

✔ **Your friends:** Spend time with the friends who support the emotionally healed you; avoid those who drag you back or remind you of old patterns of negativity.

✔ **Your family:** Your family may love you but have become used to you being the person you were. They may feel confused or uncomfortable when you want to change.

As you set your vision and goals for your future, talk with important family members about your plans and explain how they can help you. If a family member is particularly negative or pessimistic about your ability to move forward, you need to leave that person out of your life for a period while you gain the inner strength you need to make these changes. See Chapter 14.

✔ **Your passions:** Hobbies, sport and other leisure activities reflect who you want to be in the future. Surround yourself with positive, like-minded people who can support your interests and your continued healing.

Consider your options for each of the preceding areas carefully and assess the benefits of each goal you set. For example, surveys report that many people want to be rich and famous, despite the fact that the newspapers are full of stories of celebrities who are depressed or on drugs. Ask yourself what your listed goals give you in terms of your emotional happiness. If you want to move to a new location, change your work or make more money, that's fine – but what does your goal mean to you emotionally? How will achieving the goal add to your own and your family's happiness?

You can build a beautiful house in a beautiful location, but don't forget that you're still the one who needs to live in it. If your head is full of negativity and doubt, all those external pleasures may be worthless!

When you're content with your choices, split your plan down into manageable and timed steps. If you take on too much at once, you're likely to feel overwhelmed. Focusing on small, achievable steps builds your confidence, satisfaction and self-esteem.

Having dreams and hope are essential features of life; they affirm that things can be good or get better. When you're denied hope you become helpless (in addition to hopeless), which can lead to depression. So find a way to enjoy the journey itself rather than only focusing on the goal. That way if you don't achieve the precise outcome you want, or the result differs in some way to your dream, you're at least happy on the way.

Finding new meaning in life

Finding meaning in your life makes each day worthwhile. When you've been through a difficult time and are releasing past pain, you may need to reconnect with your own personal sense of purpose.

Pose the following questions to yourself:

- ✔ What makes me tick?
- ✔ What do I really care about?
- ✔ What am I passionate about?
- ✔ How do I want to make a difference in some way, great or small?
- ✔ How can I value who I am?

You can find meaning in many different ways. Just enjoying being yourself is the starting point. Then find ways to contribute something within your work or community. Volunteering your time or energy, willingly given, enhances health and wellbeing. Also, try to appreciate the small things you do. You may not be able to take your family on exotic holidays, but giving and sharing love has meaning. People in old age often look back most fondly on the small things.

If you have difficulty finding meaning, remind yourself of how much love a newborn baby receives. Babies are valued simply because they exist. You were that baby once but may have started to judge or criticise yourself ever since for not being 'good enough'. Remind yourself that your life has value and purpose in itself.

Switching your thinking

To access a different part of your brain and discover some things that are truly important to you, take a sheet of paper, sit quietly and breathe calmly. Put a pen in the hand you don't usually write with and ask yourself, 'What's meaningful to me in my life?' Then start drawing, writing or scribbling any words or images that come into your head.

Don't limit yourself or criticise yourself. Let whatever comes out, come out. Your writing may be rather weird and make you laugh. That's fine! When your mind runs out of words, stop and reflect on what you wrote.

Stepping out of your comfort zone

Life never stays the same. You must be ready to adapt to continually changing inner and outer circumstances. Yes, change can be uncomfortable. But if you're totally comfortable, you're neither growing nor changing.

Miranda came for consultation, suffering from a stiff neck and headaches. During one session, she described a choir she sang in. Her part was prescribed and her choir leader was critical if she sang a wrong note. The situation led Miranda to tense her body, which caused her neck aches. She also described how she longed to break out and sing some jazz. We encouraged her to experiment with improvising notes and style, which liberated her voice and freed up her whole body to flow and move with music as she sung. Her aches disappeared, and she found a jazz group to sing with, in addition to her choral work, which she still enjoyed because of her group of friends.

Deliberately moving yourself out of your comfort zone into a new activity can be beneficial, enabling you to discover different aspects of yourself and talents you never thought you had. See Chapter 16.

Part V
Taking Your Healing to New Levels

'Harold's gone through a physiological & behavioral change since he got involved in emotional healing, but I can't say it's been an improvement.'

In this part . . .

Envisioning a healthy and happy future requires you to integrate emotional healing practices into your daily routine. We suggest tips to prevent you from falling back into unhelpful habits and ways to switch your focus so that you continuously develop new skills for your journey through life.

You also see how your emotional energy impacts others and develop strategies to help those around you – perhaps your own partner or child – to heal emotional wounds.

Chapter 16

Planning Ahead: Handling Difficult Emotions in the Future

In This Chapter

▶ Getting ready for all that lies ahead

▶ Managing negative feelings

▶ Changing the emotional dance

▶ Embracing better times

*Y*our life is shaped by the plans and decisions you make moment by moment. As the proverb says, 'He who fails to plan, plans to fail'. Planning an event in your diary is easy, but remembering to identify the emotions that can help you manage that event is harder.

Thinking ahead is key. You need to identify potential challenges so that you can plan your preferred emotional response. The situation may not evolve exactly as you imagine, but what matters is that you feel you can manage your emotions within a challenging situation.

Managing your emotions doesn't mean that you don't feel emotions. Your emotions are powerful signals of your wellbeing and alert you to actions you may need to take in order to maintain your happiness and health. Some events may be sad or frightening; some may inspire anger, others enthusiasm. Recognise that emotional situations, however uncomfortable, provide opportunities for self-knowledge and inner growth. Knowing yourself and identifying your emotional needs enables you to make better choices in future.

This chapter prepares you for difficult situations you may face in future. We help you develop strategies to stay balanced and flexible through life's challenges.

Responding to Difficult Situations

Emotional healing doesn't have a finite end, but instead is a continuous process. Therefore, make sure that you:

- ✔ Review your life frequently (see Chapters 7 and 11).

- ✔ Check out what's working – and what's not.

- ✔ Identify potential problems and issues *before* they happen, if possible (see the following section 'Identifying potential challenges').

- ✔ Consider the options available to you.

- ✔ Decide on a plan of action (check out the later section 'Taking action').

- ✔ Work out thoughts, feelings and behaviours that support your goal.

- ✔ Act and trial out your decision.

- ✔ Review your approach and its results continuously.

- ✔ Reward effort as well as success.

The following sections detail several essential aspects of planning and responding to challenges.

Identifying potential challenges

You can't solve something that's ill-defined, and so clearly identifying current and potential future problems is vital. Giving your challenges a shape enables you to take action.

You may be someone who prefers harmony and pretending things are 'fine' even when you know they aren't. But issues continue to lurk somewhere in the subconscious shadows of your mind. Until you face up to them and address them, they're negative clutter. Negative mental clutter – like physical clutter in your home – weighs you down and makes accessing positive emotions difficult. Clutter obscures your vision of a better future and restricts your ability to act.

In order to identify and clearly define the problems you face, ask yourself some specific questions including:

- ✔ **Why is this situation causing me problems?** Spend some time figuring out whether your problems are due to actual events or how you're thinking about them.

✔ **Is the problem mine or someone else's?** Don't worry that you're shifting blame here, you're not. You're legitimately assessing who's responsible for a problem – and by extension who's responsible for solving it.

✔ **What about the situation is real – and what am I imagining?** Gather up all the facts that you currently have, as well as any assumptions you realise that you're making. Examine your facts carefully. Are any of your 'facts' actually assumptions? Furthermore, may any of your assumptions be wrong? Devise ways to test your assumptions. (See Chapter 12.)

✔ **Who else is involved in the problem and what parts are they playing?** Identify other people's issues, concerns and goals. The later section 'Managing emotions – your own and others'' offers useful tips.

Avoid mind-reading. Back up any intuitive hunches you may have about other people with facts. How do you know what these other people are thinking, feeling and planning? See Chapter 12.

✔ **What *don't* I know about the situation?** Identify any information that you must have in order to solve the problem, and devise ways to go about getting it.

✔ **What limiting thoughts may be holding me back from resolving the problem?** If you're nervous or unsure about some aspect of the situation, you may be preventing yourself – consciously or unconsciously – from responding to and dealing with the situation. Pay particular attention to the ways in which your thoughts may be influencing your emotions, your action or your inaction.

✔ **What's my emotional pay-off for holding onto the problem?** You may have to be brutally honest with yourself here. Do you get attention from others because you have this problem? Does your problem make you feel 'special' in some way?

When you know your emotional pay-off, go a step further and question whether this pay-off is helpful to you emotionally in the long-term. Can you think of a more constructive way of feeling good about yourself?

✔ **What do I need to do to solve this problem?** What different perspectives can you gain? Where can you go to seek fresh views? Perhaps going to a retreat or getting some distance can help you find new solutions.

✔ **How do I envision successfully resolving my problem?** Figure out how you'll know when you reach your desired destination. Also, how may others know that you've resolved the problem? In what ways will they see you behaving differently? What might they say? Make your goals as specific as possible and record them in your journal, including a realistic time frame.

Dealing with danger

Research shows that being realistic about potential danger can literally be life-saving. Many people freeze at times of crisis. Examples from 9/11, the London bombing of 7/7, the Herald of Free Enterprise tragedy and numerous plane crashes demonstrate that although most people become paralysed by fear, individuals who take the time to plan (identifying exit routes, rehearsing responses and so on) are able to galvanise themselves into action immediately and survive.

This information can also work as a metaphor for your emotional life. Be open and flexible – and yet prepared.

Taking action

After you've named and described your problem (see the preceding section), you need to determine how you're going to respond to it – and then do so!

When you feel overwhelmed by the problems in your life, remind yourself that you solve problems every day, such as moving house, finding a mortgage or managing a difficult relationship. Use these everyday problem-solving situations to help identify strategies that work well for you.

The following steps walk you through the process of taking action when confronted with a difficult situation. Give yourself time for the activity, or you may become overloaded. Check where you are on the performance stress curve (see Chapter 2) and take breaks as necessary to keep yourself enthusiastic and motivated about change.

1. **Define your problem and your goal clearly, in positive and solution-focused language.**

   Describe the situation as if you've already achieved the goal. For example, rather than saying 'I want to manage retirement', say 'I'm enjoying my retirement'. Instead of 'I need to address my teenager's inconsiderate behaviour', use 'I'm developing ways to help my teenager be more considerate'.

2. **Identify different ways you can achieve your goal.**

   You have many paths available to reach a single goal. Generate numerous options – as many as you can think of.

Past, present, future

Keep life in perspective in terms of what has happened to you, what's currently happening to you and what may happen to you.

Stop talking about past problems, and start talking about positive outcomes. You may gain comfort from discussing difficulties you experienced with others, but repeatedly revisiting the past can hold you back and keep you from taking action.

Pay attention to your language. The words you use give away your real intention. Saying things like 'I'm never lucky', 'I always seem to draw the short straw' or 'my relationships have never worked in the past' sets you up for more of the same. Continuing to discuss the impact of an old problem on you doesn't signify that you're resolving the situation. Talking about the actions you're taking to resolve the issue gives a strong message to yourself and others that you're focusing on change.

3. **Consider the consequences of each option.**

   As you look over your options, ask yourself which you would choose if you had no fear of failure. Future choices may be opportunities that you've never even considered before. Think outside the box of limitation and doubt.

   Identify factors that may help you and factors that may hinder you. Plan to overcome those factors that may block your progress.

4. **Choose one option.**

   Even though you choose just one solution, remember that the other solutions are always available to you if this one doesn't work.

5. **Set out actions and behaviours to achieve your goal.**

   Create a realistic time line for your actions. Ask for support from other people if necessary.

6. **Plan your desired personal state.**

   What emotions are going to help you manage and respond to this situation? What thoughts will help you to generate that emotion?

   For example, if you want to feel confident, tell yourself, 'I can feel confident and manage this situation'. Identify how you feel physically and what body language occurs when you feel confident. Practise these physical traits – and add a smile.

After you know the emotions you need to have in place, do everything you can to boost or create them. The Emotional Healing Toolkit on the Cheat Sheet offers lots of options.

7. **Execute your plan, acknowledging your setbacks and praising your successes.**

   Things may not go exactly according to plan, but give yourself credit for trying. If you manage your inner emotional state even when an event doesn't go as you want, you still have a success to celebrate.

   At each step along the path, review what worked and consider what you'll do differently next time.

Managing emotions – your own and others'

Emotions are infectious. Your own feelings impact any actions you take, and other people's emotions can trigger emotional disturbances. If someone enters a meeting angry or fearful, other people pick up on this vibe, consciously or unconsciously, and often react in a variety of emotionally charged ways. Plan in advance how you want to manage emotional situations that involve others.

Before addressing an issue with someone, plan how to manage the situation from an emotional perspective.

Start with a positive goal and then consider your desired emotional state, thoughts that can help you stay focused, the location and timing for the discussion, and any other behaviours or strategies you can employ for a successful outcome. Here's an example of the steps you may follow:

1. **Positive goal:** Help mother understand that she has dementia.

2. **Desired emotional state:** Calm, empathetic and compassionate.

3. **Thoughts that help me stay calm and focused:** My intention is to help my mother as best I can.

4. **Environment and timing (where and when):** She feels brightest in the morning. I'll go to her house so she feels safe.

5. **Behaviours and strategies:** Patience. Be ready to repeat myself several times. Listening. Loving.

Managing your own emotions as well as those of others can be challenging, but the following strategies can help you improve the outcome when confronting difficult situations:

✔ **Know the person you're dealing with.** Choose a setting and style of communication that makes the other person feel as comfortable as possible.

Some people respond better to the written word. Don't be afraid to try different methods of communicating in order to express your needs or create understanding.

✔ **Visualise the meeting going well.** Identify specifically what you would like to achieve from a situation and see yourself realising it in your mind's eye. Imagine wrapping up your difficult or negative emotions in an imaginary parcel and leaving them outside the door prior to the meeting. See Chapter 13 for more on visualisation.

✔ **Stay focused on your outcome.** Stick to the point. Don't bring up old issues. Make 'I' statements rather than blaming 'you' statements.

✔ **Identify unconstructive patterns in your own behaviour and focus on new ways of communicating.** Don't get hooked into old patterns. If you do, notice that you're doing it, take a pause and shift your approach.

✔ **Protect yourself with an invisible shield so that sharp words don't pierce you.** Don't rise to the bait of old arguments; rise above them. See Chapter 14 for more details.

✔ **Develop a positive and co-operative internal dialogue that encourages you and helps you to stay calm.** For example, 'I have a right to say what I think' or 'I can remain calm despite emotional pressure.' Give yourself loving friendship. Pace yourself. Take time out if you need to. (See Chapter 13 for a loving-kindness exercise.)

✔ **Repeat yourself when necessary to ensure that the other person hears you.** Ask the other person to paraphrase what you're saying if you're not sure that she has been listening.

✔ **Have positive expectations that the other person has the potential to solve the problem and be co-operative.** Always focus on the positive.

✔ **Conclude the conversation by summarising what you agree about and what you agree to disagree about.** Be realistic that you're simply different and can't always see eye to eye on everything.

Dealing with fear

Fear of failure can be paralysing. Some people postpone action until they reach a 'perfect and right' moment. But perfect is subjective and waiting can lead to procrastination. Even though you plan and prepare to confront a difficult situation, fear keeps you from executing your plan or going through with a particularly difficult aspect or step in the plan.

Pinning happiness on a specific series of events indicates that you're not willing to take action to enjoy the present moment. This reluctance may be due to fear of a real or imagined consequence. See Chapters 10 and 12 for more on confronting fears.

Eye of the tiger

Bill had been married for 18 years to Maxine, a forceful career lady who earned more than he did and tended to be directive and bullying. As she gained power in her work she started to criticise him and put him down. Her constant contempt caused him to lose confidence and, after trying to resolve the relationship, he decided he wanted a divorce.

Recognising that he needed support to prepare for this meeting, Bill went for coaching to help develop a plan. He identified thoughts that would help him speak up, such as: 'I have just as much right as she has to express myself and

my needs.' He visualised his fearful emotions left in his study so that he was able to focus on being calm and rational during the discussion. Bill had become physically weakened while living with his wife and so he visualised himself as a tiger. He prepared for the meeting by imagining his body taking on a tiger's strength and flexibility.

During the meeting, Maxine became abusive, but Bill managed to keep his emotions calm and concentrate on explaining that he wanted a divorce, repeating himself until Maxine finally got his message.

Tackle fear by becoming aware of your internal conversations. Most people have a range of conflicting thoughts. Here are some of the inner voices that people tend to hear when facing emotionally challenging situations:

- ✔ **The Doubter:** 'It will go wrong anyway.'
- ✔ **The Critic:** 'You screwed up again!'
- ✔ **The Fearful One:** 'It's just too frightening to have that conversation.'
- ✔ **The Victim:** 'I always end up worse off.'
- ✔ **The Couch Potato:** 'I can't be bothered.'
- ✔ **The Parent:** 'Do as I told you to.'

Do you recognise any of these voices? Hearing one, two or all these voices is quite okay because they're all you! Fortunately, they're not some marauding army who want to take over your mind; they're simply your own thoughts. Choose carefully which thoughts you pay attention to, because doing so changes your emotions and ultimately the end result.

Because *you* are in charge of your own mind, you can also develop an inner voice – the Coach – who encourages you to take action to develop your potential. Like a sports coach, the Coach helps you develop the ability to strengthen your mental and emotional muscle so as to manage situations better.

Taking One Step at a Time

Everything that happens to you gives you scope to develop. When a client was recently presented with a difficult situation at work, she ruefully told us, 'Not *another* learning opportunity!'. Her ability to view life and its challenges as opportunities to grow helped her to maintain her sense of humour as she worked through her problems.

The problem is that some emotions are so uncomfortable that you just want to get out of that feeling as quickly as possible and move on. However, if you move on too quickly, you lose the chance to stop, review and analyse what happened and what you'll do differently. The fast pace of life today can even prevent you from stopping to celebrate when things go well. Hence you may miss the chance to identify the things that you did that brought you happiness and success.

As you become the observer of yourself, you naturally start to make analysis and growth a part of everyday life. This approach makes life more interesting as you become mindful and conscious of how you're feeling and responding, instead of running on automatic.

The following sections provide insights for making the most of each opportunity that comes your way.

Reviewing what heals and what doesn't

People differ as to what they find healing. One person swears by psychotherapy, another says that the loving support of a partner is what helps, and still another believes that physical massage frees emotional pain from the body.

Attitudes to healing change. For example, not that long ago, the bodies of stillborn or miscarried children were just placed in hospital incinerators. Now health professionals understand that allowing parents to hold rituals or funerals for their lost children helps them to move on.

Work out what works for you. Ask if any other options exist whenever you're feeling uncomfortable and potentially unable to heal. Actively seek out people and situations that help you feel good.

Write down what helps you to heal and feel better, such as going for long walks by the sea or sitting in a favourite chair with soft music playing. Additionally, make a list of the things that don't help you to heal and even make you feel worse, such as feeling you have to be sociable with certain family members or being alone on a Saturday evening. Take a look around your home and see where you feel peaceful and also identify old possessions that drain your emotional energy. This is your chance to de-clutter, recycle or throw away those items that hold negative memories and associations.

Rehearsing to overcome obstacles

In Chapter 15 we talk about taking time to write a description or sketch out a picture of your ideal life – your vision for your future. In addition to devising a path that can take you towards your goal, you also need to identify events and people who may interrupt your progress, such as divorce, a difficult conversation, taking exams, caring for an ill family member, asking for promotion at work, or adjusting to the next stage of your life, such as retirement or children moving away from home.

Plan *now* how you're going to manage these obstacles by rehearsing ways to overcome difficulties and manage your feelings. You can use rehearsal in various ways, including:

- ✔ **Mental rehearsal:** Neuro-scientists have now demonstrated that you can trick your brain into believing that the situation you imagine is actually happening. So if you visualise positive events, your brain releases good chemicals that relax, energise your body and support your immune system.

- ✔ **Verbal rehearsal:** Without practice, difficult conversations can trip you up. You may be saying things and using words for the first time. Rehearsing helps you gain confidence and also become aware of the emotional impact of your words.

- ✔ **Role-play rehearsal:** Involve another person to help you prepare for a conversation in advance. Encourage the other person to challenge what you're saying so you can then practise how you respond and possibly try different scenarios. The other person can also give you feedback as to whether your strategy is effective.

- ✔ **Emotional state rehearsal:** Choose the emotional state you want to be in for the situation you face and practise feeling that emotion. As you register a challenging event in your diary, decide in advance what emotional response best helps you to manage the situation.

All emotions are stored in your memory bank so you can recall them. Imagine a video store in your head where you can take feelings of calm, authority or assertiveness off the shelf and experience them again. Use the techniques of recall, anchoring and trigger words in Chapters 3, 12 and 13.

Facing a challenge – together

Paul and Ingrid were expecting their first baby but were told that the baby had died just 24 hours before she was due. Sadly, Ingrid had to go through labour knowing that their baby was dead.

As a devoted couple, Paul and Ingrid talked about what would help them to manage this sad situation. They decided that they wanted to be alone for the labour but that their parents should be nearby to support them when the baby was born. Then each of them wrote a letter to their unborn daughter, thanking her for the nine months in which she had existed, because they felt she had already become a part of their family life. They also thanked her for bringing them so closely together in love as a couple. The family were present for the funeral and they read the letters out.

Working together

You can plan a future as a couple – as well as prepare for the inevitable bumps in the road.

If you're about to settle down with a new partner, begin living together or get married, take time to visualise some scenarios together or answer some open-ended questions such as:

- What is our vision of a life of love?
- What values do we want to base our relationship on?
- What makes us feel loved?
- How do we manage differences and difficulties?

The responses you and your partner come up with aren't just for special occasions. The more you make them a part of everyday life, the easier you find applying them when you feel you need to manage your life and your feelings.

Visualising success

You may have a vision and plan for your future. You may identify ways to work around any obstacles. But the real challenge is often to just keep going. Being able to see yourself in the future, successfully responding to challenges, will keep you motivated.

Find a quiet place to relax where you'll be undisturbed, and do the following exercise to visualise yourself successfully meeting your goals:

1. **Take 6 breaths, and for each breath count silently to yourself to 4 on the in-breath and 6 on the out-breath.**

   Move your breathing away from your upper chest and into your abdomen, so that when the diaphragm descends with the in-breath, the tummy expands. See Chapter 2 for more on healthy breathing.

2. **Close your eyes and begin to imagine some scenes of your future where you feel content, confident and healed of disturbing emotions.**

   Whether you're in a beautiful place or going about your ordinary life you're feeling happy and in control of your own responses.

3. **Notice the skills and resources you have to help you feel resilient to manage the ups and downs.**

   Notice how this sense of self-determination and enjoyment feels. Take that feeling inside you.

4. **Put yourself in the pictures that you create of a resilient you.**

   Experience the feelings as if they're really happening.

5. **Build up images gradually of yourself in the future.**

   See yourself with your family and friends. See yourself at work, at study and at home. In all these situations, visualise yourself managing situations confidently.

6. **Think of a word that reminds you of this feeling, for example 'happy' or 'fulfilled'.**

   This word can act as a trigger to remind you of these feelings any time.

   Gradually open your eyes, stretch and smile.

Staying out of the rut

Emotions can become habits. Even unpleasant emotions such as depression or anxiety can feel comfortable and normal. Thus, focusing on feeling good can feel strange at first. The old groove is familiar, even when it's no good for you.

Become vigilant so that you don't fall back into old ways. Your old patterns of behaviour can creep up on you unawares. Notice the signals – such as a fear response with butterflies, anger with tension in your neck, helplessness with fatigue or withdrawal from friends – that draw you backwards. Negative emotional habits can be like a magnet to conflict, pain and complication.

Identify the pay-off that old behaviours give you and find a more constructive pay-off to associate with change. Be prepared to ask and answer some difficult questions. For example:

- ✔ You may intend not to be a victim, but suddenly find yourself feeling like one. Being a martyr makes you feel special and worthy, turning the other person into the persecutor. Ask yourself: how can I feel special without being a martyr?

- ✔ You want to move away from rescuing other people, but can't resist helping when a friend is in need. This behaviour makes you feel needed, but in fact your behaviour requires the other person to remain needy in order for you to feel okay. Ask yourself: how else can I feel needed and yet know when to let others help themselves?

- ✔ You want to get better from a physical illness, but realise that your symptoms give you attention and absolve you from certain activities. Ask yourself: how else can I get attention and feel safe?

- ✔ You intend to allow others to solve their own problems, but find yourself hooked into your colleague's messy affair. Trying to help her solve her problems makes you feel rather superior. Ask yourself: which of my own problems need solving?

Acknowledging, releasing and growing again

You gain power through acceptance. Admitting 'Yes, I am angry' or 'Actually I *am* feeling totally fed up at the moment' gives you the integrity of honesty. Denying the existence of difficulty or a problematic emotion just doesn't work. You may pretend that you're sorted, but your mind still churns the problem over in your unconscious. Over time, this inner struggle can impact your blood pressure and immune system (see Chapter 2).

Making decisions and taking action to address an issue creates space in your mind and frees you up for your new endeavour – it's energising. Procrastination, by contrast, simply holds you stuck and frozen. Be willing to make things happen, make some mistakes and grow emotionally.

Acknowledge that life is challenging and that you've experienced some pain. Accept what you can't change. Be ready for what you can. Come to understand the nature of your emotions. For instance:

- ✔ **Anxiety** signifies that you're imagining something in the future, making some kind of negative assumption that things are going to go wrong. Yet your fearful negative assumption may never happen, and so your speculation spoils the day. If you experience fear, step back, calm yourself and check whether the fear is justified. Stay in the present moment, breathing quietly and think through what's actually happening rather than what may happen so that you can then take appropriate action based on facts.

- ✔ **Anger** signifies that you feel threatened and need to re-establish your sense of safety. Express anger appropriately in words. If you're angry, find ways to support yourself and recognise that you're probably not in a good emotional state to make a major decision. Feel safe that you can speak up assertively and manage yourself, even if you can't change the external events that you experience.

You're going to feel difficult emotions in the future, but you can view them differently – not as an invading, alien force but as something rich and deep that allows you to continue growing.

Let go of the past and see yourself going forward in greater strength as a result of having been through these events. No one gets everything right or perfect, and so value the knowledge you gain along the way.

How can you be pleased with what you've experienced, particularly if a lot of painful emotions are involved? Try any or all the following exercises:

- ✔ **Appreciate those who've been your teachers.** The people around you – parents, children, partners, ex-partners, bosses or strangers – may have been difficult, but interacting with them led to you developing skills and having experiences that you may not otherwise have had.

- ✔ **Keep a gratitude diary.** At the end of each day remind yourself of all those things for which you can feel grateful. Instead of continuously chasing new and shiny things, be happy with what you've got. Build the future on today's joys.

- ✔ **Love yourself.** You've survived so far and there's every reason for you to be able to create an enjoyable life in future.

Chapter 17

Inspiring Healing in Others

· ·

In This Chapter

▶ Understanding emotional energy

▶ Resisting group-think

▶ Enabling others to heal in their own ways

▶ Shifting stuck emotional patterns

· ·

The way you're feeling immediately influences other people around you. You have to take responsibility for how you make others feel and also be attentive to the ways in which you can absorb their emotions, for better and for worse.

Becoming more aware of your impact on others enables you to support friends, family and colleagues who may be going through hard times. Being mindful can also help you to avoid becoming a rescuer or caretaker, and instead become someone who encourages other people to develop skills to take care of their own life, health and wellbeing.

In this chapter we examine the emotional dynamics of healing that occur between two (or more) people. We believe everyone has the capacity to help others to heal by developing the necessary emotional energy and intention. In generating healing energy for others, you can also become more aware of how you can apply the same strategies to heal yourself.

Understanding that Emotions Are Infectious

Allowing the mood of those around you to influence you is all too easy. If you spend time with a negative colleague, you may have to work very hard to keep your own spirits up. A focus on negative emotion can drain the energy from a whole group of people.

Human nature draws people to bad news or difficulty like metal to a magnet. In the same way that people slow down on the motorway to look at an accident, you can get drawn towards a person who's going through a divorce, being made redundant, or feeling just plain miserable and pessimistic. This pattern, particularly if you're not aware of it, can become your default way of communicating and result (quite literally) in forgetting how to access good feelings.

Of course, you can use your own emotions to good effect. You need to find a balance between empathising with someone else's problems and getting sucked into them. You can maintain a sense of control over your personal emotional state so that you can help other people find their own way to manage a situation. By sharing loving friendship, compassion and optimism you can inspire positive emotions that remind others of the good feelings that strengthen coping abilities.

Feeling as a group

Sociologists and business consultants talk about *group-think* in which a collection of people seem to lose their ability to reason individually and end up following one another as a pack. In its extreme version, the pack response is known as *group* or *mass hysteria*.

The group-think experience can more accurately be called *group-feel*, because the underlying emotional feelings are what really drive the behaviours. Individuals in the group may feel that something is wrong but they aren't strong enough to stand up for what they believe in.

People feel and act in a pack for a variety of reasons, including:

- ✔ They want to belong to the group.
- ✔ They seek the approval of others.
- ✔ They fear the risk of saying, doing or feeling something different.
- ✔ They fear failing alone.
- ✔ They fear responsibility; being invisible means that they merge into the group and have limited individual responsibility.
- ✔ They don't want to be different or stand out.
- ✔ They are overwhelmed by the emotions of fight, flight or freeze (which we describe in Chapter 2) and lose the capacity for rational thought.
- ✔ They come under the influence of an authority figure, who overrides their individual thought and reduces their confidence, even when this person's beliefs are incorrect or inappropriate.
- ✔ They are overwhelmed by the pressure to meet a specific goal, which compromises their common sense; in these instances, people often focus on a narrow result and ignore the rest.

Certain personalities inspire pack responses. In the 1960s, teenage girls were 'taken over' by emotion and screamed at their pop heroes. You can see similar group emotion at present-day football matches. Some commentators described the response to the death of Princess Diana as a type of pack response, although many people were genuinely moved by the tragic loss of a beautiful young mother. Throughout history, many dictatorships have used fear to control the behaviour of large groups of people.

Likewise, certain events stimulate group behaviours. People get emotionally aroused, losing the ability to think rationally as individuals. A fundamentalist mindset may underlie these experiences, such as with present-day examples of terrorist groups. The power of suggestion and uncertainty can also lead to group behaviour, as happened with Orson Welles' 1938 radio broadcast of the fictional play *War of the Worlds*; panic spread through the United States as people became convinced that Martians had invaded.

Emotion can even inspire illness; some people genuinely feel the symptoms described by another person, even though they don't have the same ailment.

Breaking with the pack

Group emotions are powerful influencers of behaviour; try the following actions to take care of yourself:

- ✔ Stepping back, observing and analysing what you yourself think about the situation. Ask yourself, 'What do I feel?' and 'What is right for me?'.

- ✔ Standing up for your own beliefs, with the understanding that you may be right and you may be wrong.

- ✔ Accepting that others may criticise you and disapprove of your stance.

You can also encourage others to take individual responsibility and break from the pack by:

- ✔ Making others aware that group emotions can lead a pack thoughtlessly in the wrong direction or (more often) paralyse individual thought. See the preceding section for details.

- ✔ Helping others step back and consider the situation for themselves. For example, suggest they stop, breathe quietly and gather their thoughts before acting.

- ✔ Encouraging others to determine the right action for themselves. For example, young men in a gang may blindly follow their leader for fear of looking stupid. Suggest that they stop to ask themselves whether this behaviour is worth spending the rest of their lives in prison.

✔ Being prepared to act with authority to lead others to safety when people are in real danger. For example, many people freeze with fear in catastrophic events, such as plane crashes or road accidents; you may need to direct them to take action.

You're most likely to be influenced by your *peer group,* your closest friends or contacts at home, school or work, who share similar interests and life situation as yourself. Belonging is a human need, but you can end up limiting yourself when you put belonging above your own need to develop your unique potential. You can help others understand this dynamic and release themselves from the chains of conforming to group pressure.

Taking responsibility for your emotional message

When you're in a group setting, or talking one to one, work on becoming aware of the emotional message that you're sending out. Words represent only a minority of the meaning of your communication. You may say one thing, but the other person may pick up your underlying emotional message. For example, if you're trying to support a friend with terminal cancer and say, 'I'm sure you'll be better soon' and yet feel emotionally that he won't recover, you may just confuse and even frustrate him.

Identify situations where other people are in difficulty. Consider how your own emotions may make them feel. Your feelings and *emotional energy* emanate from your thoughts and expectations. To understand what exactly you're putting out there, turn your attention to your internal dialogue:

✔ If you're trying to be supportive but your thoughts are 'Why doesn't he just pull himself together?', you probably aren't helping much!

✔ If you're endeavouring to smooth over a problem while angrily thinking 'How could he be so inconsiderate of my feelings?', these negative emotions are very likely to bubble up in some way.

Try to align thoughts and feelings to give a coherent and consistent message. For example:

✔ Instead you may think, 'Whilst I'd prefer him to pull himself together, I can accept that he finds this difficult. I can find a way to support him anyway.'

✔ You can think, 'Even though I'm angry that he was inconsiderate in this situation, this one event doesn't make him an inconsiderate person. I can focus on times when he was kind and considerate to me.'

Denying or blocking emotions may interrupt honest communication between you and another person. Certainly, being 'the strong one' and supporting someone for a period of time can be appropriate, and a stiff upper lip can get people through emergencies. But being strong can seem cold when someone you love is in pain or grief, and people ultimately need to experience feelings of sadness, loss, grief and uncertainty.

Julian's mother had a massive stroke. He and his brother went to the hospital together and as she lay on a stretcher, Julian held her hand and told her he loved her. His brother immediately remonstrated with him and said, 'Don't say that; it'll make her think she's about to die.' Julian reflected on this advice and decided that his brother could behave however he wanted. But Julian felt that telling his mother he loved her was important, because he wanted to share this emotional message regardless of her prognosis. So he continued doing so.

Helping Others to Heal

You don't have to be trained in order to help others to heal. Everyone has the potential to comfort people through touch, words and actions. So believe in the goodness and nurture you bring to your friends, family and colleagues and be proactive with ideas about how you may be able to support them. As Dante wrote, 'He who sees a need and waits to be asked for help is as unkind as if he had refused it.'

You can help others by sharing:

- ✔ **Affirmations:** Empowering others to believe in themselves by acknowledging their own strengths and resources to resolve the situation.

- ✔ **Compassionate attention:** Exchanging feelings empathetically.

- ✔ **Kind words:** Enquiring about other people's needs and wellbeing.

- ✔ **Laughter and levity:** Helping others rise above problems and experience some joy again, lightening up conversations.

- ✔ **Loving kindness and friendship:** Being there with love and support.

- ✔ **Touch:** Comforting people with kisses, hugs, gentle touch and massage, when appropriate.

- ✔ **Positive thoughts:** Sending healing thoughts, even from a distance. Even though scientists haven't proven telepathy, individual accounts indicate that people can sometimes pick up these good messages.

- ✔ **Practical help:** Offering to babysit, clean, shop or drive. Each of these gestures is an offer of care and love.

✔ **Problem-solving:** Helping others solve problems, see new perspectives or find ways forward.

✔ **Visualisation:** Helping others paint a picture of happiness and fulfilment in their future.

Know when to stop. You can get caught into another person's dramas or difficulties as if they are your own. You may end up trying to solve their problem or alleviate their feelings – and you may be able to do neither. In fact, you may even disempower them by taking on too much yourself. Your good intentions can backfire and they can feel controlled. Watch out for this tendency in yourself; it can come from a need to be needed.

Treat other people as if they're the ones with the best solutions for themselves. Don't take over. If you're interacting with very vulnerable people, physically or emotionally, gradually help them to own their recovery and encourage them to take the reins of their life again.

Also, be watchful for misguided loyalty on your part. Sometimes you can put yourself out for another person who doesn't value your support. You may even do so for someone who has, in the past, been abusive towards you. Be honest with yourself; the person may not deserve your support.

Whilst you can help and offer support, people heal at their own paces and in their own ways. They may not accept what you offer. If they don't take your advice, you may feel like you've failed. Instead, accept that you don't have all the answers and that the ultimate decisions are theirs. You don't need to take the situation personally. Support them in their choices with generosity.

Making time to listen

The feeling of being truly heard and understood is powerful. Life moves at a fast pace and people's ability to concentrate for any period of time has been eroded by interruptions such as email, mobile phones and a general expectation that you should be available 24 hours a day.

This tendency has resulted in a low boredom threshold and people being physically in one place but mentally in another. You may even answer your mobile phone or respond to emails while supposedly listening to a friend or colleague talk to you. (Of course the other person can always hear and see when you're not really listening!)

If someone you know needs support and healing, do take real time to stop and be with them. You want the very best for that person, and so give them the very best listening you can. See Chapter 13 for tips on being present.

Listening is a five-sensory experience of being present. Be all there, not half-in half-out of the situation. In order to truly listen, notice:

- ✔ Who you are with
- ✔ What expressions you're seeing
- ✔ Where you are
- ✔ What you're hearing
- ✔ What you're feeling and sensing about what you're hearing, which tells you about the other person's real issues and emotions

Don't allow your mind to wander off elsewhere or jump to conclusions. And don't feel that you have to solve problems. Don't finish sentences, interrupt or feel you have to say anything unless something pops into your head that you feel is truly worth sharing.

If you do share, make sure that you do so for the other person's sake, not just to make yourself feel better or smarter. If you feel that your idea or solution is genuinely helpful, share it. Otherwise just listening can be enough to help others gain greater understanding of their own feelings and needs. In discovering how to listen in this way, you become aware of other people and what they're really saying and needing.

Giving love and empathy

Love is an essential human need. Without it you shrivel and wither away, becoming less than the person you can be. When you give love, you enable other people to blossom and feel that they have permission to behave honestly, even if at that particular moment being themselves means sharing their misery, depression or pain.

We're not talking here specifically of romantic love, although romantic love is healing when given and shared in a mutually loving way. Love can take many other forms, and a good number of these ways can heal other people.

Loving attentiveness between two people crosses boundaries of gender, age, hierarchy, culture or race. Love takes away the judgement and accepts others as they are, with all their quirks, fallibility and vulnerability. They don't get everything right – but then neither do you. And love doesn't mean that you sugar-coat things. For example, you can be helpful and analyse a friend's specific behaviour while being loving and accepting of him as a person. ('You're a great guy, but being so rude and angry with your boss may do you no favours!')

Andrew's brother Vince committed suicide when they were both in their early 20s. Andrew was devastated but didn't know how to express his feelings because his parents were so consumed in their own grief. Even though Vince was in his own world of depression before he chose to end his life, Andrew kept asking himself what he could have done differently to save his brother.

At the time of the funeral, Andrew had recently moved to a new area to start his first job on leaving university. He felt miles from anyone loving and became depressed. After nearly a year of trying to cope, Andrew took the decision that he needed to move back to be with his friends. He chucked in his job and found a flat back with his old group, who loved and accepted him as he was, understanding his grief and supporting him through it. Andrew felt comforted and better able to re-build his life.

Empathy is not the same as sympathy. *Empathy* is understanding another person's pain but keeping your separate objectivity so that you're able to help him. *Sympathy* is feeling the other person's pain so deeply that you can get swamped by the problem and can't see a way out. Sympathy is less helpful.

Changing Emotional Patterns in Relationships

All human relationships develop certain patterns that can become habitual. For example, if a friend has been through a hard time, you may take on a caring role, for a period of time, to support your pal through this situation. However, at some stage you need to become aware of this pattern and take steps to let go and allow that person to take charge of his own life again.

Whatever the relationship, pay attention to patterns in the following areas:

- ✔ What you talk about
- ✔ Who has more power
- ✔ Who has most of the 'answers'
- ✔ Who talks more
- ✔ How you feel with – and about – the other person

When you observe a pattern, consider whether it's helping the other person to heal from emotional pain or physical sickness. You may have heard of the concept of *tough love,* in which you hold back from helping or even refuse a request for help in order to assist others in discovering how to manage situations themselves. Sometimes people need to be encouraged to do more than they feel able to do, so as not to set up a pattern of dependency on another person.

Tim was in the Army and returned from Iraq disabled. His fiancée was sup-portive and looked after him while he had several operations and skin grafts. He was in a great deal of pain, but as he recovered she had to steel herself not to do everything for him because otherwise his muscles would continue to waste away. Although it hurt him to move around, they agreed that he would do some cooking and housework in order to regain a sense of independence and the ability to look after himself.

Become aware of the fact that you can hold people in their emotional pain by continuing to respond in habitual ways. A time does exist for talking about a problem or trauma, but the time also comes when you need to help the person move on.

Recognising (and not reopening) old wounds

People's pasts don't have to define their futures: however difficult or trau-matic your experiences, you're able to move on. You don't always have to keep raising old issues and rehashing old problems.

When supporting people with old emotional wounds, discover how to see them as healed, not as people who are still in pain. Believe in their ability to recover and make life good again. Although support groups can help in the immediate aftermath of an event, evidence suggests that continuing to belong to a support group for months or years gives people labels – abused child, single parent, accident victim and so on. A sense of support and belonging helps in the short term, but a long-term label simply holds the person in that stuck position.

Dennis's 25-year-old daughter had been badly disabled in a car accident and later died. During this traumatic time, he confided that one of the things he found hardest was that his friends felt that they should continually refer to the accident and her death. He felt that he was now labelled 'the man who had this awful event happen to him' instead of being allowed to move into another stage of his life. He knew the memory would never disappear, but he wanted to have ordinary conversations with people again, not discussions about sad-ness and grief.

Be sensitive and empathetic for a period of time and then allow people the ability to be seen in whatever new and positive light they choose for themselves.

Similar problems, tough problem-solving

If you share a similar but unrelated difficulty with a friend, such as both caring for dying parents or both having unruly teenagers, your ability to sympathise with each other too much when discussing your problems can hold you both back.

Mandy and Kate were old friends. Mandy's daughter was staying out late and indulging in binge-drinking. Every time they met, Mandy brought up the subject and Kate ended up giving advice. Nothing changed and Kate realised that

ultimately she wasn't helping because Mandy was leaning on her and not resolving the problem with her daughter. Eventually Kate suggested Mandy see a child guidance specialist, along with her husband. Mandy was advised to apply principles of tough love with her daughter, which included setting clear rules for behaviour and sanctions. Mandy found administering tough love very difficult but came to see that she had to in order to help her daughter face up to the consequences of her own action.

Helping others move on

Some people do need a nudge to help them move on to new ground. Knowing when to offer help or advice is always difficult, as is judging when to hold back and let people recognise for themselves that they're stuck in old patterns.

We can't offer a perfect answer here, but you may well benefit from letting go of your 'need' to help others move on. Allow for the fact that your innate wisdom and intuition are going to speak up if and when the moment is right.

Paolo had experienced a harrowing childhood. His mother committed suicide, his father died young and his brother was taken into a mental hospital. So, aged 22, he found himself truly alone in the world. He leapt into a relationship and an early marriage, blocking out his feelings for some 20 years. Although people suggested he may benefit from counselling, he was deaf to the idea.

When his marriage broke down, he met another woman and, when their relationship hit difficulty, she said that she thought it would be helpful for him personally and for them as a couple to have therapy. By this time Paolo was ready to hear the suggestion of counselling because she offered it with genuine care and in his best interests. Going to therapy changed his life for the better.

From a more objective standpoint as a friend or colleague, you may be able to observe negative patterns or sense when a relationship is bad for a person. People can easily break up one relationship only to recreate an almost identical one with a new person.

Telling people about the patterns you observe may not be helpful, but you can ask some useful, non-judging questions that may enable them to stop and reflect on what's happening. For example:

- ✔ In what way is this relationship similar or different to your previous one?
- ✔ How do you know whether this relationship is heading into the same territory as your previous one?
- ✔ I can see that you love this person. Do you feel that the relationship is good for you in the long term?
- ✔ What would it take for you to feel healed of your past pain?

A person has to be ready to hear a suggestion or see a new opportunity for happiness and health. You may well notice that some of your friends or family moan about a relationship, a marriage, a job or a home and yet take no major steps to alter the situation. This lack of action signifies that the pain hasn't yet become bad enough to make a move.

Enable others to see what they're doing and that their actions – or inactions – are contradicting their words. You can help by using the following strategies:

- ✔ Explain that you're not helping them by listening to their problems and wish to hear about solutions for change.
- ✔ Point out that if they are, in fact, accepting the current situation, what's the point in complaining about it. They may as well just get on with things and find a way to be happy within the situation.
- ✔ Ask whether they really want to change the situation. If so, help them to visualise a better future. Help them to build feelings and pictures of the next stage of their lives, encouraging them to associate more pleasure with moving forward than with the comfortable but unhelpful pleasure they currently associate with not changing (see Chapter 15 for more on embracing change).
- ✔ Ask them what skills, emotions or resources they require in order to move forward in their lives. Then ask them to imagine that they have these things: what would be the first action they would take?

Wisdom can come from surprising sources. Benita had been struggling to know how to assert her independence within her relationship. Her partner, Simon, was a perfectionist and very controlling. He thought that he knew best how to live life. He criticised her taste in food and clothes. One day Simon was arguing with her about how to cook a recipe when their four-year old daughter piped up saying, 'We're not all the same you know, Daddy.' Benita looked at her daughter in wonder, amazed that she had been able to express the simple words that had failed Benita as an adult. Her daughter's words altered Benita's relationship with Simon for the better; she felt she had been given permission by her daughter to express her own tastes.

ANECDOTE

A dramatic response to negative memories

Judy was 32 and single. She had just started to date a new man when she suddenly developed an auto-immune disease that meant she had to be treated in hospital and became paralysed with fear. Her GP, who knew her well, visited her in hospital, recognised that her illness had a strong emotional aspect and referred her for counselling.

Prior to the onset of her condition, Judy had been asked to marry. She had previously been jilted just before her wedding and now was trapped in intense fear that the same was going to happen again. Through an exploration of her emotional state, Judy realised that her illness was a result of this memory of being jilted. The new relationship literally froze her body into fear at the prospect of being hurt again.

As she understood how her brain had pattern-matched her current situation with her past one, she unlocked her old feelings. This experience was very uncomfortable for her but she was encouraged to accept and go with the emotions that arose. Going through this process, Judy was able to separate her emotional attachment to the pain of the previous situation. She re-framed her new relationship in a different light, associating it with pleasure rather than fear.

Her new partner was very supportive, and gradually Judy recovered full mobility and health. Healing her emotions through counselling moved her on to heal her emotional paralysis.

Chapter 18

Helping Your Child Heal

· ·

In This Chapter

▶ Recognising the effects of loss

▶ Encouraging healing

▶ Exploring and expressing feelings

▶ Developing self-care for you and your child

· ·

*L*ife can be confusing and challenging to children. They have to face many new experiences and they're going to encounter hurt, disappointment, rebuff and rejection: children can be notoriously unkind to one another. Alongside these everyday events your child may face specific, more traumatic losses – a death in the family, divorce, separation, disability or illness.

Whether great or small, each change or loss equates to a mini-death. Your child experiences a sense of loss that may trigger grief, anxiety, insecurity and anger. Such events can ignite negative emotions that may slowly burn inside and affect future happiness. In this situation, your child also loses a *stabilising anchor* – the person, place or situation to which she feels an emotional attachment. Life as your child knew it has changed, and a process of adjustment is inevitable.

Children respond differently depending on their age and development, but your love, understanding and support can be invaluable to the healing process. As with adults, healing occurs when your child comes to terms with the change, acknowledges its significance and allows the negative emotions to slip into the past. The goal is for you as the parent to renew your focus on enjoying the present for your child and look forward to creating happiness in the future.

In this chapter we give you strategies to create an atmosphere of acceptance, love and quality time, which helps your child heal and adjust to change, however great or small the situation.

Creating Time to Accept and Grieve

Creating love and attachment to people, things and places is a natural part of children's development. They're dependent and vulnerable, and reassurance that they're loved and safe is essential to their survival.

When your child's routine is disrupted, her stability may feel undermined for a period of time. This instability can affect various aspects of life including:

- ✔ **Attachments to other people:** Bereavement, parental separation or divorce; moving away from certain family members, losing contact with friends.

- ✔ **Attachments to places:** Moving house, leaving a familiar neighbourhood, changing schools.

- ✔ **Connections to themselves:** Injury, illness, changes to self-image, disfigurement, puberty.

- ✔ **Connections with objects:** Loss of toys, cuddly animals, dolls, digital games, watches, presents.

- ✔ **Trust:** Abuse (physical, emotional and sexual), criticism that seems unfair, adults not following through on what they promise.

Any change or loss can trigger anger, sadness, guilt and hopelessness. Although your child's response is unique, the process of adjustment involves moving in stages through the grief process towards acceptance and healing. We cover the phases of grief in Chapter 10.

Feeling the feelings

The key for you is to help your child acknowledge emotions, regard these feelings as normal and, where possible, talk about the feelings that the situation brings about. Until the age of about five, children's capacity to use words and process information is limited, so adapt your approach depending on the age of your own child.

Because you yourself may also be upset, your child may consciously or unconsciously protect you by hiding her feelings. For example, a young child dying of leukaemia told her mother: 'Don't cry. I'll be fine.' As an adult, you need to find your own help and support with your feelings so that you don't look to your child for sympathy. By doing so, you're able to explain that you're getting help for your own upset feelings and are therefore open to how your child is feeling.

Use the following tips to create an environment in which your child feels safe enough to share what she's experiencing:

✔ **Explore similar stories to the situation through imagination, pictures and metaphors.** Choose books and games that encourage children to identify with the experiences of other children going through similar situations, involving animals or imaginary friends. Identifying with someone other than yourself is an important step for children to be able to see that others have been in their situation and got through it.

✔ **Use play or art as a means of expression, particularly with very young children.** Play together with cuddly toys or puppets. Draw and paint to illustrate what happened and how you're feeling and explore how your child is feeling.

✔ **Just relax.** Playing a game, reading a book or poetry, going to the cinema or sharing time in a favourite sport or hobby are all enjoyable ways to spend time together. Let your child suggest or choose activities that she considers fun. Real intimacy often occurs during an informal time together. When feelings and concerns surface, be ready to talk through them.

Don't push a grieving child to talk. Just be patient and allow a conversation to evolve. Be there and show that you care. The words eventually come.

✔ **Talk about your own emotions in ways that may reflect your child's feelings.** For example, after the death of a pet dog, you can say, 'I wake up every morning imagining I can hear Bella wagging her tail. Do you ever feel like that?' Or if you recently moved house, you can say, 'I sometimes wake up and can't remember where I am, do you?'.

✔ **Involve extended family.** Siblings grandparents, aunts, uncles, trusted teachers and other members of your family may be experiencing grief too, and so encourage them to express loving support. Children often talk to grandparents in more intimate ways than to their own parents, a dynamic that can provide love and security as well as a continuity of routine.

✔ **Communicate feelings non-verbally.** Even a brief touch with a look of love and compassion tells children they're loved and understood. With young children, touch, stroking and massage reconnect with memories of being held and loved.

Be sensitive to children's response to any of the preceding activities. If they're feeling angry or guilty, they may brush adults off. Accept this phase for a time. Allow them space and don't pressurise them into feeling they must respond in order to satisfy your own needs. However, denial and suppression can lead to the emotions surfacing in unhealthy ways later in life in the form of drugs abuse, self-harm or depression. Encourage sharing as far as is possible.

ANECDOTE

Mind your words

John was ten when his mother died. He was away at an all-boys boarding school and although he came home for the funeral, he didn't cry, and his father was too distraught to be available and open to John's feelings or even to share the experience of his own grief. He soon returned to school, carrying on as usual.

On the first anniversary of his mother's death, John felt angry, tearful and sad. His housemistress told him that he 'should be over it by now', which left him feeling even more isolated and misunderstood.

He became aggressive at school, and his academic performance fell. At 14, he started to smoke cannabis and in his early 20s developed severe depression. In therapy he was able to bring back and release old memories of abandonment and loss. He eventually made a complete recovery, but his life journey may have been less difficult had a few people compassionately expressed feelings and asked about his own more than a decade earlier.

Knowing what's normal

Children who are grieving may at first experience complex and difficult feelings. These emotions often result in withdrawal, apathy, sadness, helplessness, guilt and anger. Become knowledgeable about normal grief behaviours (reading Chapter 10 is a good start) so that you can gently observe your child's progress. You can also turn to *Raising Happy Children For Dummies* by Sue Atkins, which provides information on the stages of a child's development.

REMEMBER

Both adults and children change when under stress, so pay attention to your mood. Being more impatient, irritable or vulnerable than usual has an effect on your child. We're not recommending that you become a Pollyanna here! Be natural, and yet conscious of your behaviour. Acknowledge your own emotions, too.

Here are some common behavioural changes that children may go through while grieving losses:

✔ **Children may become very anxious about their own safety and security – or the safety and security of loved ones.** Children may cling to you for a period of time because you represent security. They may not be able to express anxiety in words until after the age of five, but they still may not want you out of their sight. This behaviour is normal for a short time, so give as much comfort and reassurance as you can.

✔ **Children may not want to do things on their own for a period of time.** They may not play alone or they may want to sleep in your bed or sit close to you in order to feel secure. Again, this behaviour is normal, but as they regain trust in you and in life, they'll be able to tolerate separation from you without distress. Clinging behaviour is normal until a sense of security returns. Building security is a child-led process that depends on your ability as an adult to feel strong in yourself and to know when being firm is appropriate. No set schedule exists. Be sensitive to your own child.

✔ **Children may have difficulty going to school or participating in other activities outside the home.** Be prepared for tears at the school gate. Giving children a sense of security and love enables them to feel secure enough to carry this feeling into school or other places where they need to become independent. You can demonstrate your love by being reliable and clear about what time you'll return, telling them you love them and being available to share experiences of the day when you reconnect. The important message and example is that you're emotionally resilient enough in yourself not to need your child with you.

✔ **Children may revert to earlier stages of development.** They may experience bed-wetting, thumb-sucking, head-banging or talking 'baby' talk. As a parent, you need to balance between accepting and treating your child in age-appropriate ways. Remind yourself that the regression is temporary, and avoid anger. Your child's actions are an appeal for love and security; respond to them with love rather than rejection.

If these behaviours continue, consider raising the subject with your child. For example, 'Sarah, you're talking like a much younger child, and I have difficulty understanding you. How about going back to being the big Sarah again?' Head-banging can damage a child so if this behaviour continues, we advise you to see a child psychologist.

✔ **Children may be unable to sleep alone or may experience nightmares.** Be responsive, not dismissive, of their fears and anxieties. Build up their bedrooms as havens of security and safety. Consider placing a nightlight in the room, adding an intercom that connects to your bedroom or incorporating restful colours and music. A bedtime ritual involving favourite stories can help as well.

✔ **Children's emotions may become extremely physical.** Temper tantrums, screaming and physical anger can represent a release of pent-up and unexpressed emotions that children can't deal with or articulate. Allow these to happen and provide as much safety as possible. Physical expression of emotion can be healthy and your child may naturally reach a state of calm afterwards. Gently hold your child afterwards and, depending on age, encourage your child to put feelings into words.

✔ **Children who experience sudden deaths, accidents and traumas may be dealing with Post-Traumatic Stress Disorder (PTSD).** Like adults, children dealing with PTSD have flashbacks and anxious memories. See Chapter 8 for more on this type of behaviour.

Tricky teens

Adolescence is an awkward time of transition and can exacerbate the emotional response to loss or grief. Teenagers may demonstrate challenging behaviour, including the use of drugs and sexually inappropriate actions. They may refuse to discuss or share their feelings, or their feelings may leak out through rudeness and lack of co-operation with you and their schoolteachers.

Teenagers need to be individuals while also feeling safe enough within their families and other groups. This tension requires you as a parent to maintain firm boundaries while simultaneously creating time to be together and to allow their feelings to be explored naturally. Consider with whom and how your own teenager most easily feels relaxed and open to expressing feelings. This may be you or your partner, but it may also be a grandparent, aunt, best friend, school counsellor or close adult friend. Think about going shopping, going to a football match, playing a digital game, watching a film or pop concert together – any activity that your teen enjoys. Just be sure to build in time to talk and share emotional experience.

Boys and girls may respond differently to loss and grief. Boys may feel they can't be sad, cry or ask for help, and yet research shows that young boys need hugs as much, if not more, than girls do. Girls may be more able to share emotions with their friends but benefit from mature discussion with adults, and so you need to encourage honest conversation where possible.

Be ready and willing to ask for advice and support from a trained therapist if you're concerned about your child or if you personally need support. Find contact details in the Appendix.

Guiding your child along the path

Regardless of a person's age, healing is a process; it doesn't happen overnight. At times your child seems fine, but then regresses or has an emotional outburst. Be patient with your child, and at the same time be compassionate with yourself. This time is difficult for your child and for you as a parent or carer. You may be grieving too. (Chapter 10 has lots more information on grief.)

Help yourself and your child to accept her feelings and stay with the emotions that arise – however uncomfortable they may be. Focus on creating a future where happiness can occur again. (See the later section, 'Looking forward'.)

Pay attention to your child's words, actions and moods. Look for signs of unresolved distress that may not be talked about in words but still require healing, including:

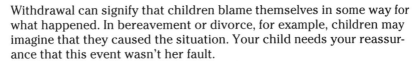

✔ **Alcohol and drug use.** You may notice withdrawal, change of personality, stealing, secretive behaviour or residual smells. Confront your concerns head on because experimentation can lead to long-term addiction and severe behavioural consequences. This is a specialised area where you need to seek help. We list details of professional organisations in the Appendix and you may also like to read *Addiction and Recovery For Dummies* by M. David Lewis, Brian F. Shaw PhD, Paul Ritvo PhD, and Jane Irvine D.Phil.

✔ **Behavioural challenges.** Examples are aggressive behaviour for a child who externalises distress, or withdrawal and loss of energy for a child who internalises distress.

Withdrawal can signify that children blame themselves in some way for what happened. In bereavement or divorce, for example, children may imagine that they caused the situation. Your child needs your reassurance that this event wasn't her fault.

✔ **Signs of increased stress.** Your child may reach the limit of her ability to manage feelings, and experience poor sleep, irritability, tiredness, fatigue, headaches, skin irritation and abdominal pain.

Make time to be with your child during the healing process. Create a loving space to talk about things you may notice. Help your child unearth and express emotional concerns with the following strategies:

✔ **Choose a relaxed place for any talk.** Your child, regardless of age, needs to feel physically comfortable in order to open up. Consider spending time in her bedroom, the garden, the kitchen as you cook a meal together, or the park.

✔ **Start the conversation by discussing a subject your child cares about.** Include a positive remark about something specific you appreciate in your child. For example, 'I love the way you helped me carry the shopping in today; you're so kind. Have you got everything you need for your camping trip next week?'

✔ **Introduce your concern.** Present what you observed that worries you about your child using 'I' language phrasing (see Chapters 8 and 9). For example, 'I've noticed that you stay in your room every evening these days. What are you thinking about?'

✔ **Allow your own feelings to emerge as concern and express your desire to understand what's happening.** You don't know exactly what your child is going through (even though you may think you do). So put your feelings out there and ask questions. For example, you can say something like, 'When you stay in your room, I feel concerned about whether you're okay. I've been feeling quite sad since Dad and I split up . . . how are you feeling about it all?'

✔ **Listen and – whatever the situation – be prepared for your child to direct some blame towards you personally.** Your child may need to project her feelings and may also have her own view of your part in events.

Try to not take these comments personally, even through they may be directed at you and about your behaviour. Prepare yourself by being present for your child. Breathe into your stomach and collect yourself so that you pay full attention and respond in ways that are loving rather than aggressive or defensive (see Chapter 8).

✔ **Allow her feelings to emerge in the knowledge that you're open and empathetic to what has happened.** Openness and empathy allow trust to evolve again, so let your child have her say and emphasise that you're in this together.

✔ **Reaffirm that you're with your child on every step of the journey.** Remind your child that you're available to answer questions and offer support wherever you can. Encourage your child to share whatever's on her mind – no subject is taboo!

If you sense that your child is still holding in information about potentially damaging behaviours, such as drinking, gangs or drugs, you must be open about your concerns. If necessary involve professional help, which we list in the Appendix.

Avoid 'saving up' concerns for a special time, because these conversations often feel forced and put pressure on both parent and child.

✔ **Talk about happy memories of the time before the event.** Childhood objects, photos and toys linked to times of comfort and happiness help your child to build on positive memories of the past and realise that she can be happy again.

✔ **Empower your child by sharing ways to manage her moods.** Help the child create a mantra such as 'Stay calm' or 'Don't worry, be happy' to remind her to remain in the present moment. Or share one of your favourite breathing techniques (see Chapters 2 and 13) to help manage emotions when they become overwhelming at school or elsewhere.

Helping Your Child Express Feelings

Having emotional needs met is central to your child's wellbeing. Just as with adults, when a child's needs aren't met, the mind-body system stays in its alert state, encouraging the brain to send out distress signals that promote physical or emotional symptoms (see Chapter 2.) But how do you know what your child's really feeling?

Listening to questions – rather than looking for feelings

Children don't always consciously understand or express their feelings. Instead, they may experience and express a whole jumble of questions. Being attuned to children's questions can help you make sense of their concerns. For example:

- **Questions surrounding a death:** What happened? Why did this person die? Did I do something wrong? Am I going to die as well?

  Underlying concern may be: I'm not sure that I can manage this. I feel small and helpless. I'm frightened.

- **Questions surrounding a divorce or separation:** What does this mean to me? Where will I be living? Who's going to look after

me? How can I make sure that I see Dad if I'm living with Mum? Who will do my lunch box? Who'll pick me up from school?

Underlying concern may be: I don't feel safe. I'm worried about losing my family life. I want things to stay the same.

- **Questions about moving house:** What's going to happen to my friends? How will I get to see them? I don't know anyone at my new school. How will I make new friends? Who am I going to play with?

  Underlying concern may be: I worry that I'm going to lose touch with my friends. I'll miss them. I'm not sure that I'm likeable or that I can make new friends.

Children's emotions and emotional needs differ, and some children are more sensitive than others. If your child seems happy, well adjusted and without obvious disturbance, despite the changed situation or loss, your child may be well. You may not need to push your child to express feelings. Evidence suggests that even after major trauma, rushing in with counselling may not be particularly helpful to your child. However, when your child's natural coping mechanisms are overwhelmed, you must explore the situation in more depth to help the child to heal.

The following sections help you explore your child's emotions and emotional needs.

Getting down to those feelings

How you help children express feelings depends on their ages. If you're concerned that your child has underlying emotions that need expression, get to the heart of the matter:

✔ **Encourage your child to write a diary, journal or creative story describing the event and how she is feeling about it.** You can also draw pictures or make a collage together, combining words and pictures. This can be a fun activity. Put some music on, have a snack and share your own interpretations so that you heal together.

✔ **Suggest that your child write a letter to the person who's now gone, expressing whatever she likes.** You can also write a letter to someone who's still alive but has moved away or caused some pain or misunderstanding. Depending on whether the person is alive or dead, you can help your child decide whether she wishes to send the letter. The main intention of this exercise is for her to express her feelings in words.

✔ **For younger children, look together at illustration books about nature's cycle of birth, living and death.** Playing with puppets and dolls may also enable the feelings to emerge safely. Look for special books that include pictures of children experiencing a variety of emotions which you can talk about together. We list some books in the Appendix.

Releasing anger and guilt safely

Anger is a natural emotion that shows up at some point in the healing process. Both you and your child may be experiencing grief and change, which can put extra pressure on your relationship. You may both be on a shorter fuse than usual. Anger hijacks your ability to think.

Neither you nor your child can think clearly when you're upset because your emotional brain is signalling that your physical or emotional security is threatened. This signal leads to the automatic physical response of fight, flight or freeze (see Chapter 2). The fight response can kick in within a fraction of a second, overriding your thinking brain and resulting in you or your child causing hurt to others or yourself.

You and your child must rehearse ways to do the following:

✔ Recognise the feeling of anger

✔ Switch on a thinking response (rather than a feeling response)

✔ Respond mindfully and with full attention to address the situation

For more information on how specifically to do these three things, turn to Chapters 8, 9 and 13.

Most importantly, rather than telling your child what to do when she feels angry, share your own experiences of responding to feelings of anger. For instance, you may say something like:

Special days, simple rituals

Anniversaries, such as birthdays, Mother's Day or Father's Day can be especially difficult for children who have lost parents or other loved ones. Their school friends may be making cards and presents, and they can feel totally lost. One child told her teacher, 'It's hard to think I'll never be able to call someone Mummy again.'

Use these special times to return to memories of love in simple, structured ways. Help your child honour loving memories in mutual healing by visiting a grave, passing by an old house, looking at a photo or baking a cake.

I know that I get angry with people who push past me on my commuter train. I can feel it because my heart starts racing and I get hot and flushed. But I know I can calm my thinking down and manage the situation so I don't do something I regret like hitting a fellow commuter! I take a gentle breath and find a space to clear my head. I change my thoughts from 'I can't stand this!' to 'I'd prefer it if they weren't pushing past me, but I can manage it and keep calm.' I change the word 'angry' to 'a bit annoyed'. And all that helps me calm down my temper.

Then ask your child if this type of situation sounds familiar. Ask whether your child thinks that a process such as the one you describe can help.

Whatever anger-related techniques you and your child agree to try, the important message to remind yourself is: 'I can stay calm, and I can manage without losing my cool'.

Facing guilt as a parent

Your child's intense feelings – particularly anger – can be upsetting for you as a parent because you may not be able to change the situation or help her.

As a parent you want to protect your child, but when loss or change occurs, you can't turn the clock back or bring back a person. If your child has been injured in some way, you may not be able to remedy the situation. You may feel powerless to comfort or support your child, which can sometimes trigger defensive or aggressive reactions, as well as feelings of guilt.

Guilt signifies that you've broken some moral code. Ultimately you have an underlying feeling that you should be punished. Guilt can play out in unhealthy ways during stressful periods, leading you to unconsciously punish yourself or others.

To deal with your feelings of guilt, ask yourself whether a particular situation or action was illegal in the eyes of the law. What may others have done in your shoes? Did you respond in a natural – although not perfect – way to a difficult situation? Remind yourself that you're not perfect or omnipotent! You may not have had the power to alter events.

Finding support for children

Your child may need extra support in order to come to terms with loss. She may demonstrate signs such as a deterioration of school performance, truancy, phobias, fears or withdrawal.

Your child is going to benefit from talking about her responses to an event in a loving environment with someone who has knowledge of the bereavement or grief process. This person may be you, a grandparent, a teacher or a professional, such as a family doctor, counsellor, family bereavement support group, or mental health professional. We list some organisations that offer support in the Appendix.

Many organisations also offer trained facilitators who bring children together to share their experiences and feel supported.

Moving On from Traumatic Events

Emotional wounds can heal. The scars may remain for the rest of life, but they no longer hurt so intensely. They can remind you and your child of the joy of the original situation and of the pain of losing it. Without joy, the loss wouldn't be painful.

Help your child to focus on the richness of who or what existed before. As healing occurs, the ability to be happy returns. This feeling doesn't mean that you forget the person or situation that has changed. Photographs of a lost loved one, for example, are important because otherwise a child may think it was all a dream. One girl, who lost her mother when she was five years old and moved into her stepfather's house began to doubt her memories because her new home included no photographs of her mother.

So focus on the joy and richness of the past – as well as acknowledging and accepting the pain of loss.

Daring to discipline

Children may continue to show some disturbances as they heal. Children of all ages push the rules. Be ready to state what is unacceptable behaviour:

- ✔ **Set clear boundaries that provide security.** Topics to address include bedtimes, mealtimes and (for a teenager) times to be in at night and requirements about texting or calling if delayed for unavoidable reasons. Mutual consideration, respect and politeness may also be a part of what you agree and expect.

- ✔ **Separate the behaviour from the person.** For example, you may say: 'I love you, but being rude to me is not acceptable even if it is a difficult time.'

- ✔ **Be specific about the feelings your child's behaviour generates in you.** Say things such as 'I feel angry' or 'I'm annoyed' rather than 'you're self-ish' or 'you're impossible'.

  You may have a mixture of feelings, so describe each feeling and what the feelings are about. This approach helps your child gain understanding of another person's emotions as well as her own.

- ✔ **Suggest specific ways that you can get on better in the future.** Point out how being respectful of each other's needs is beneficial to everyone. For example, 'If you're able to respect my need for privacy in my room to do my mindfulness exercises, I can respect your need to keep your room in the way you wish as long as it's not unhygienic.'

Looking forward

Emotional responses depend on your child's age, personality and maturity. Children process and remember loss in their own unique ways as they grow up.

Keep an observing eye and help point your child towards the future:

- ✔ **Be honest and factual in answering questions:** Doing so encourages honesty in them and gives you the opportunity to share your own experiences. Saying something as simple as 'I feel sad that Grandad has died. How are you feeling?' demonstrates that talking about emotions is natural and also that you're ready to listen.

  If you don't know something or have no answer, say so. For example, 'Grandad died suddenly today. We'll bury him after the funeral next week. I don't know why he had a stroke and I know we'll all miss him. We love you and are here for you.'

✔ **Share future plans:** Talk about what's going to happen. Reassure your child that you're going to look after her.

✔ **Keep the painful situation in the conversation:** In this way, your child knows that you haven't forgotten. Like any wound, the pain needs to be aired and cleansed.

✔ **Acknowledge your own spiritual and religious beliefs:** Your own response to a death or loss is inevitably coloured by your personal beliefs. The decision to share your beliefs with your child is completely yours. In our own experience, children often find comfort in a concept of heaven and a life after death. You may explain that beliefs differ from facts. For example 'Grandad died of a stroke' is a fact whereas 'Grandad is in heaven' is a belief. In the longer term, open expression of beliefs can help children both accept the reality of loss and develop their own belief systems.

You and your child are building a new life – without a loved one following death, as part of a new family after divorce or with changed circumstances following disability. Allow your child to express lingering feelings such as sadness, anger, guilt or fear at the altered situation. Help her realise that she can build happiness again.

Discuss together ideas about how to make life good again. Ask her what can help create a good life going forward. She may want to paint a picture or tell a story of what this life may be like. Help her see that, like a story, life is a continual process of change, of birth, renewal and death.

Part VI
The Part of Tens

'While my client was practising his 6-breaths -a-minute technique, he didn't realise he was holding a telelphone — He <u>categorically</u> denies he is the Huntingdon Heavy Breather.'

In this part . . .

*H*ere are our favourite tips and stories for staying positive through life's challenges. The personal stories we share in this part are among the most inspiring we've encountered, and we encourage you to reflect on how the experiences of others can enhance your own life.

You also find a host of activities to try. Adapt these methods and models to suit your goals and take control of your life. Think of this part as your easily accessible resource guide of ideas to keep moving forward in life.

Chapter 19

Ten Ways to Heal Emotional Wounds

· ·

In This Chapter

▶ Releasing held-in emotions

▶ Paying attention to your body's signals

▶ Starting anew

· ·

*Y*ou need to tend emotional wounds if they're to heal. Just as a doctor investigates a physical wound, so you need to attend to your emotional wounds in order to address and heal them. Some wounds may be easily visible and on the surface; others may be held somewhere deeper and require exploration in order to understand their root causes.

You may have avoided looking at your deeply buried wounds for years because you fear returning to a painful place that you'd rather forget. Unfortunately, untended wounds can fester and have a toxic influence in your life, resulting in physical and emotional illness.

The paths towards greater emotional health are numerous. Listening to the stories of other people who've worked through difficulty and achieved resolution can help and inspire. In this chapter we share ten stories of people we've worked with in our practices and who addressed issues in their lives and found ways to heal.

Setting Your Own Agenda

Sally suffered repeatedly with depression. She traced the cause of her first bout of depression to her mother, who constantly criticised her housekeeping skills. Her mother's high standards of cleanliness, tidiness and neatness drove Sally to strive for maintaining perfect order – in the hopes of receiving her mother's approval. Sally worked compulsively day and night, never attaining her mother's idealistic expectations.

Feeling criticised by her mother, Sally had a breakdown and was admitted to hospital, where she was treated with medication and obtained temporary respite. Sally eventually recognised that medication alone didn't address her problem. She needed to investigate the underlying pattern of being unable to detach from her mother's demands.

Through coaching Sally recognised that she was working to her mother's agenda and not her own (see Chapter 3). She realised that she was able to choose to review her own needs and stop working compulsively to keep the house clean. She also began turning down the nagging voices in her mind that previously drove her to exhaustion (Chapters 3 and 12). She began to recognise that her symptoms were signals that she needed to ask others for support. When she started getting anxious, Sally instead asked herself: 'What do I really need now?'

Reflecting Before Acting

Although married with a wife and family, Richard worked long hours in an unenjoyable job. On returning home, his wife Penny frequently made demands of him before he caught a breath. He came to coaching feeling overloaded and resentful about what Penny was asking of him, as well as guilty because he didn't like to refuse her.

Through coaching, Richard was able to step back, acknowledge his frustrations, observe the situation and then work out the best way to respond. He realised that he sought approval from Penny and his boss, and feared that refusing them would lead to rejection (see Chapter 10). He planned to pause before responding in future so as to reflect on his own needs first.

He identified physical signals such as neck tension and headache that warned him he was overloaded (Chapter 2). He worked to accept that he couldn't please everyone and prepared himself to accept their anger. He rehearsed saying no in ways that weren't aggressive (Chapters 8 and 11).

In addition to agreeing to listen to his wife's concerns and arrange evenings together, Richard negotiated with Penny that he would go for a 20-minute run after work before starting the domestic round. Running allowed Richard to release the stresses of the day and respond to his family's needs in a more loving way, without feeling burdened.

Developing Better Sleep Patterns

Sheila developed sleep problems after she lost her job. She churned over her concerns at night, unable to rest. By morning she felt exhausted, irritable and unable to think clearly.

Following her coaching sessions, she decided to take a ten-minute rest space every ninety minutes throughout the day to re-balance herself and calm her emotions. She also spent ten minutes at the end of her day listing outstanding tasks and concerns. This activity enabled her to identify those activities she had achieved during the day, set aside persistent worries, and shift from daytime responsibilities to winding down for the evening.

She developed a routine to help her relax progressively through the evening – slowing her pace gradually, avoiding stimulants such as caffeine and alcohol, and turning off her computer and television an hour before she went to bed (see Chapter 5). She treated herself to a warm bath, a healthy snack and a milky drink (Chapter 4), with gentle music to relax her mind and body. Before sleep, she wrote any lingering concerns on a to-do list for the next day, which allowed her to let go of worries and calm her brain further. In bed she practised a relaxation routine to switch herself from 'drive' mode to 'sleep' mode, gradually releasing tension from each part of her body (Chapter 13).

As she integrated these various techniques into her evenings, Sheila established a more restful pattern for herself and started to sleep well again.

Moving towards Acceptance

Steve harboured resentment about how his mother Sylvia attempted to control him as a young adult. Even after he was married, Sylvia refused to talk to Steve's wife and attempted to put Steve and his wife in separate rooms when the couple visited. Steve avoided returning home except for essential family occasions, but his anger at his mother festered.

When Steve had children of his own, he realised that the root cause of Sylvia's behaviour was her difficult relationship with his father, as well as the fact that she missed the level of closeness with Steve that they enjoyed when he was young. He came to understand what led to Sylvia's unconscious behaviour patterns and saw that her possessiveness and controlling side were ways of filling the emotional gaps in her own life (see Chapter 7).

He was able to adjust his response to his mother's behaviour. Rather than remain angry, he explained that he loved his wife and wanted Sylvia to accept that they were now married adults. Steve told his mother that whilst he loved her, unless she honoured their marriage, he would not be able to visit her in future. Sylvia was upset but realised that her son was serious and that she needed to change her behaviour. By asserting his needs, Steve gradually re-established a healthy relationship with his mother and his wife felt supported and loved.

Quietening Your Breath for Ten Minutes

Wendy became severely anxious and depressed when she divorced. Treatment with antidepressants helped, but she found herself even more depressed when several new relationships broke down. She stopped working and experienced obsessive thoughts of 'I'm no good' and 'I'll never have a loving relationship ever again'.

Recovery occurred when she began to take ten minutes a day for quiet, meditative breathing (see Chapter 13). Engaging in daily breathing practice helped her release her anxiety and feel peaceful. During her calm, non-judgemental breathing practices, Wendy came to recognise that the unsettling voices she sometimes heard in her mind were coming from her parents. Memories of their unhappy marriage and arguments fuelled her current anxiety and continued to unsettle her.

Combining various techniques during her daily meditation practice allowed Wendy to accept, quieten and let go of the old voices (see Chapter 3). She started introducing positive affirmations (including 'I love myself as I am now') and connecting with images that reinforced her ability to create a better life in future (such as seeing herself confident with life, regardless of whether she had a relationship).

Scanning Your Body

Matthew was persistently tired with depression and severe pain in his right shoulder. Doctors were unable to identify a physical cause, despite multiple tests and physical therapies.

Matthew eventually identified the cause of his pain by using the Body Scan Technique (Chapter 2). When he focused on his right shoulder and breathed gently into the region, he became conscious of memories of being with his dying mother and holding her hand in his right hand ten years earlier.

Matthew hadn't wanted to let go, and he held an awkward position for many hours while his mother was unconscious. She died without regaining consciousness and so Matthew was unable to express his love for her. He felt sad and guilty that he had previously ignored her symptoms.

As he became aware of how his mind and body were associating this memory with physical pain in his shoulder, Matthew was able to work consciously on releasing the emotions that his body had been holding unconsciously. He realised that his body was signalling to him to take notice of his unresolved feelings, accept them and let go of his guilt from the past. (Chapter 10 contains more on handling grief, and Chapter 18 tackles recovering from guilt.) Matthew eventually decided to visit his mother's grave and his express love, sadness and regret.

Keeping Your Body Flexible

Molly began attending a Pilates class and became aware of persistently restricted mobility and low-back tension. During the physical examination during a mind-body consultation, gentle pressure was applied to her lower back. We asked Molly to remember the onset of her pain. She instantly reconnected with memories of abuse by her stepfather when she was a young teenager and was overwhelmed by sobbing.

Talking about her experiences later, she was able to devise a strategy to release the physically held pain, working with an osteopath and additional Pilates movements. Through this additional touch and ongoing stretching, Molly's body unlocked the held-in trauma that needed to be addressed and healed. In Chapter 6, we discuss various forms of exercise and bodywork that aid in emotional healing. (In her mind-body sessions, she also released her emotions by writing a letter to her stepfather, now dead, which enabled her to fully express and let go of her feelings.)

Finding Your Relaxation Response

Paul was constantly anxious, and his friends advised him to 'just chill and meditate'. So Paul went to a meditation class complete with candles, mats and tranquil music, but he found that his mind continued to be agitated.

He was relieved to discover that people respond differently to various relaxation methods and decided to explore his options. Because he always enjoyed sport, he decided that movement and physical activity might help him relax (see Chapter 6). He chose to go swimming three times a week and found that he was able to calm his mind while in the water. By swimming mindfully, he focused his attention away from anxious thoughts and towards the physical sensations of the water against his body. Swimming reduced his anxiety levels and he was able to gain insight into the sources of his anxiety.

Improving Your Breathing Chemistry

Upon his death, Patricia's father left her as executor of his estate and asked her to support her mother and three younger siblings in managing their financial affairs. In order to focus on this duty, she put her grief on hold and neglected her own needs. After a time, she became overloaded with responsibility and felt too tired to respond to her family. When her husband developed a heart condition, she suffered overwhelming anxiety and depression and eventually broke down. She was admitted to a mental hospital, and yet on release failed to recover and had two further admissions.

In coaching sessions as part of her treatment, she was introduced to a *capnotrainer*, a device that measures the level of carbon dioxide in out-breaths. She discovered that her exhalations had a severely reduced level of carbon dioxide, a condition associated with chronic hyperventilation (see Chapter 2). Unprocessed emotions following her father's death were combining with her husband's illness to create a continuous stressed state.

Patricia practised regular breathing with diaphragmatic control and was able to raise her carbon dioxide level to normal. As her breathing regulated, her brain gradually switched out of emotional arousal and she began to think clearly again.

Taking Action

Peter married young and found himself dominated by his wife Kate. She criticised him continuously and sometimes physically slapped him. Expressing his needs always led to a row and more criticism, so he ended up holding in his emotions. Over time, he lost confidence and suffered inflammatory bowel disease.

In hospital, Peter's symptoms quickly improved. However, the medical team recognised that after each of Kate's visits, Peter's condition declined. In discussion with his doctor. Peter came to understand that his symptoms were connected to his emotional state (see Chapter 2). He realised that he needed to address his relationship with Kate in order to recover.

Peter expressed his unhappiness to Kate and explained how her continuing verbal assaults were causing him ongoing stress, impacting his health and immune function. He asked her for couple counselling, but she refused and continued to demean him. He realised that he needed to take action to protect himself, and eventually he asked for and obtained a divorce.

Chapter 20

Ten Ways to Stay Positive

● ●

In This Chapter

▶ Shaping your emotions and responses

▶ Acknowledging your successes

▶ Living in the moment

▶ Checking your perceptions

● ●

*T*he focus of your attention determines your quality of life now and in the future. You can choose to dwell on pain and disappointments – or switch the focus towards making the future positive. The saying 'Every cloud has a silver lining' suggests this truth, but even more importantly, the onus is on you to find that silver lining.

Your past experiences, however difficult, are always a part of you, but you can move through them to a place where they no longer incapacitate you. Simply put: you can feel happy again. This fact doesn't demean in any way the emotions that you've been feeling, but a time comes when you need to be ready to take an active part in shaping a positive future and living life to the full.

In this chapter we share some ideas and strategies to help you become and remain positive – and avoid sinking back into the emotional wounds of the past. Not only can the techniques in this chapter help you heal old troubles, but also they can enable you to feel better prepared to manage life's inevitable future ups and downs.

Recognising Your Emotional Needs

Be clear about what makes you feel happy and secure and take direct action to bring this situation into your life. Unless you take time to consider these factors, you may find yourself in a situation, career or relationship where you're not meeting your security and happiness needs. You can end up feeling not only unhappy but also a victim of circumstance. Find more about identifying your needs in Chapter 1.

You need to act in order to feel happier and more secure. Take responsibility for creating the positive actions that provide the fun, love and enjoyment that you require to feel good. Here are some positive actions you can take, and chapters where you can find out more:

- ✔ Being heard, recognised and seen for who you are (see Chapter 15).

- ✔ Being assertive – not aggressive – in expressing your needs to others (see Chapter 8).

- ✔ Enjoying a physical environment and home that provides nurture (see Chapter 7).

- ✔ Feeling loved and supported by partner, family, friends and work (see Chapter 9).

- ✔ Following a life path that's meaningful to you and gives you a sense of purpose (see Chapter 15).

Creating a good life is up to you. Speak up when your needs aren't being met Explain to others the part that they can play to help you.

Accepting Your Need to Belong

Everyone needs friends, so actively seek connection with others. When you're feeling bruised by life, you can easily withdraw into yourself. Avoid doing so, because you need to belong to, and feel included within, a social group (see Chapter 12 for all about social networks).

Connecting with other people includes accepting invitations, joining new groups, nurturing old relationships, smiling at people in the street or starting conversations. Sometimes you can make a friend for life with a chance exchange on a train!

Use technology wisely and recognise that the sense of belonging you may gain through email and mobile phones can be addictive and illusionary. Just like in the real world, discriminate between those online relationships with people who really know you and are going to remain loyal and those based on superficial connections. Whatever the venue, spend your time and energy on relationships with the people who matter most to you.

Take a piece of paper and draw a web of connections to all the people in the world whom you hold in affection and feel connection to. Keep the drawing in a safe place and feel held by those relationships as you look over it. Take time to keep in touch with the individuals you include on this drawing.

Focusing on Your Strengths

Empower yourself to feel positive by focusing on what you have rather than on what you don't have.

Stop now and remember those things of which you can feel proud. Draw up a record of your achievements, whether from education, or in professional or personal life. Begin by listing your work and life skills. Then go beyond diplomas and outstanding performance appraisals. For instance, keeping a life-long school friend, maintaining a comfortable home, or ensuring your finances are in good order are all achievements worth acknowledging.

Consider your personal qualities as well, including kindness, patience and determination. Keep this record stored in your mind so you can take a sense of pride with you wherever you go.

Detecting Prolonged Stress and Taking Action

Don't accept a lifestyle that puts overwhelming pressure on you: do something about it! As people rev up into their aroused state, they forget how to relax and can feel trapped by their habitual routines (see Chapters 2 and 7). The balance between doing and being is lost. Although you may become accustomed to experiencing stress, feeling this way constantly isn't good for you physically or emotionally.

Watch out for stress signals, such as tiredness, colds or sleep disturbance. Stop and create breathing spaces in your day to review your life and your work. Figure our what would help take the pressure off you. Make a plan to avoid unnecessary challenges, alter how you handle difficult situations, and feel more in control. Finally, relax, breathe and accept those things you can't change. See Chapters 12 and 13 .

Rehearsing Best Outcomes

Imagining and mentally rehearsing a successful result moves you forward. Don't get stuck in old problems. Notice when you tend to grumble about work or life, and then switch the focus to a positive outcome. Visualise what a positive alternative may look like and think strategically about what needs to happen in order to achieve that outcome.

Always focus on what you *can* do to change the situation. For example, if you have a problematic relationship, think about what you can possibly change if you work to create good communication. What steps do you need to take to bring that about?

To begin creating a vision of how to change your life, ask yourself:

✔ What is my new life going to look like?

✔ Where am I going to live, work or travel?

✔ Who's going to be with me?

Use your answers to create a mental video that depicts your journey from today to the desired end result. See yourself as the hero in a movie, meeting challenges and succeeding at whatever you attempt. Notice how you feel emotionally and physically as you watch your mental movie. Add captions or dialogue to the scenes to include motivating words or phrases to remind you of your intention.

Moving Beyond Old Traumas

A traumatic event – such as a car accident, divorce or sudden death of a loved one – can be devastating but doesn't have to ruin your whole life. Nurture yourself gently towards recovery. Whatever happened, recognise that you also developed certain skills and strengths in the process of moving through the situation. Acknowledge these strengths and pat yourself on the back. (Chapter 8 has more on recovering from traumatic events.)

Identify how you may feel when you're recovered. How will life be different? In what ways will you look and feel differently? What will you be talking about instead of dwelling on your traumatic event? Fade the trauma into the past and bring your future life into sharper focus. Each time you experience a flashback or memory of the event, change the picture to one of you feeling happy and confident about life again.

Other people may not realise that you continue to need support during your recovery, and so be direct in explaining what you need in order to release past trauma.

Switching to Supportive Emotions

You can choose how you feel by recalling positive emotions. Identify and make a list of which emotions help you to enjoy life. Then make a list of those emotions that don't help you to move on so that you can be alert to these feelings creeping up on you unawares. Notice which thoughts help you to stimulate supportive emotions. Become aware of how your behaviours and actions change when you're focusing on constructive thoughts rather than negative or doubtful thoughts.

At the beginning of each day choose the dominant emotion you want to experience. If you have a difficult situation coming up during the day, identify:

✔ The desired positive outcome.

✔ The specific emotion that can help you to achieve this outcome.

✔ The supportive thought that inspires that emotion.

✔ The actions you need to take.

Switch on the feeling of content, happiness or confidence just by reminding yourself what these emotions feel like. Carry this positive emotion with you into the event. Find out more about this technique in Chapters 8 and 16.

Living in the Now

Each day is precious. No one knows whether today is going to be the last, so don't fritter away the moment. Even if you have difficult or boring tasks to do today, choose to do them wholeheartedly so that they're enjoyable. Love the person you're with today.

Open your eyes, ears and senses to the beauty that exists in your surroundings: leaves on the trees, sky and cloud formations, small details on houses and buildings, birdsong, the voices of small children, music, love. Don't waste a minute of life by allowing negativity, resentment or another person's anger to spoil your day. Don't wait to be happy; be happy now.

Expressing Feelings in Words

Emotions need expression. Tune into your feelings and consciously choose how to express these emotions in words. Determine for yourself whether talking to someone can help – or whether you just need to get something off your chest (for example, by writing down your feelings in a journal).

If you need to express your feelings to another person, balance criticism or negative remarks with positive affirmation and appreciation. Connecting on a positive level first lowers defences and opens up others to listening. Remember: good relationships have a ratio of five positive statements to one negative comment.

Express problems in positive terms of what you both can do differently. Focus specifically on the behaviour rather than on the person. For example, instead of saying 'You're so inconsiderate', say 'Thanks for cooking tonight though can you clear up the kitchen afterwards next time? It would really help.' See Chapters 14 and 16 for more ways to express feelings in productive ways.

Changing Your Thinking

Your mind is your emotional compass. Your thoughts shape your feelings and experience of life. When you focus on the negative, you feel negative; when you focus on doubt, you feel doubtful. Focus on your confidence and competence, and you feel powerful.

You have the control switch to decide which thoughts you listen to. Tune in to your inner dialogue and start to analyse which thoughts are helping you to live a happy and fulfilling life and which thoughts are limiting you.

As you listen to your thoughts, understand that your mind can twist the way it interprets situations, which can sometimes result in more pain than may be necessary. In particular, seek to avoid the many forms of distorted thinking that we cover in Chapter 12.

Chapter 21

Ten Activities for Emotional Healing

In This Chapter

▶ Gaining and shifting perspective

▶ Setting healthy boundaries

▶ Finding peace of mind

---

*A*ctive participation in your healing is essential for you to integrate change into your life. Healing theories and case studies are useful, but you must apply them as practical actions and new behaviours in order to achieve change in your own life. For this reason, we include many activities throughout the book that give you the opportunity to stop, review your personal situation and develop your own solutions to problems as you go forward.

In this chapter we provide you with ten activities to help you develop new ways of thinking, feeling and behaving in future. We've found in our respective practices that the activities in this chapter are among the most powerful techniques for change.

Every activity in this chapter merits a Try This icon. Instead of sprinkling dozens of little pictures throughout the chapter, we recommend that you try any and all the ideas on the following pages.

Treating Emotions as Friends

Instead of running away from emotions and seeing them as scary, think about your emotions as friendly guides. Even those uncomfortable feelings of anxiety and anger provide you with essential information that something isn't right in your life.

List the emotions you experience most frequently. Then identify the body signals that accompany each emotion; these signals alert you to feelings of threat (flip to Chapter 2 for more on understanding your emotions). Consider whether you can give each feeling a symbolic image that reminds you that your emotions are on your side, guiding you to make good life decisions by restoring your thinking and purposeful action. For example:

Emotion: Fear.
Physical symptoms: Tightness in my tummy, stiff jaw, shortness of breath, heavy feeling of dread.
Friendly image: My grandfather. He sailed the Atlantic. I see him standing on a ship's deck saying, 'Hello, don't freeze! Just think.'
Message this emotion may be giving me: Check what's so frightening about the situation. Ask myself whether my fear is real or imagined. Would I feel better if I took action?

Practising Loving Kindness

When you're facing a difficult period of your life or are in conflict with others, stop and focus on the feeling of loving kindness towards yourself, and then flowing this feeling out to others. Practising loving kindness helps you soften and be gentle with yourself and others.

To locate and increase feelings of loving kindness, think of someone you love: a partner, family member, spiritual figure, friend – even a pet. As you think about this person, bring in the emotional and physical feelings that you associate with loving kindness. Your eyes may soften, your heart open and your body relax.

Transfer these feelings to yourself so that you imagine the sensation of compassion and warmth enveloping you. Feel truly loved. Practise this activity by breathing in the remembered sense of love and as you breathe out release struggle. Do this regularly throughout the day. You only need a minute or two. With practice you may be able to open your heart again to those you dislike or have done you harm. See Chapter 13 for more meditation practice involving loving kindness.

Taking Time for Morning Mindfulness and Journaling

Starting your morning well – with a sense of calm and control – sets you up with the greater likelihood of having a good day. Buy a good pen and journal or notebook to have beside your bed. Set your alarm for 20 minutes earlier than usual and do the following:

✔ **During the first ten minutes,** tune into your body. Focus on your breathing (see Chapter 2). If your mind wanders, gently bring it back to the breath, without judgement. Gradually your mind and body quieten.

✔ **During the second ten minutes,** free-write in your journal. Jot down anything that comes to your mind. Don't think about a right or wrong way to do this, just allow the thoughts to flow from your brain onto the page. Don't stop. In the final minute, review what you wrote. Don't criticise, just ask yourself:

- Where is the focus of my feelings and thoughts? Are there any themes?

- How do the words I wrote make me feel?

- Do I seem to be optimistic and positive or negative and pessimistic? Underline the negative phrases and consider what you can do to change the negatives into positives.

- Thinking of the day ahead, what thoughts and affirmations can help me stay mindful and calm?

Releasing Pain and Finding Compassion

Past hurt and pain just weighs you down, spoiling your day. Make a decision to free yourself of old resentments and problematic thinking so that you walk on with a lighter step (Chapters 6 and 7 have more about physical and emotional healing).

All human beings are fallible and make mistakes. No one gives you an official 'Book of Life' when you arrive in the world. Everyone muddles along and sometimes, in that muddle, you or others may have been hurt. You may also inadvertently – or intentionally – hurt others.

Gather together two different colour self-adhesive note pads, a waste-paper basket and a large page of blank paper. On one colour of note, write the hurts that you want to release; one hurt on each note. As you do this, scrunch up each piece of paper and throw it in the waste-paper basket.

When you finish with the hurts, take the other colour pad and write, one person at a time, the names of people to whom you want to show compassion. Stick these notes on the large piece of paper. Spend as long as you like writing notes.

Pick up the waste-paper basket and say, 'I let all these hurts go so that I can now live a happier life'. Throw the crumbled papers in your outside dustbin to recycle. Hang the large piece of paper with the names in a prominent but private place. Each time you look at these people, remember that you can choose to show them compassion, recognising that they're just human beings.

Brushing Away Negative Thoughts

You probably don't think twice about brushing your teeth each day, but how often do you consider the negative 'plaque' that may be building up in your mind from negative thoughts? Just like dental health, you need to think daily of your mental health.

Each time you brush your teeth, imagine you're not only cleansing your teeth but also brushing away negativity, so that you can create an environment for positive thoughts and good feelings to come in.

Adopting Healthy Eating Choices

Eating the wrong things is easy when you're feeling low. Unfortunately, a lousy diet often just makes you feel worse (see Chapter 4). Your emotional healing may include creating good habits that help you to eat better.

Take a month to track what you eat from morning to night. Write down each item in your journal or a special notebook. Jot down how you feel following each meal. Which foods help you to feel healthy, lively and energised? Which foods leave you feeling bloated, tired and uncomfortable?

Look over your lists and then look through your fridge and cupboard. Give or throw away foods that don't add to your feeling of wellbeing. Stock up with those foods that make you feel good. You may need to change your behavioural habits – for example, going down different aisles at the supermarket or changing your Internet shopping list.

Gaining Perspective

In a busy life, you can easily lose perspective of what's important. Establish a mental gauge to measure the intensity of your feelings of stress, irritation, fear or other negative emotions. Rate emotions on a scale of 0 to 10, with 0 being low intensity and 10 being high-impact intensity. Use this scale to acknowledge, assess and adjust your emotional responses.

Gain perspective by stopping and thinking of something worse that could have happened, for example an accident to your child. Remind yourself that he's going to be safe and his carer will wait for you. You can regain perspective and reduce the measure of stress on your mental gauge.

Ask yourself questions about how important the event is going to seem in six months. This may in itself reduce your stress level on the mental gauge. If you can do something to alter the situation, take action; if not, accept that what's happening is happening, flow with it and make the best of it. This may enable you to lower levels on your mental gauge even further.

Creating Boundaries

Everyone has emotional and practical needs. Sometimes your needs are in conflict with other people's. This difference can be okay at times – for example, you may be happy to help out a friend who's having a bad week even though you have a major project wrapping up at work. But always monitor how you feel physically and emotionally to detect imbalances between giving and receiving. You may need to reset your boundaries and take care of your own needs.

Many people think that saying 'no' is impolite, but all you're doing is negotiating different priorities. You aren't being rude, just practical. Taking care of your own needs is responsible, not selfish. If you don't do so, perhaps no one else will. Think of the safety instructions on a plane where they tell you to fit your own oxygen mask before fitting it to others; if you don't help yourself first, you can't be of use to other people!

Take a piece of paper, create two columns and list your acceptable and unacceptable demands. For example

- ✓ **Acceptable demands:** Working late for a special project deadline; babysitting to let your partner go out; accepting that your partner chooses the holiday from time to time.

- ✓ **Unacceptable demands:** Working late out of habit; always hiring a sitter because your partner is busy when you want to go out; your partner insisting on specific holiday destinations without negotiation.

Next, identify the aspects of your life that you consider to be priorities – things you want to ensure time to focus on – in your home and at work. For example:

- ✓ **Home priorities:** Getting home on time to read a story to my son; sitting down to a meal as a family three nights a week.

- ✓ **Work priorities:** Making time for my direct reports; responding to all emails within one work day.

Finally, decide how you express your boundaries (turn to Chapter 15 for some helpful suggestions) to enable you to achieve your priorities.

Accepting Your Body

Many people berate their bodies for not being 'perfect' and make themselves miserable in the process. But what is perfection? Models often don't feel confident of their bodies, and the vast majority of images you see in movies and print are specially lit, air-brushed and altered so as to be nearly artificial. Bodies come in all shapes and sizes – you don't necessarily judge a tiny baby's body.

Take ten minutes in the next week to go and stand in front of a mirror. Release judgement and draw in the feeling of loving kindness (see the earlier section 'Practising Loving Kindness') as you look at yourself. Allow your eyes to soften. Focus on what you can be grateful for. For example, your heart beats and keeps you alive, your lungs work, your legs take you from one place to the next, your eyes see the beauty of a child's smile, your ears can hear music.

Each day offer your body love and respect and honour it by taking care of it with exercise, good food, touch and love.

Finding Patience and Peace

You may feel that your life is on a treadmill and you want to get off sometimes. Whatever is happening on the outside, you can find a way to slow down on the inside by creating mental space to re-balance yourself.

Spend tomorrow deliberately slowing down. Carry out the same routines but keep in mind the saying, 'more haste, less speed'. Instead of feeling rushed and pressured, find your inner space to relax and be patient. Try any and all the following activities to find patience and peace in the midst of your life:

- Become aware of your breath from time to time during the day.
- Change the words you use. Don't say 'I'm in a rush ' or 'I'm hectic'. Instead, say 'I'm just pottering' or 'I can take my time'.
- Slow your walk, be at peace and enjoy the view as you move from place to place.
- Focus on your senses. Enjoy what you see and the air you breathe.

Appendix

Useful Contacts and Resources

● ●

*Y*ou may find that reading this book makes you want to work on emotional issues with extra support. We have created a list of resources and recognised organisations in this Appendix for support and information.

To contact the authors: We are practitioners in Emotional Healing and are happy to hear from you if you feel that you have a situation with which you desire professional support. Helen is a Cognitive-Behavioural Coach and David is a Doctor of Medicine, now specialising in Mind-Body and Behavioural Medicine.

> **Helen Whitten**, BABCP, MCIPD, AC Accredited Coach, CEDR Accredited Mediator, Managing Director, Positiveworks Ltd: www.positiveworks. com. Personal and professional development and emotional healing through coaching, facilitation and mediation.

> **Dr David Beales, FRCP (UK), MRCGP, DCH, DRCOG, Dip Psych**; www. mindfulphysiology.co.uk. Mind-body and behavioural medicine; Physiological assessments including breath chemistry using capnography; Personally tailored programmes for emotional, cognitive and behavioural change.

Professional Bodies that Offer Support

A variety of organisations offer information to individuals seeking emotional healing. We list those that support the specific areas we cover in the book. You can call these organisations or visit their websites any time for information and support.

> ✔ **Alcoholics Anonymous:** 0845 769 7555; www.alcoholics-anonymous. org.uk. Support for alcoholism and drug addiction.

> ✔ **Beat: Understanding Eating Disorders:** Youthline: 0845 634 7650; Adults: 0845 634 1414; www.b-eat.co.uk.

- **Biofeedback Foundation of Europe (BFE):** www.bfe.org/breathpacer.htm. Resource for the Ez-Air Plus breath pacer.

- **Carers UK:** 0207 378 4999; www.carersuk.org. Offering information and advice for carers, as well as campaigning for change.

- **Childline:** 0800 11 11; www.childline.org.uk. Free and confidential helpline, giving support and information relating to concerns of abuse, domestic violence and self-harm for children and young adults.

- **Cruse:** 0844 477 9400; www.crusebereavementcare.org.uk. Bereavement support.

- **Daily Strength:** www.dailystrength.org. Internet addiction support.

- **Disordered Eating:** www.disordered-eating.co.uk. Help and information for eating disorders and treatment.

- **Foundation for the Study of Infant Deaths:** 0207 802 6868 www.fsid.org.uk. Support and research into cot death.

- **Grief Encounter:** 0208 446 7452; www.griefencounter.org.uk. Offers support for children experiencing bereavement.

- **HealthWorld Online:** www.healthy.net. Links to general mind/body topics including medicine, health, exercise, and links to specific mind-body therapies such as bodywork, guided imagery, and more.

- **Macmillan Cancer Support:** 0207 840 7840; www.macmillan.org.uk. Dedicated to improving the lives of people affected by cancer with nursing assistance, support and guidance.

- **NHS information:** www.patient.co.uk/find_me.asp. Organisational information for patients.

- **OnHealth:** www.medicinenet.com. Provides easy-to-read, in-depth, authoritative medical information for patients, including mind-body medicine, biofeedback, guided imagery, hypnosis, meditation and yoga.

- **Penny Brohn Cancer Care:** 0845 123 2310; www.pennybrohncancercare.org. Support for individuals affected by cancer at any stage of their illness, and their families and supporters.

- **Refuge:** 0808 2000 247; www.refuge.org.uk. Support and helpline for women and children experiencing domestic violence.

- **Sane:** 0845 767 8000; www.sane.org.uk. Provides help and information to those experiencing mental health problems, their families and carers.

- **Supportline:** 01708 765200; www.supportline.org.uk. Confidential support line for children, young adults and adults, for any emotional issues.

- **The Child Bereavement Charity:** 01494 446 648; www.childbereavement.org.uk. Provides specialised support, information and training to individuals affected when a baby or child dies.

- **Walking the Way to Health:** 0300 060 2287; www.whi.org.uk. Information on local natural spaces and the benefits of health walks. They offer loans of pedometers.

- **Winston's Wish:** 08452 03 04 05; www.winstonswish.org.uk. Offers support for children experiencing bereavement.

- **Young Minds:** www.youngminds.org.uk. Offers young people contact details of health and mental health organisations.

Professional Organisations

In the UK, you can get support with mental health and medical issues through the NHS, so you may wish to visit your GP to discuss your emotional healing needs. Our approach for this book is based on Mind-Body medicine, Mindfulness and Cognitive-Behavioural psychology. All organisations we list here can provide additional contact details of practitioners in your area:

- **Association for Coaching**; 01795 535430; www.associationfor coaching.com; Membership association for professional coaches and organisations involved in coaching or related training.

- **British Association of Art Therapists (BAAT):** 0207 686 4216; www. baat.org. Information about art and music therapy and directory of therapists.

- **British Association for Behavioural and Cognitive Psychotherapies (BABCP);** 01254 875277; www.babcp.com. Provides details of accredited therapists.

- **Centre for Mindfulness Research and Practice;** www.bangor.ac.uk/ mindfulness. Research and information on mindfulness practices and practitioners.

- **The Centre for Stress Management:** 0208 228 1185; www.managing stress.com. An international training centre and stress consultancy. Carries out stress management and prevention programmes, stress audits and research, stress counselling, coaching and training.

- **EMDR Association:** www.emdrassociation.org.uk Lists therapists who specialise in EMDR, an effective treatment of trauma.

- **Find Me A Professional:** www.patient.co.uk/find_me.asp. NHS health information as provided by GPs and nurses.

- **LifeCoach Directory:** www.lifecoach-directory.org.uk. Directory of coaches by area and specialism.

Books

You can gain healing insights by reading books. We chose the following because they've been useful to our clients. All are available in bookshops or online.

- ✔ *The Artist's Way: A Course in Discovering and Recovering Your Creative Self:* Julia Cameron (Pan Books, 1997)

- ✔ *The Bristol Approach to Living with Cancer:* Helen Cooke (Robinson Publishing, 2003)

- ✔ *Cognitive-Behavioural Coaching Techniques For Dummies:* Helen Whitten (Wiley, 2009)

- ✔ *Cognitive-Behavioural Therapy For Dummies:* Rob Willson and Rhena Branch (Wiley, 2005)

- ✔ *The Compassionate Mind:* Paul Gilbert (Constable, 2009)

- ✔ *Counselling for Stress Problems:* Stephen Palmer and Windy Dryden (Sage Publications Ltd, 1994)

- ✔ *Emotional Blackmail:* Dr Susan Forward and Donna Frazier (Bantam Press, 1997)

- ✔ *Emotional Freedom Techniques For Dummies:* Helena Fone (Wiley, 2008)

- ✔ *The Feeling Good Handbook:* David Burns, MD (Plume, 2000)

- ✔ *Future Directions, Practical Ways to Develop Emotional Intelligence and Confidence in Young People:* Helen Whitten and Diane Carrington (Network Educational Press Ltd, 2006)

- ✔ *Heart of the Mind: Engaging Your Inner Power to Change with NLP:* Connirae and Steve Andreas (Real People Press, 1989)

- ✔ *Human Givens: A New Approach to Emotional Health and Clear Thinking:* Joe Griffin and Ivan Tyrrel (HG Publishing, 2004)

- ✔ *Hyperventilation Breathing Pattern Disorder:* Dinah Bradley (Kyle Cathie, 2007)

- ✔ *Mind over Emotions:* Les Carter (Baker Publishing Group, 1985)

- ✔ *The Mindful Way through Depression:* Mark Williams, John Teasdale, Zindel Segal, Jon Kabat-Zinn (Guilford Press, 2007)

- ✔ *Mindfulness: Full Catastrophe Living:* Jon Kabat-Zinn (Piatkus Books, 2001)

- ✔ *Monkeyluv: And Other Lessons in Our Lives as Animals:* Robert M. Sapolsky (Vintage, 2006)

✔ *Muddles, Puddles and Sunshine: Your Activity Book to Help when Someone Has Died:* Winston's Wish (Hawthorn Press, 2000)

✔ *Neuro-Linguistic Programming For Dummies:* Romilla Ready and Kate Burton (Wiley, 2004)

✔ *Overcoming Anxiety:* Helen Kennerley (Robinson, 2009)

✔ *Overcoming Low Self-Esteem:* Melanie Fennell (Robinson, 2009)

✔ *Rescuing the 'Inner Child': Therapy for Adults Sexually Abused as Children:* Penny Parks (Souvenir Press, 1994)

✔ *Sad Isn't Bad: A Good-Grief Guidebook for Kids Dealing with Loss:* Michaelene Mundy (University of Massachusetts Press, 2004)

✔ *Sunbathing in the Rain: A Cheerful Book about Depression*: Gwyneth Lewis (Harper Perennial, 2006)

✔ *The Power of Now: A Guide to Spiritual Enlightenment:* Eckhart Tolle (Mobius, 2001)

✔ *Time to Think: Listening to Ignite the Human Mind:* Nancy Kline (Cassell Illustrated, 1998)

✔ *Transitions: Making Sense of Life's Changes:* William Bridges (Perseus Books, 2004)

✔ *Why Zebras Don't Get Ulcers:* Robert M. Sapolsky (Saint Martin's Press, 2004)

Index

• S •

FOR DUMMIES®

Making Everything Easier!™

UK editions

BUSINESS

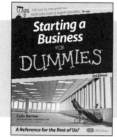
978-0-470-51806-9

978-0-470-74381-2

978-0-470-71382-2

British Sign Language
For Dummies
978-0-470-69477-0

Business NLP For Dummies
978-0-470-69757-3

Competitive Strategy For Dummies
978-0-470-77930-9

Cricket For Dummies
978-0-470-03454-5

CVs For Dummies, 2nd Edition
978-0-470-74491-8

Digital Marketing For Dummies
978-0-470-05793-3

Divorce For Dummies, 2nd Edition
978-0-470-74128-3

eBay.co.uk Business All-in-One
For Dummies
978-0-470-72125-4

Emotional Freedom Technique For
Dummies
978-0-470-75876-2

English Grammar For Dummies
978-0-470-05752-0

Flirting For Dummies
978-0-470-74259-4

Golf For Dummies
978-0-470-01811-8

Green Living For Dummies
978-0-470-06038-4

Hypnotherapy For Dummies
978-0-470-01930-6

IBS For Dummies
978-0-470-51737-6

Lean Six Sigma For Dummies
978-0-470-75626-3

FINANCE

978-0-470-99280-7

978-0-470-71432-4

978-0-470-69515-9

HOBBIES

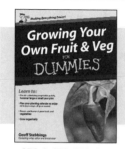
978-0-470-69960-7

978-0-470-74535-9

978-0-470-75857-1

8041_p1

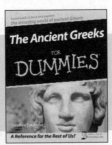

FOR DUMMIES®

The easy way to get more done and have more fun

LANGUAGES

978-0-7645-5194-9

978-0-7645-5193-2

978-0-471-77270-5

MUSIC

978-0-470-48133-2

978-0-470-03275-6
UK Edition

978-0-470-49644-2

SCIENCE & MATHS

978-0-7645-5326-4

978-0-7645-5430-8

978-0-7645-5325-7

Art For Dummies
978-0-7645-5104-8

Bass Guitar For Dummies
978-0-7645-2487-5

Brain Games For Dummies
978-0-470-37378-1

Christianity For Dummies
978-0-7645-4482-8

Criminology For Dummies
978-0-470-39696-4

Forensics For Dummies
978-0-7645-5580-0

German For Dummies
978-0-7645-5195-6

Hobby Farming For Dummies
978-0-470-28172-7

Index Investing For Dummies
978-0-470-29406-2

Jewelry Making & Beading
For Dummies
978-0-7645-2571-1

Knitting For Dummies, 2nd Edition
978-0-470-28747-7

Music Composition For Dummies
978-0-470-22421-2

Physics For Dummies
978-0-7645-5433-9

Schizophrenia For Dummies
978-0-470-25927-6

Sex For Dummies, 3rd Edition
978-0-470-04523-7

Solar Power Your Home For Dummies
978-0-470-17569-9

Tennis For Dummies
978-0-7645-5087-4

The Koran For Dummies
978-0-7645-5581-7

Wine All-in-One For Dummies
978-0-470-47626-0

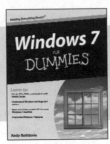

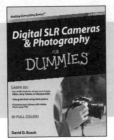